ERICH DONNERT

RUSSIA

IN THE AGE

OF ENLIGHTENMENT

EDITION LEIPZIG

W9-BVQ-555

Translated from the German by Alison
and Alistair Wightman

© 1986 Edition Leipzig
Lic. No. 600/7/85
Design: Ursula Küster
Production: INTERDRUCK Graphischer Grossbetrieb Leipzig
Manufactured in the German Democratic Republic
Order No. 594 282 7

CONTENTS

PREFACE

THE AGE OF ENGLIGHTENMENT, as a social movement in the 18th century, marks the beginning of a new historical era. The development of national cultures, the great intensification of interrelations with Europe in terms of society, education, science, literature and art, and the internationalization of cultural and intellectual life in Europe all followed in its wake. The humanistic idea of the coexistence of European peoples and cultures on a basis of equal rights became firmly established in Enlightenment thinking. Thus the Enlightenment was synonymous with the emergence of the European peoples into a new age.

For Russia, too, the 18th century signified the final breakthrough into modern times. The absolute monarchy played an active role in the renewal of the social, cultural and political life of the country. It paved the way for the transition to a capitalist social order from a mediaeval feudal order, and gave Russian society the basis for further development. This trend was recognized even by contemporaries. Changes and developments excited great interest and aroused a passionate response. There was scarcely an intellectual, artist, scientist or writer who did not try to contribute, in some form or another, to solving the social problems which it entailed. The task of this book is to cast light upon the struggle to win acceptance for the new in the cultural development of the tsardom, taking as the principal examples social thought, education, science, literature and art.

RUSSIA BECOMES A WORLD POWER

RUSSIA'S DEVELOPMENT was noticeably inhibited by hundreds of years of Tatar rule, and by the warlike activities of Swedish and Polish forces in the tsardom at the beginning of the 17th century. This was compounded by the fact that the state authorities gave a legal foundation to the serfdom of Russian peasants with the Imperial Code of 1649, the *sobornoye ulozheniye*, thus increasing the backwardness of the country in relation to the more advanced states of Central and Western Europe. The fact that the tsardom had practically no access to the oceans of the world was also a key factor: for not only was the White Sea far from the urban centres, it was also navigable for only four months of the year, being frozen over for the remaining eight. Nevertheless, the unity of the country, which became steadily stronger from the 17th century on, and the growth of manufacturing production, paved the way for more rapid development in Russia.

In constitutional terms the Russian Empire was superior to politically divided countries such as Germany and Italy at the end of the 17th century, although in social terms it lagged behind countries such as the Netherlands and England which had already experienced bourgeois revolutions. This was especially true of industrial development, foreign trade, shipbuilding and many other fields of the economy, society and the state. Its backwardness also represented a threat to the independence of the country and the further development of the Russian Empire.

As early as the second half of the 17th century, Russia's future development was the theme of social criticism. Contemporaries believed that far-reaching reform was an urgent necessity. Russia's access to the Baltic was of the greatest significance, since this was vital for the social and cultural renewal of the country. Those who demanded economic, social and cultural reforms in Russia included the statesmen Afanasi Lavrentevich Ordyn-Nastshokin, Count Artamon Sergeevich Matveev, Prince Vasili Vasilievich Golitsyn and the scholars and writers Yepifani Slavinetski, Simeon Polotski and Silvester Medvedev. They all recognized the importance of finding a rapid solution to Russia's backwardness. Their plans for reform, and the practical measures they had already taken in various fields, paved the way, to a certain extent, for the changes introduced by Peter I.

The historical merits of Peter Alekseevich (Tsar from 1682 and Emperor Peter the Great from 1721), the most attractive and talented ruler in Russian history, consist in his recognition of the social needs of his time and his attempts to take account of these in his work. Peter's rule completed the transition to absolute monarchy in Russia. The changes he introduced during his reign, the "Petrine" reforms, led to important changes in all sectors of social life, although they did not overstep the boundaries of the old order with its system of serfdom. On the contrary, the nobility was able to consolidate and extend its power. Although it is true that Peter's peasant reforms enabled some serfs to progress to other classes, in general the privately-owned peasant remained in a position of wretched social need which was only aggravated by the introduction of the poll-tax.

In the early 18th century, the nobility owned about 60 percent of the land as well as the serfs who worked it. As the previous tsar had also done, Peter I gave his associates and generals large estates, extending the property of the nobility to the northwest, south and southeast margins of the empire. Landowners demanded soccage and rent from the peasants on their land. This was compounded by the demands of the state, which were an additional burden on the shoulders of the peasantry. At the beginning of the 18th century, the peasant population of Russia fell into three main categories: privately-owned serfs, state peasants and appanage or court peasants. Labourers and domestic servants also made up a large percentage of serfs.

Privately-owned serfs, who were tied to the land and were the property of their master, lived in the most wretched conditions. Their situation was similar to that of rightless slaves, and they were totally at the mercy of their masters. Accordingly, their work was relatively unproductive. State peasants, who not uncommonly exercised a trade or business, and who were free countrymen in the eyes of the law, were in a much better position. They managed their own farms on state land, and had to pay quitrent, or *obrok*, to the treasury. These peasants were free, and could dispose of their la-

1 Inside a Russian peasant's cottage.
Etching by Jean Baptiste Le Prince, 1768.
Staatliche Bücher- und Kupferstichsammlung,
Greiz

bour as they saw fit. The appanage peasants, who worked the land of the Tsar's family, were in a similar position. Although, like the privately-owned serfs, they did not enjoy the rights of citizens, they were better off in economic and legal terms than the former. They were not liable for soccage, but instead paid a tax to the state appanage administration. The largest category of peasants in numerical terms was that of privately-owned serfs, followed by the state peasants. Until the abolition of serfdom in 1861, the former could be found mainly on the estates of European Russia, especially in the black-earth belt, where serfdom was predominant. State and appanage peasants, on the other hand, could be found mainly in the southern, eastern and northern extremities, which had been colonized at a later stage and had not been shared out among private landowners.

Thus there were few privately-owned serfs in Siberia, and no appanage peasants at all.

There were no legal standards regarding the extent of the peasant's obligations under Peter I. One of the most oppressive of duties to the state was liability to military conscription. Tens of thousands of young, healthy men of the peasant class were faced with a lifetime of service in Peter's army and navy. Losses, which were particularly high in times of war, were met by drafting fresh peasant recruits. Countless other peasants were put to work in

2 Loom and press.
Detail of the mark of the large manufactory in Yaroslavl, engraving by Aleksei Ivanovich Rostovtsev, mid-18th century. State Museum of History, Moscow

construction, building canals and fortresses. At any one time, 40,000 peasants would be engaged in the building of Russia's new capital, St. Petersburg; they were replaced at regular intervals. Similarly, tens of thousands of serfs helped to complete roads, dockyards and other projects.

According to statistics of 1722, Petrine Russia had 13 million inhabitants. Of these, 97.7 percent lived on the land. By 1742 the population of the Russian Empire, whose territory had increased dramatically, had risen to 16 million, and by 1796 to 36 million. No matter how much the energies of the nobility were put to use by Tsar Peter I, the heaviest burdens of his policies and reforms fell on the shoulders of the peasant population, whose importance he fully recognized, to the extent that he described the peasant serfs as the "arteries of the state", and demanded that they should be looked after and cared for, and not unduly burdened. He was also sharply critical of their being sold "individually like domestic animals". But of course, Peter's reform policies meant a further deterioration in the social position of the peasant serf, leaving him totally at the mercy of his master.

In contrast to the sad lot of the serfs, the Petrine state promoted the development of trade, commerce and manufacturing. It was under Peter I that mining was introduced in the Ural mountains. The economic policies of the Tsar had a strong fiscal character; they were based on mercantile principles and designed to meet military needs. Peter set about consolidating the economic base of the merchant class by taking measures to expand trade and industrial enterprise, to secure a trading surplus for Russia, to transfer part of state manufacturing into private hands, to grant subsidies to businessmen, etc. A special trade bureau, the "College of Commerce" as it was later known, was created. Consulates were also set up in other countries. Tsar Peter gave active support to annual fairs, which were important for domestic trade, dealt with the regulation of the stock exchange and market trade, built canals to improve freight transport, signed beneficial trade agreements with Persia and extended the exchange of goods with China and Central Asia.

Because of the increased military and economic role of the state, Peter I showed an extraordinary interest in the industrial development of the country. Consequently, his government was prepared to provide financial support from the treasury for merchants who wished to set up workshops. The serf economy, with its restricted social division of labour, could not develop into a large market of mass consumption, but the state bought increasing quantities of weapons, munitions and armaments for the army and navy from home manufacturers. This resulted in a close link between manufacturing and the state, a situation which assumed specific characteristics in the tsardom.

Manufactories in this period had their roots in peasant crafts and cottage industry, as well as in the soccage trades of the 17th century. There were over 200 manufactories in Peter's time, and a special "college" was created for them. Some were state-owned, others private. The latter belonged to noblemen and merchants, and included possessional manufactories. Most used serf labour for production, with the exception of those owned by foreigners and merchants, who did not have a labourforce of serfs.

State-owned factories produced weapons, sailcloth and saltpetre, but also encompassed cannon foundries and, to a large extent, the iron industry in the Urals. In the mid-18th century, this latter secured Russia the first place in world pig iron production, although this position soon had to be surrendered to England, since the Ural works clung to the use of a serf workforce, and consequently remained technically backward. A lack of financial means, and administrative difficulties in those enterprises which produced for the market, meant that the organization of industry in the form of state-owned factories soon had to be abandoned, resulting in the expansion of the private sector.

Peter I tried to compensate for the lack of workers, the main problem facing merchant manufacturers, by creating the category of so-called possessional serfs, by an *ukaz* of 1721. Their obligations included both farming the land and working in factories. The *ukaz* allowed merchants to purchase entire villages complete with serfs, on condition that those villages retained their connection with the factory in perpetuity and could only be sold together with the factory. Furthermore, the entire

Construction d'une Maison

Tartares du Kouban.

production of the possessional manufacturers was under the control of the government, to the extent that the government determined the volume of output, the number of articles, the quality of goods and so on. Thus the possessional manufactories were unwieldy institutions. Only a few noblemen were engaged in manufacturing in Peter's time, with the exception of cloth production.

This position changed only in the second half of the 18th century, when the nobility was granted extensive privileges by the government which were used in part to set up industrial enterprises.

The development of private manufacturing companies was closely linked with the evolution of the bourgeoisie. By transferring factories and works which had been built at the cost of the state to private individuals, the foundations were being laid for the private ownership of industry on a massive scale, as illustrated by the activities of the founding father of the industrial Demidov family, Nikita Demidovich Antufyev. The Demidovs built up a powerful financial empire in the Urals by means of state support. By the mid-18th century, 40 percent of Russian cast iron production came from works owned by the Demidov family.

Tsar Peter also called upon the support of merchants and entrepreneurs in the execution of state projects. Special bodies for mercantile and municipal self-government were created by administrative reform to improve the economic position of the cities; for example, the town councils *(ratusha)* and the mayoralties, and later the main municipal council, to which the two guilds of "regular" citizens—merchants, doctors and guild craftsmen—were subordinate. The population of the cities declined steadily in the face of recruitment campaigns and continually rising taxes. Like the peasants before them, the urban dwellers began to flee to the extremities of the empire. This meant a considerable increase in the size of the working population in the towns and settlements of the Ural area and Karelia. Such people represented the vast majority of the urban population there. However, as "common" citizens they were not entitled to work in the offices of municipal administration. Thus, alongside the old classes and strata of the nobility, the peasantry and the urban bourgeoisie, Russian society saw the beginnings of the modern bourgeoisie and the working class, which clearly heralded the bourgeois age in Russia.

State administrative reforms occupied a special place in the system of changes under Peter. These were directed towards strengthening the state apparatus and further centralizing power in Russia, and culminated in Russia's transformation into an empire in 1721. The governing senate took the place of the boyar *duma*, to which the boards which replaced the old *prikaz* (government office) system of administration were subordinate. More and more representatives of the aristocratic bureaucracy took up leading positions in state institutions. They were no longer chosen because of their noble lineage, however, but according to how well their personal abilities met the needs of the state. Peter also set up control bodies consisting of a procurator and the apparatus over which he presided. These measures included regional reform, dividing the country into *gubernii* (governments), provinces and districts.

These Petrine reforms favoured and strengthened the economic and political position of the Russian nobility. Decrees conceded to noblemen in the emperor's service the right to bequeath their property to their descendants. At the same time, it was stipulated that property

5—11 Genealogy of the Tsar's family. From Büsching, Magazin, *part 1, Halle 1767*

5 Tsar Aleksei Mikhailovich (1645—1676), father of Peter I, with his second wife, Natalia Kirillovna Naryshkina, mother of Peter I

6 Ivan Alekseevich, Peter I's half-brother and co-ruler (1682—1696), and Petr Alekseevich, later Tsar Peter I (the Great), and Emperor from 1721

7 Tsarevna Sofia Alekse-evna (regent 1682—1689), half-sister of Peter I

should be left to only one son and not shared out. The other sons were to serve the state in the civil administration, army or navy. The reason given for this order was that the division of property increased the burden on the peasants and increased their poverty even further, while at the same time leading to the decline of respected noble families. This *ukaz* completed the process of assimilation of inherited and earned wealth, and also led to the creation of an aristocratic class which no longer owned land.

In the Russia of Peter I, one's degree of nobility was measured by one's diligence. The Tsar and his aides created new ranks, and ennobled and advanced those whose achievements were great. The Table of Ranks of 1722 comprised 14 ranks, bringing civil and military grades into line with each other. State and military service opened up the prospect of elevation to the nobility to gifted commoners, so long as they were prepared to serve the state of Peter I. These individuals also became owners of land and the peasant serfs who worked it, and became typical representatives of the nobility, as shown by the examples of General Field Marshal Count Aleksandr Danilovich Menshikov, who sold pastries as a boy, Baron Petr Pavlovich Shafirov, Aleksei Aleksandrovich Kurbatov and Vasili Semyonovich Yershov: they all advanced in status from serfs to vice-governors.

Many new authorities emerged in the reorganization of the state administration. Thus the central departmental administrative councils,

with their many officials, replaced the older *prikaz* administration. The senate and councils were the second stage in the development of Russia's central administration.

One of the earliest and most important of Peter's reforms was that of the army, which was prompted by the defeats at Azov in 1695 and Narva in 1700. The reform led to the creation of a regular army and the construction of a Russian ocean-going fleet. Unlike the armies of mercenaries which existed in Western and Central Europe, Russia had compulsory military service. According to military regulations, military service was also compulsory for the nobility. Every nobleman had to begin his service as a common soldier. Domestic armaments factories, especially in Tula, made the Russian army independent and enabled a standing army to be established. With its thirty-two ships of the line, sixteen frigates and some one hundred smaller vessels, the Russian fleet was the largest in the Baltic by 1724. During the Northern War (1700—1721), Russia was allied with Denmark and Saxony-Poland against Sweden for vital access to the Baltic and, with its victory at Poltava in 1709 and the Peace of Nystad in 1721, it secured itself a position of dominance in the Baltic, destroying Sweden's position as a European great power.

Resistance to Peter's reforms was expressed in a conservative opposition. These opponents placed their hopes in Peter's incompetent son Aleksei; but his plans were to come to grief. Social protest against the regime of Peter I was expressed in the uprisings of the Bashkirs

(1705—11), the revolt of poor city-dwellers, conscripts and lowly Cossacks in Astrakhan and the surrounding area (1705/6), and in the peasant movement under Kondrati Afanasevich Bulavin (1707/8) on the Don and in the Ukraine.

Other important economic, social and cultural changes followed during the reigns of Peter the Great's successors, who occupied the Russian emperor's throne until the end of the 18th century. Capitalist elements became more pronounced. At the same time, serfdom was intensified. Important measures taken by the government in the second quarter of the century included the elimination of the state's monopoly on foreign trade and the abolition of internal customs duty. Trade and commerce increased, while new roads and canals were built. In the immediate aftermath of 1725, the landowning nobility succeeded in extending its privileges, which Peter had tried to restrict. Various regulations increased the financial burden on peasant serfs, while their obligations and duties increased. The peasants stepped up their resistance to social oppression. Unrest also became apparent amongst manufacturing workers, and in 1747 and 1755 the Bashkirs revolted again.

After the death of Peter I, the domestic scene was characterized by power struggles amongst groups of nobles. Under a rapid succession of emperors, each new emperor's protegées dominated the scene, and favouritism became all-important. In the period 1725 to 1761 alone, seven governments were overthrown. The em-

8 Empress Catherine I,
Peter I's second wife
(1725–1727)

9 Emperor Peter II,
son of Aleksei and grandson of
Peter I (1727–1730)

10 Empress Anna Ivanovna,
daughter of Ivan V Alekseevich,
step-niece of Peter I and widow
of the Duke of Courland
(1730–1740)

11 Empress Elizabeth
Petrovna, daughter of Peter I
(1741–1761)

peror's throne was occupied almost exclusively by women. Thus it was held by Catherine I (1725–1727), the wife of Peter I; Peter II (1727–1730), his grandson; Anna Ivanovna (1730–1740), the daughter of Peter I's half-brother Ivan Alekseevich; Ivan VI (1740 to 1741), a year-old infant; Elizabeth (1741 to 1761), the daughter of Peter the Great, and Peter III (1761–1762), the Duke of Holstein-Gottorp and grandson of Peter I.

Until the early 1760s, Russian foreign policy was dominated by its close contacts with Austria, Prussia and Saxony-Poland, with intensive economic, cultural and dynastic interrelations. Russia gained a dominating influence over Poland and Courland, which belonged constitutionally to the Polish crown. In the War of the Polish Succession (1733–1735), Augustus III of Saxony became King of Poland with Russian support. General Field-Marshal Burkhard Christoph Münnich finally conquered the Crimea and Ochakov for the first time in the coalition war with Austria against the Turks (1735–1739). The Treaty of Belgrade in 1739 finally ceded Azov to Russia.

Under Empress Elizabeth, i. e. in the forties and fifties, Russia's foreign policy developed along the lines of European cabinet policy. The events of the greatest import were the intervention of the Empire in the War of the Austrian Succession (1740–1748) and in the Seven Years' War (1756–1763). Sweden's war of retaliation against the tsardom (1741–1743) was a failure. The Peace of Åbo gave Empress Elizabeth southeastern Finland.

Russia's participation in the Seven Years' War as an opponent of Prussia greatly increased her prestige as a major European power.

By the second half of the 18th century the clear outlines of bourgeois society were already apparent in the country. Russian works and factories were still often reliant upon serf labour, because capitalism was developing more slowly than in other parts of Europe, and clinging to the feudal order and to the system of serfdom.

Capitalist methods of manufacture, and the use of free wage-labourers, were highly significant, particularly in cotton processing. The development of peasant manufactories was also important.

Increasing the serfs' output was the main means of improving the productivity of the nobles' estates in the second half of the 18th century. The *obrok* was increased almost five-fold, and the sale of serfs, as recruits or otherwise, became commonplace. The economic basis of the nobility was reinforced by massive loans and gifts of state and appanage land together with the peasants living thereon to noblemen and the favourites of the ruler. This meant a significant increase in the number of rightless privately-owned peasants. Even the state peasants' independent farms began to fall into decline, and itinerant landworkers became a common sight.

All in all, serfs made up more than 50 percent of Russia's total population. (At the end of the 18th century the percentage of people living in the towns was 4.1%.)

12 Peter III
(Tsar 1761/62), son of Anna Petrovna and Duke Karl Friedrich of Holstein-Gottorp, husband of the Princess of Anhalt-Zerbst, later to become Catherine II. Reduced facsimile of the mezzotint engraving by Johann Stenglin after the painting by G. C. Grooth

The incipient crisis in the serf order and the intensification of social struggles led to mass unrest among the peasants and revolt by manufacturing workers in the sixties, culminating in the great Peasants' Revolt under Emelyan Pugachev in the Ural and Volga region (1773–1775). This was the greatest peasant movement in Russian history. The rebels, who demanded the abolition of serfdom, were recruited from various sectors of the population; from Cossacks, miners and factory workers, peasant serfs and from numerous non-Russian

13 Proclamation of the
coronation of Catherine II
in Moscow.
*Engraving by Aleksei
Yakovlevich Kolpashnikov,
drawing by Jean de Velly*

14 Gala dinner of Cather-
ine II in the Throne Room
of the Moscow Kremlin.
*Engraving by Aleksei
Yakovlevich Kolpashnikov,
drawing by Jean de Velly*

Russia becomes a world power

15/16 Medal commemorating the accession to the throne of Catherine II.
Reverse: St. Petersburg presents the Russian crown to Catherine. From Brückner, Katharina II, Berlin 1883

17 Prince Repnin is granted an audience by the Turkish Sultan, 1775. Engraving by Ivan Bugreev

peoples. The *Pugachevshchina* also had a marked influence on Russian intellectual life. It was crushed by the military, and Emelyan Pugachev, who had been masquerading as Tsar Peter III, was executed in Moscow in January 1775.

The pressure of these social uprisings and revolts led to the development of a revolutionary-democratic ideology in Russia in the second half of the 18th century whose main proponent was Aleksandr Nikolaevich Radishchev. Empress Catherine II, who was born Princess Sophie of Anhalt-Zerbst, became the wife of Tsar Peter III and ascended the imperial throne in 1762, initially represented the so-called enlightened absolutism, for she and her advisers initiated projects to alleviate serfdom, although there were no fundamental social reforms. Neither did Russia receive the promised constitution under Catherine II. The reform of the *guberniya* in 1775 increased the power of the nobility and the tsarist autocracy. The municipal statutes of 1785 brought only the beginnings of communal self-administration, which proved to be impracticable. In the same year, 1785, Catherine II published the *Charter to the Nobility* proclaiming the freedom of the nobility. In her peasant laws, the Empress gave noblemen the right to banish, deport or subject to forced labour any disobedient peasant serf. Subsequently peasants could be sold, pawned or auctioned independently of land and separated from their families.

In terms of foreign policy, it was under Empress Catherine II that Russia rose to the position of a world power. Following the successful solution of the Baltic question under Peter I, the tsardom had achieved dominance in Poland and became a force to be reckoned with in European politics. The integration of Russia's economy with that of the rest of Europe increased, and the economic necessity of exporting the tsardom's grain in particular made access to and control of the Black Sea a principal objective of Russian foreign policy. Russia's struggle against Turkey encouraged the national liberation movement of the Balkan peoples, who drew closer to the tsardom.

Catherine's troops won major victories in the Russo-Turkish Wars (1768—1774 and 1787—1792). The Danube principalities of Moldavia and Walachia were occupied and the coastal regions around the Sea of Azov, as well as the Crimea, were annexed. Russia consolidated her right to free shipping on the Black Sea and unhindered passage through the Bosphorus. At the same time, Catherine II made East Georgia a protectorate of the Russian Empire. The German colonists of the Volga summoned to the country by the Empress were granted personal freedom, self-administration and other privileges when they settled. The situation in the steppes of southern Russia and around the Black Sea was similar. Here, Russian and Serb settlers founded numerous cities and villages, such as Nikolayev, Odessa, Sevastopol, Yekaterinoslav, and others. Russian settlements even sprang up in Alaska during the eighties.

As for Russia's Western policy in the second half of the 18th century, Catherine II's troops

18 Emelian Ivanovich Pugachev.
The leader of the greatest uprising of Cossacks and peasants in Russian history, from 1773 to 1775 in the Ural and Volga regions, he was executed in Moscow in 1775 on the orders of Catherine II. Pugachev claimed to the people to be Peter III, and demanded the abolition of serfdom. Contemporary handbill

19 *Authority of Catherine II to conclude the agreement on the third partition of Poland in December 1794. Zentrales Staatsarchiv, Merseburg*

20 *Russia in the early 18th century. General map of the Russian Empire from the Atlas of Johann Baptiste Homann, Nuremberg 1725. Forschungsbibliothek, Gotha*

imposed the election of Stanislaw Augustus Poniatowski as King of Poland in 1764. In 1772, the first partition of Poland took place between Russia, Austria and Prussia, with the second in 1793 between Russia and Prussia and the third in 1795 between Russia, Austria and Prussia. Russia's mediation in the War of Bavarian Succession (1777—1779) between Austria and Prussia culminated in the Peace of Teschen. In 1780 Catherine II supported the American War of Independence with her declaration of "armed neutrality". Russia's war against Sweden (1788—1790) ended in the Peace of Vârala, which confirmed the status quo. In 1794, Russian troops under Field-Marshal Count Aleksandr Vasilievich Suvorov crushed the Polish uprising under Tadeusz Kościuszko. Catherine's Polish policy was also directed against the French Revolution. The new emperor Paul (1796—1801), son of Catherine II, continued Russia's campaign against revolutionary France.

All in all, the 18th century signalled the beginning of a new epoch in Russia's evolution. The historian Heinrich Storch wrote in the first part of his *Historisch-Statistisches Gemälde des Russischen Reiches am Ende des achtzehnten Jahrhunderts* (Historic-statistical table of the Russian Empire at the end of the eighteenth century), published in 1797: "We are approaching the end of a century which will remain a curiosity for ever in the annals of mankind because of its many extraordinary events. One of the most important phenomena of this period is without doubt the moral and

political transformation of a vast and powerful people, whose latent powers were awakened as if by an electric shock, and were transformed into the most astounding activity. Russia, which had previously been a little known and little feared empire, suddenly made an appearance among the European states at the beginning of this century and, after a short test of its strength, became the arbiter and decisive power of the north. The entire state system of Europe has assumed a different form; the in-

fluence of the Nordic eagle has spread to the Adriatic Sea and the Tagus, while the terror of its thunderbolts makes the Hellespont and the Caucasus tremble. European culture has been extended to a new, immense region and is rooted on the Neva and the Irtysh; a new world is being opened up to trade, and the arts, mores, luxury, virtues and burdens of Western Europe are being given a willing reception in the steppes of Eastern Asia and on the inhospitable shores of the Arctic Ocean."

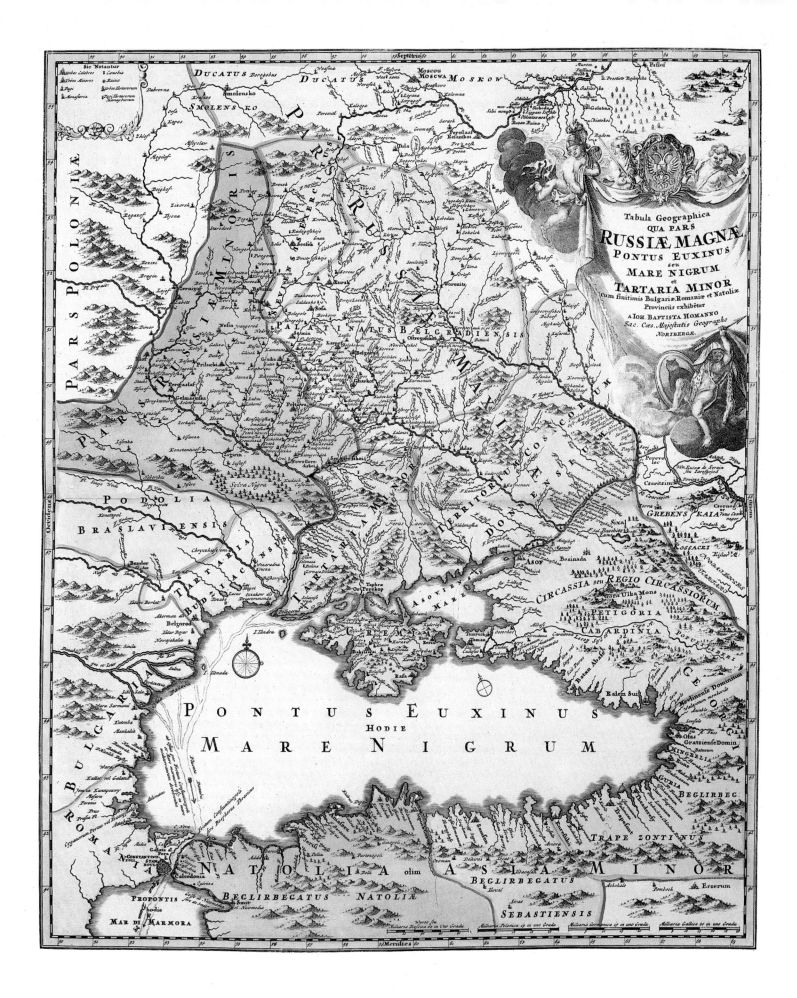

21 *Russian peasant's cottage.*
Etching by Jean Baptiste Le Prince, 1768.
Staatliche Bücher- und Kupferstichsammlung,
Greiz

22 *A Russian peasant woman taking eggs, butter*
and fruit to sell at the market.
Etching by Jean Baptiste Le Prince, 1764.
Staatliche Bücher- und Kupferstichsammlung,
Greiz

de Prince 1764.

23 Russian peasant
in traditional rural dress. From Weber,
Die Russen, Innsbruck 1787

24 Pavel Nikolaevich Demidov.
He belonged to one of the first capitalist families of industrialists in Russia,
which used Petrine reforms in the field
of manufacturing to build up an
enormous industrial empire. Painting
by Dmitri Grigorievich Levitski, 1773.
State Tretyakov Gallery, Moscow

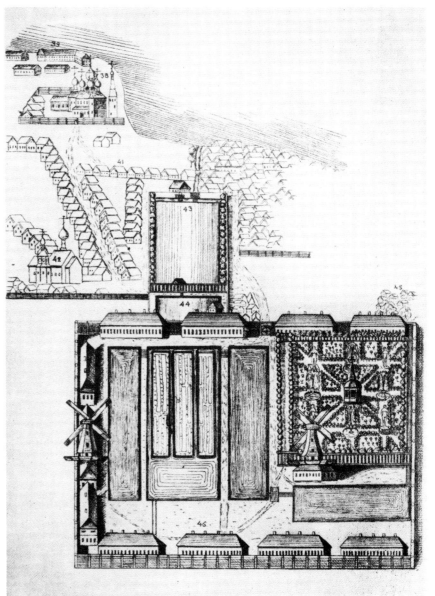

25 Metalworks.
Watercolour from Georg Wilhelm von Hennin,
Beschreibung der Werke im Ural und in Sibirien,
1735. State Museum of History, Moscow

26 The great manufactory in Yaroslavl.
Engraving (detail) by Aleksei Ivanovich
Rostovtsev, 1731. State Museum of History,
Moscow

27–29 *Worker at the arms factory in Tula. Late 18th century. State Museum of History, Moscow*

30 *Ivan Satrapezny, factory owner. Chromolithograph by an unknown artist, 18th century. State Museum of History, Moscow*

31 *The bazaar in Simferopol.*
Engraving by Geissler, ca. 1804

32 *Selling frozen meat at market.*
Engraving by Geissler, ca. 1804

33 *At the Battle of Narva on 19th (30th) November 1700, the Russian troops were soundly defeated by the Swedish army, led by Charles XII. Copper engraving by Peter Schenk after Romoyn de Hooghe, 1700. Staatliche Kunstsammlungen Dresden, Kupferstichkabinett*

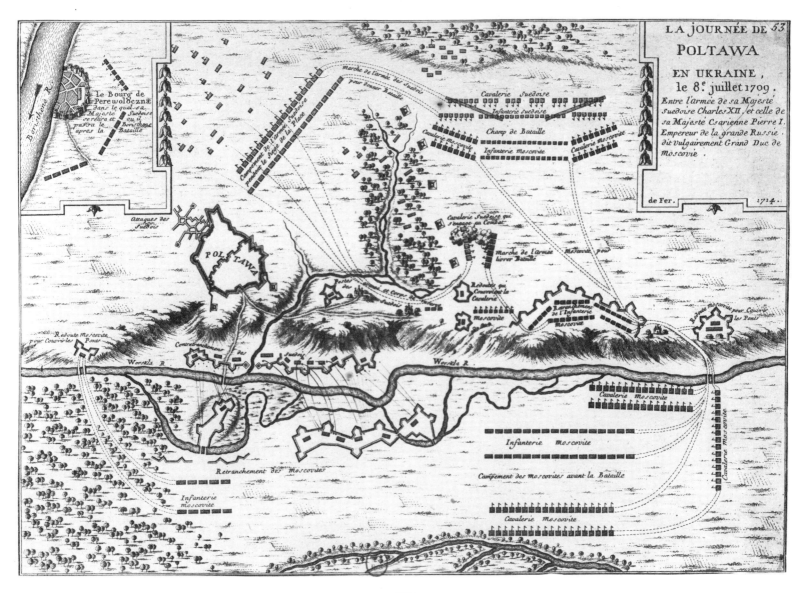

*34 Plan of the Battle of Poltava
on 27th June (8th July) 1709.
Contemporary copper engraving by Nole
de Fer. Bibliothèque Nationale, Paris*

*35 Medal struck to commemorate
the victory of the Russian troops over
the Swedish army at the Battle
of Poltava in 1709. Bibliothèque
Nationale, Paris*

36 *Peter I Alekseevich (the Great), 1672–1725.*
Together with his half-brother Ivan V Alekseevich,
he became joint Tsar at the age of ten, and in
1689 he became regent. His step-sister Sofia was
banished to a convent. He pursued his programme
of reforms, which laid the foundations for
Russia's later status as a major power, with
inexhaustible energy and determination, coupled
with impatience and a violent temper. Painting by
Gottfried Kneller. Staatliche Schlösser und
Gärten, Potsdam-Sanssouci

37 *Empress Catherine II Alekseevna*
(1762–1796),
née Princess of Anhalt-Zerbst, wife of Peter III.
As a representative of enlightened absolutism, she
corresponded with leading French rationalists and
implemented reforms in Russia. After the French
Revolution in 1789, she took draconian measures
to suppress progressive movements at home. Her
aggressive foreign policy helped Russia to become
a world power.

38 *Aleksandr Vasilievich Suvorov,*
the unvanquished generalissimo of the Russian
army in the wars waged by Catherine II.

39 *Grigori Grigorievich Orlov,*
a favourite of Catherine II. Together with his
brother, he was responsible for the violent death
of her husband, Peter III, who had previously
abdicated the throne. Engraving after a painting
by Fedor Stepanovich Rokotov

40 *Field-Marshal Grigori Aleksandrovich*
Potemkin,
an adviser and favourite of Catherine II. Medal
struck to commemorate the journey to the Crimea
of Catherine II and the German Kaiser Joseph II
in 1787, which prompted Turkey to declare war.
Engraving after the obverse of the medal by Carl
Leberecht (original size), from Brückner,
Katharina II, 1883

41 *Brilliant victory of the Russian fleet over the Turks in the Bay of Chesme on 25th/ 26th June (6th/7th July) 1770. This victory gave Russia free navigation in the Black Sea. This was put in writing in the Treaty of Küchük Kainardshi of 1774, which also guaranteed Russia free passage through the Bosphorus, and allowed it to become the most influential and powerful force in the politics of southeastern Europe by ceding to it Kerch, Yenikale and the Kabardas. Copper engraving by Pierre Charles Canot and William Watts after a painting by Richard Paton*

42 *Storming by Potemkin of the Turkish stronghold of Ochakov on the northwest coast of the Black Sea on 6th (17th) December 1788. Engraving by Adam von Bartsch after a painting by François Casanova*

Following page:

43 *Dividing up the cake. Allegoric sheet on the first partition of Poland in 1772. Copper engraving by Noël Lemire. Deutsche Staatsbibliothek, Berlin*

THE EARLY ENLIGHTENMENT AND PETER'S CONCEPT OF THE STATE

DURING THE REIGN of Peter I, Russian history began to quicken its pace. "We are no longer growing in centuries, but in decades", Karamzin was later to write. This was particularly true of cultural development, which penetrated all spheres of Russian society after Peter. It was the Tsar himself who recognized, as no other, the importance of the economy, trade, education and science for Russia's development. From the outset, the cultural measures taken by his government were very closely related to the economic and social needs of the country. One of Peter's exploits was the scientific exploration of the eastern vastnesses of his enormous empire. Tobolsk in Siberia and Astrakhan where the Volga flows into the Caspian Sea did not become mere administrative centres, but expanded principally into major economic and trading centres. Important schools and training institutes sprang up in quick succession, and these were the bases for major scientific expeditions to the south and east, reaching as far as China.

The monarch directed his attention particularly to the promotion of Russian city life and the establishment of new communities. One example of this is the founding of the Empire's new capital, St. Petersburg. In addition, innumerable new roads and canals were built. The new schools, institutes, scientific institutions and centres of the arts which were established transformed the philosophy, emotions and the taste of the Russian people and encouraged the emergence of modern architecture, painting and literature. Scientific writing and belles let-tres gained particular significance. His journeys to Central and Western Europe strengthened Tsar Peter's resolve to give as many as possible of his Russian countrymen the opportunity of studying and training abroad. To this end, he charged young noblemen with the task of learning languages in the West and becoming thoroughly conversant with the sciences, medicine and technology. Consequently, Russian students were matriculated at many foreign universities; at first, in places of learning such as Amsterdam and Venice, but later also in Wittenberg, Halle, Jena, Leipzig, Göttingen and elsewhere. The foreign study ordered by Peter's government was very closely linked with the duty prescribed for the nobility to serve in the administrative sector, army and navy. When they returned from foreign parts, the former students were bound to accept, without delay, the tasks to which they were assigned.

As early as 1696, sixty-one young noblemen, including twenty-three sons of princes, were directed to travel to the West, at their own expense, and in particular to Holland, England and Italy, and to seek detailed instruction there in shipbuilding and other related technologies. As for the Tsar himself, all through his life he made it a principle never to ask anyone to do anything he would not do himself. He observed and learned passionately as no other Russian tsar or grand duke had done before him. From the outset, there was resistance to this conception of the role of the ruler. The horror in conservative boyar circles was all the greater when it was rumoured that the Tsar himself wished to go abroad. This signified a complete break with ancient tradition. On 6th December 1696 the Tsar announced that a mission would travel to Germany, Holland, England and Venice, and on 9th March 1697 the delegation set off on its great expedition to Europe. Its declared intention was to create a strong coalition to fight the Turks. This Grand Embassy, which was to last eighteen months, caused a sensation in Europe and aroused very strong emotions.

Tsar Peter tried to keep his trip to Europe secret, not only in Russia, but also abroad. The first stops made by the Russian ruler were in Swedish Livonia and Polish Courland, then in Prussia. From Prussia, he made a brief stop in Hanover before moving on to Holland. The Tsar clearly wished to arrive there without delay. In Zaandam he took lodgings with a blacksmith whom he had met in the foreigners' quarter in Moscow. Tsar Peter apprenticed himself to the Rogge firm as a ship's carpenter. This work gave him an opportunity to take a good look round the shipyards. Predictably, he was surrounded by numerous admirers and curious onlookers who had realized long since that he was none other than the Tsar of Russia. Peter did similar work in Amsterdam, where he was able to acquaint himself with the shipyards of the East India Company.

Tsar Peter spent a total of four-and-a-half months in Amsterdam. During this period, he took part in fleet manoeuvres, visited artisans' workshops, hospitals and the Botanic Garden,

44 Peter I gives young noblemen instructions regarding their study abroad (1697).

45 Arrival of the Russian legation at The Hague on 25th September 1697. Engraving by Daniel Marot, early 18th century

46 Natural history collection in The Hague, which was visited by the Tsar on his first trip to Europe in 1697/98. Peter I was passionately fond of such institutions. The collection which he himself made is today housed in the art gallery of the Academy of Sciences in Leningrad. Copper engraving by Andries van Buysen after Bernardi Picart, ca. 1700. Staatliche Kunstsammlungen Dresden, Kupferstichkabinett

and attended the anatomy classes of Professor Frederik Ruysch. He also visited Utrecht, The Hague, Delft and Leyden, where he met the famous anatomist Hermannus Boerhaave and also became acquainted with the well-known naturalist Antonius van Leeuwenhoek. On other occasions he was instructed in copper-engraving and the use of fire-extinguishers. Leeuwenhoek introduced the Tsar to the wonders of the microscope, and the architect Simon Schynvoet showed him his natural science collection. The Russian ruler spent many hours in the workshops of the mechanic van der Hey-

den. The engineer and military writer van Coehorn introduced the Tsar to Dutch engineers who entered Russia's service. At the same time, Coehorn arranged for Russian students to be instructed in military science. Peter also established contact with Dutch merchants, for example with members of the Thessing family, which had commercial ties with his homeland. It was thanks to the Thessing firm that Tsar Peter succeeded in establishing a Russian printshop in Amsterdam.

Peter arrived in England in January 1698. There the Russian ruler was to see and learn much that he had missed in Holland. In contrast to the Dutch, who built their ships according to age-old traditions, the English placed a high value on a knowledge of mathematics and physics and on technical instruments. The shipbuilder Admiral Carmarthen took the Tsar all over the country, and told him everything he wished to know. They inspected iron works, bridges, docks and other structures. In Deptford the Tsar was also visited by the famous Quaker William Penn, who tried to win him over to his way of thinking.

The Tsar once again worked in the docks during his stay in England, and attended fleet manoeuvres. He showed an apparent lack of interest in the English Parliament. At the beginning of May, he returned to Holland, and by the end of the month he was already on his way to Vienna via Kleve, Bielefeld, Hildesheim, Halle, Leipzig, Dresden and Prague, arriving in the Imperial City on 26th June 1698.

The Russian monarch abandoned his final destination of Venice because his plans for Turkey had failed, once and for all, at the Viennese court. This was what decided him to return home. His hurried return to Russia was made all the more urgent by the news that the streltsy palace guard in Moscow had mutinied. Peter's "Grand Embassy" was more successful as a scientific and technical voyage of discovery than as a diplomatic mission. It not only aroused controversy at home, but was also a great talking-point in the West. Countless legends were born; it was, after all, the first time that a Russian tsar had visited foreign countries to serve an apprenticeship. Albert Lortzing was later to erect a permanent memorial to Peter's visit to Holland with his popular opera *Zar und Zimmermann* (Tsar and Carpenter).

Despite the significance for Russia's cultural development of Peter's first foreign journey in 1697/98, his subsequent trips, especially that of 1716/17, which took him to Paris, were much more important. The shorter visits of 1711 and 1712/13 which were sandwiched between these two major expeditions took him exclusively to Germany and Bohemia, and particularly to the waters at Carlsbad. Their scientific and historical significance resides mainly in the fact that it was here that Peter I and Leibniz were to come face to face.

In February 1716 the Tsar set out on what was to be his longest and most important journey, in terms of both cultural and scientific history, to Western Europe. At this point in his life, the

The early Enlightenment and Peter's concept of the state

forty-five year old could look back at the great success, not only in politics, but also in the field of finance and culture, of his reforms. The somewhat youthful wonder of the Russian monarch on his first trip to Europe in the face of the technical and scientific achievements of the advanced countries of the West had given way to a genuine, purposeful and much more extensive thirst for knowledge.

The travel diary of Peter I gives us an indication of the work which occupied him on his second visit to Holland. On one occasion he saw "East and West Indian shells and birds", while on another he visited the country retreat of his chargé d'affaires Christoffel Brant, in whose park he strolled, he also went to the theatre. State politics were apparently forgotten: it was as if the Russian ruler were seeking peace and relaxation and intellectual contemplation. Even the art galleries he had scorned in England began to attract him. Similarly, Peter occupied himself greatly with garden designs with a view to those which were to be laid out at Petrodvorets. He left Amsterdam for The Hague, going on to Leyden, where he attended the university as he had done twenty years before; he took note of its syllabus and the way it was laid out. In Brussels he visited the Cathedral of Ste. Gudule. He then travelled to Ghent, Bruges and Dunkirk, reaching Calais on 25th April 1717, where he set his sights on Paris.

Peter's stay in Paris was of major importance for his conception of science and his cultural policy. The Tsar attended the Sorbonne, and declared himself much impressed. Immediately before his departure, he was invited to attend a special session of the Paris Academy of Sciences held in his honour. The assembled scholars were at pains to show Peter everything new and extraordinary which was to be found in the field of experimental science. A model of a water pump was demonstrated, chemical experiments were performed, the illustrations for a publication on the history of

47 *Execution of the streltsy
at a convent near Moscow, 1698. From Korb,*
Diarium, *Vienna 1700*

art were exhibited, and much more. In its session of 22nd December 1717 the Paris Academy agreed unanimously to adopt the Tsar as a member.

This last great foreign expedition of 1716/17 greatly broadened the intellectual horizons of the Tsar. He was now familiar with almost all fields of contemporary culture and science. His interest in all the wonders of nature and his pleasure in art collections and curiosities which were clearly discernible in 1697/98, had given way to more profound insights. The spontaneous visits of the first expedition had evolved into purposeful examination and learning. Peter demonstrated clearly his taste and his enjoyment of beautiful works, as witnessed by his viewing of painting and architectural works. Building in Russia was to reveal how strongly he was influenced by French Baroque. His vastly increased understanding of culture and science was reflected in his greater association with leading scholars and artists, in his large-scale purchase of books and in other ways too. In the face of these increased cultural and scientific needs, even the important requirements of practical politics and diplomacy in the tsardom were overshadowed; Peter handed over responsibility for these to his associates and advisers, to a large degree. When he first came to power, Peter was without doubt inspired to a large extent by the hardworking, active and practical Dutch, as well as by the Germans. But what he missed in Holland and Germany he found in abundance in France: a highly developed, vibrant, creative cultural and scientific world which was unequalled in Europe at the beginning of the 18th century.

In order to ensure that Russia kept abreast of economic and social developments in the advanced countries of Europe, the necessary measures had to be introduced. Peter I was assisted in the implementation of his educational and scientific policies by experienced advisers. These included Russians, Ukrainians and non-Russians, many of whom had been born in the tsardom. They had names like Prokopovich, Shafirov, Bruce, Blumentrost, Areskin, Tatishchev, Kirilov, Vinius, Matveev, Gordon, Lefort, Sheremetev and Apraksin. The services of many experts were needed to improve the economy, trade, industry, education and science. A large number of these had to be recruited abroad and committed to Russian service. This practice of recruiting foreigners for the work in the tsardom demanded religious tolerance in particular on the part of the state; of course, the patriarch and the orthodox bishops wished to have nothing to do with such tolerance. The Church authorities felt that, if the assistance of foreigners was absolutely vital in Russia, their activities should be strictly controlled. To make this task easier, foreigners working in Russia were settled in areas apart from the towns, in foreign quarters, at the instigation of the ecclesiastical prelates.

But the regency of Peter's half-sister Sofia Alekseevna (1682—1689) had already spoken out for tolerance towards aliens working in Russia. Thus the *ukaz* of 26th January 1689

invited the French Huguenots to Russia, with a guarantee of complete religious freedom. In 1692, then again in 1702, Peter I upheld this decree, extending it to cover all creeds. The Tsar's encounter with the Quaker William Penn, and his stay in England, obviously convinced him that in Russia, too, the Church had to take second place to the needs of society and the State. Along with Switzerland and the Netherlands, England was one of the first countries in Europe to overcome denominational absolutism, not least thanks to Thomas Hobbes, who prepared the ground for this. In the tsardom, on the other hand, Church and State proved still to be closely allied. Just as in the past, the patriarch occupied a throne of equal importance to that of the tsar in the Kremlin Coronation Church in Moscow, and prelate and monarch governed Russia together. As soon as a tsar found himself in difficulties, he would seek refuge, as the young Peter had done, in the monastery at Zagorsk, not far from Moscow.

Peter I recognized at an early stage the importance of religious tolerance for Russia's development into a modern state. He was helped to reach this conclusion by Lefort and Gordon, later to become generals, who had a lasting influence on the young monarch in Preobrazhenskoye. François Lefort, who was a latitudinarian Calvinist, and Patrick Gordon, a staunch Catholic, advocated far-reaching religious tolerance, despite their different religious views, in sharp contrast to the dogmas of the Orthodox Church. Ioakim, the Patriarch, and

48/49 Diary of Peter the Great
on his experiences abroad. Title page and
frontispiece.

his advisers regarded the exercises, war games and exuberance of Preobrazhenskoye, which were organized by men of other creeds, as a threat to the one true faith, and accordingly warned Peter repeatedly of their misgivings. But even then the young ruler, of whom much was being anticipated, had a vision of a new Russia preparing to do battle with the rest of Europe in finance, culture and science.

In his edicts of tolerance, Peter I used all his power as a ruler against the Orthodox Church. It was not religious considerations which moved the Tsar, but the economic, social and political needs of the new age which was dawning even in Russia. Naturally enough, the supporters of the old order and of the autocratic Church had no intention of accepting these edicts without a show of resistance. They prepared for battle; after all, for the high clergy it was also a matter of holding on to their former positions of power in old Russia. In this, all the rich prelates found the support of broad sections of the powerful families of boyars and princes. Even members of the Tsar's own family, such as his first wife Yevdokiya and his son Aleksei, defected to the growing opposition, whose spokesmen tried to discredit Peter as a heretic.

The rapidly growing antagonism of these conflicts represented a life and death struggle. "Bearded men"—representatives of the all-powerful Church and of the *starshina*, of all that was traditional, used every means to thwart Peter's intention of subordinating the Church to the needs of society and the State; it was they who were behind the streltsy uprising of 1689 and,

even more openly, the uprising of 1698. But even before his first foreign trip in 1697/98, the Tsar had succeeded in imposing state control on the income and expenditure of the Church, and in compelling prelates to keep annual records of their expenditures. This allowed the ruler to introduce financial control over the Church by the State, and the *ukaz* of 30th December 1701 transferred the administration of monastery estates to a special monastery *prikaz*.

Peter's strict command that all beards should be shaved was a particularly symbolic element of his struggle against the ideology of the Orthodox Church. After 1705 a tax was levied on bearded men, in proportion to their income. The patriarchate was the focus of resistance to Peter's measures; he was described with increasing frequency by the high clergy as an "Antichrist" on the imperial throne. A militant patriarch at the head of the opposition which was rising up against the ruler might have been a dangerous antagonist, so after the death of Adrian in 1700 the monarch left the patriarchate vacant. He merely appointed a *locum tenens*, an exarch. The man selected for this task was Yavorski, the learned rector of the Mohyla College in Kiev, who was at the same time created Metropolitan of Ryazan.

Stefan Yavorski enjoyed an international reputation as a scholar, and his interests as a clergyman were many. He seemed to Peter to be the most suitable man for the office of exarch. But soon even he stood up in opposition to the Tsar. In an attempt to bind Yavorski, as far as

50 *Meeting of Peter I and the French King Louis XV on 11th May 1717 in the Louvre. Bibliothèque Nationale, Paris*

possible, to the State and to his own will, Peter left him at the head of the Orthodox Church until his death in 1722, rejecting his many attempts to resign his office. In comparison to the strict, old orthodox opposition, Yavorski, who was pro-Catholic, appeared to the ruler to be the lesser of two evils.

Of the intellectual conflicts which were fought out during the reign of Peter I, the attitude to scholasticism was central. Thinkers and theologists such as Yavorski and Feofilakt Lopatinski, the rector of the ecclesiastical academy in Moscow, were very careful to ensure that no enlightened thinking penetrated the ideology of the Orthodox Church. Such men made it impossible for Peter to realize his aim of clearing the way for social progress in Russia. In order to push through his plans for reform, however, the monarch needed the cooperation of high Church prelates who would place themselves unreservedly in the service of society and the State. What Peter needed was an intellectually outstanding colleague and ideologist, who had not only to be a convinced supporter of tsarist absolutism, but also a scholar in many fields and a talented writer. He finally found such a man in Bishop Prokopovich.

Feofan Prokopovich, of Ukrainian origin like Yavorski, and a pupil of the latter, attended the Jesuit Gregorian University in Rome for a time. He became professor of poetry, rhetoric and philosophy at the Kiev Academy in 1704, where he was rector from 1711 to 1716. The monarch's attention was drawn to him by his tragicomedy *Vladimir*, produced in 1705, a

work which attacked social injustice and ignorance, and the sermon he delivered in 1709 on the occasion of the victory at Poltava showed quite unmistakeably the enlightened attitude of this theologian. Feofan was able to win the Tsar's trust in a very short time. Once he was appointed to direct the Kiev Academy, the new rector began to work for social progress throughout Russia. In 1718 Peter promoted him Bishop of Pskov, entrusting him with the elaboration of a Church order corresponding to the state collegiate system.

Unlike Yavorski with his catholicizing tendencies and plans, Prokopovich proved to be a radical opponent of the Papal Church. He was an outspoken champion of reform, drawing his inspiration from Protestant literature, and displayed a clear affinity for an Established Church in which enlightened ideas were predominant. Here Prokopovich's theological and social ideas underwent a noticeable change. While his main concern in the Kiev speeches had been the metaphysical, the St. Petersburg period saw a shift to preoccupation with

worldly affairs. In Peter I, Prokopovich saw a ruler who was striving to improve the lot of his subjects and who was concerned with the salvation of his people. He appeared to him as the embodiment of the victorious power of man, freed of mystical hero-worship, and endowed with human features. This image of the ruler was to have a not insignificant impact on the ethical and political consciousness-building of that and the subsequent period of history. "Many rulers", said Prokopovich to Peter, "rule in such a way that the common people cannot understand the function of the ruler. But you alone have shown that it is a matter of the highest rank and dignity to take all the labours and burdens onto your own shoulders, and even if you were to tire of your high station, we should still see you as a master of all trades and a working man in imperial guise."

Prokopovich's sermons in St. Petersburg comprised an appeal to all to cooperate with Peter's reforms, and extolled the virtues of work, glorifying him as the supreme worker. Idleness and indolence were condemned. Prokopovich made it clear that only through an enormous effort would Russia be able to overcome her economic and technological backwardness. But forward-looking plans were also needed to bring the country onto the road to progress.
It is clear from all of Prokopovich's writings that Peter and his associates saw the raison d'être of Peter's enlightened social ideology in overcoming Russia's economic and technological backwardness. One of their main postulates, apart from the promotion of science and technology, was the education of the people. Prokopovich drew his ideas from a wealth of learned works in his library, and not merely

51 Colonel of the streltsy.
Etching by Jean Baptiste Le Prince, 1768.
Staatliche Bücher- und Kupferstichsammlung,
Greiz

52 Streltsy soldier.
Etching by Jean Baptiste Le Prince, 1768.
Staatliche Bücher- und Kupferstichsammlung,
Greiz

53 Moscow Kremlin.
From Olearius, Reisebeschreibung, *1656*

from actual conditions in Russia. His main task as Peter's associate was to lay the ideological foundations of absolute monarchy. He put forward the view that, in the current situation, the necessary reforms could only be carried out under a strong absolute monarchy. Thus in his sermon on the *Power and Glory of the Tsar* in 1718, and in the tract on *The Right of the*

Monarch's Will in 1722, he defended the unrestricted power of the absolute ruler, which was derived from the Bible and natural law.

As early as 1718, Peter commissioned Prokopovich to write a memorandum on the effectiveness of an Ecclesiastical College. This *Description and Assessment of an Ecclesiastical College*, as it was first called by Prokopovich, was a long tract which outlined the advantages of collegial Church government, proposed official and administrative regulations and listed countless basic guidelines for a reform of the school system and of education. After it had been approved and personally revised by Peter I, Prokopovich's draft of a new Church order attained the force of law, and appeared on 25th January 1721 unter the title *Ecclesiastical Regulation*. It bore the signatures of the Tsar, several senators and many high clergymen, most of whom had been forced to sign against their will.

The regulation decreed that an "Ecclesiastical College" was to take the place of the patriarchate as head of the Church. This college was later to be known as the "Most Holy All-Ruling Synod". In its capacity as a leading council of bishops and archimandrites with supreme clerical authority, whose functions included the regulation of Church affairs, religious education and the supervision of the clergy, the Synod represented to a certain extent the principle of orthodox conciliarity and accordingly was recognized as demanded by the Tsar, by the patriarchs of Constantinople and Antioch. In accordance with the structure

of the other colleges, the Synod had a president and two vice-presidents. The first president was the former exarch Stepan Yavorski, who was succeeded after his death in 1722 by Feofan Prokopovich. Like officials and the military, the members of the Synod had to sign an oath which committed them to serve the Tsar as "loyal, upright and obedient servants and subjects".

The *Ecclesiastical Regulation* of 1721 clearly reflected the spirit of Peter's concept of the state. For example, apart from overseeing orthodox doctrine, pressure was put on the Synod to combat superstition, and the sciences were defended against accusations of heresy. The *ukazy* on monastery reform, which Peter

personally introduced to complement the *Ecclesiastical Regulation* between 1722 and 1724, pursued the same objective. He demanded that monasteries and convents be given over to profitable work, and obliged their former inmates to tend the sick and poor, care for orphans, do handiwork or take up scientific study. The monarch had no sympathy for ascetic ideals and meditation by the monks. Even the measures taken to reform the monasteries, then, were carried out entirely so as to be of obvious benefit to society and the state. In almost every detail, this was a forerunner of Josephinism. Peter I's claim to a direct power of disposal over the human productive

forces of society was even more forceful than that of Joseph II in Austria sixty years later.

The Patriarch Nikon's earlier claim that the Church, or sun, was superior to the state, or moon, evaporated in the lifetime of Peter I and Prokopovich. The Tsar and his religious advisers had forced through the integration of the Church into the absolutist state with a heavy hand. The sudden death of Peter in 1725 was a severe blow to Prokopovich. But regardless of the troubles which thereafter plagued Feofan's life until his death in 1736, he was able to pass on his ideas to his pupils and their successors. One of these was the Ukrainian Cossack and wandering philosopher Grigori Skovoroda, who was able to say what Prokopovich, hindered by his dignity as a bishop, was unable to express openly. Skovoroda, who lost his personal freedom towards the end of his life and became a serf, propagated "understanding, peace, harmony, love and joy" and dreamed of a world free of misery and indolence. The self-taught writer Pososhkov, who was something of an outsider, made a definitive contribution to the new concept of society and state represented by Peter I and his associates. Ivan Tikhonovich Pososhkov was of peasant origin, but advanced from the position of a serf craftsman in a village to become an independent factory owner with his own land and property. His career is a clear indication of the opportunities which the state in Peter's time offered for members of the lower classes. The fact that Pososhkov belonged to two different centuries was plainly reflected in his world

view and in his concept of society, both of which were marked by strong contradictions. Although he remained within the framework of the religious dogmatism prescribed by Stepan Yavorski in his theological and didactic treatises, such as the *Mirror* of 1708 and the *Father's Testament to His Son* in 1719, and although he was sharply opposed to heretics, Raskolniks, Lutherans and foreigners in general, his proposals on the reform of the military, the economy and legislation were bold, and their objectives went beyond Peter's official social ideology, with the result that he spent the last days of his life imprisoned in the Peter and Paul fortress. His writings were not to be published during his lifetime.

As early as the Russian defeat at Narva in November 1700, Pososhkov proposed reforms to increase the striking power of the army, as is made clear in his memorandum to General Artamon Mikhailovich Golovin and his letter to Peter I *On Military Organization* in 1700/1701. Here he delivered a damning critique of conditions in the Russian army. His *magnum opus, Book on Poverty and Wealth* of 1724—also addressed to Peter I—displayed the remarkable independence of mind and boldness of his critical social and economic thought. With this work, Pososhkov entered the ranks of those European economic thinkers who had been considering the problems of poverty and wealth at regular intervals since the 16th century. In 1667, for example, Johann Joachim Becher presented his *Political Discourse on the Real Causes of the Rise and*

Decline of Cities, Countries and Republics. Like Becher before him, Pososhkov put the greatest emphasis on the origins of poverty and wealth. In earlier works he had selected problems of religion and the Church. *Mirror*, for example, dealt exclusively with problems of religious dogmatics, and in the *Testament*, too, he turned to worldly and practical problems of everyday and professional life only at the end of the work. These same problems were emphasized so much in his last and most important work, in the *Book on Poverty and Wealth*, that this comprehensive treatise is rightly considered as the first Russian study in political economy to be written from a bourgeois point of view. The fact that such a work could even be published in the Russia of Peter I proves that the social importance of the merchants and entrepreneurs who formed the nucleus of the bourgeoisie at the beginning of the 18th century in the tsardom should not be underestimated. Pososhkov was not only the mouthpiece of his class, of merchants, tradesmen and entrepreneurs, but also used his book to articulate what moved and concerned millions of the Tsar's subjects. He was not afraid to parade the needs and concerns of the people before the eyes of Peter the Great. Yet Pososhkov was only too aware of the difficulties which the Tsar faced in implementing his orders and laws, as these now famous words express, which are almost resigned: "He (Peter I) may be climbing the mountain with nine others, but millions are climbing down the mountain: so how can he succeed?"

ѠБРАZ ВЕЛИКАГО
ГДРѦ ЦРѦ ИВЕЛИКАГѠ
КНZѦ · АЛЕ ЗѢѦ МІХАЙЛОВИЧѦ
ВСЕѦ ВЕЛИКІѦ ІМАЛѦ
ІБѢЛЫѦ РОСІЇ САМОДЕРЖЦѦ ·

59 Tsar Aleksei Mikhailovich,
Peter I's father (1645—1676). State Museum
of History, Moscow

60 Tsar Fedor Alekseevich,
half-brother of Peter I (1676—1682). State
Museum of History, Moscow

61 Ivan V, Peter I, Aleksei Petrovich,
the Patriarch Adrian and the Metropolitan of
Kiev. Copper engraving after Weber,
Russland, 1721

62/63 *Peter I Alekseevich (right) and his son,*
the Tsarevich Aleksei Petrovich. Enamel portraits,
bordered with rubies, by Georg Friedrich
Dinglinger, pre-1714. Staatliche
Kunstsammlungen Dresden, Grünes Gewölbe

64 *Golden drinking cup of Ivan IV.*
Gifted to Augustus the Strong. Grünes Gewölbe

65 *Peter the Great. Medallion of Böttger*
stoneware by Christian Kirchner in about 1712.
Dresden, Porzellansammlung

66 *Johann Melchior Dinglinger. It was in the*
house of this famous goldsmith that Tsar Peter I
stayed during his visit to Dresden in 1712.
Etching by Antoine Pesne. Staatliche
Kunstsammlungen Dresden, Kupferstichkabinett

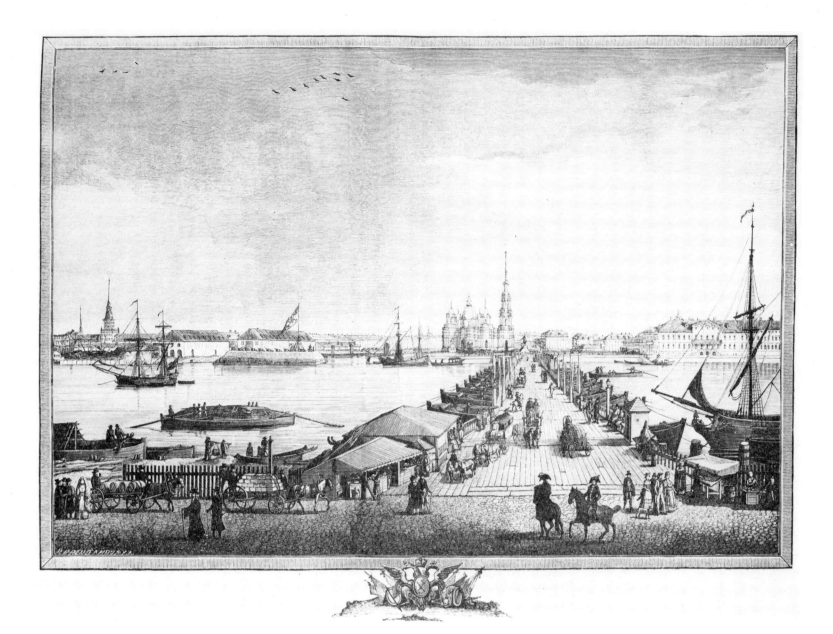

67 Map of St. Petersburg and the River Neva
immediately after the foundation of the city. From
Festung und Stadt St. Petersburg, 1714

68 The Russian fleet at Azov, 1695.
The defeats at Azov in 1695 and at Narva in
1700 made the need for basic army reforms only
too apparent. His visits abroad, and to Holland in
particular, gave Peter I many new ideas on how
to modernize his fleet. Engraving from Korb,
Diarium, Vienna 1700

69 View of St. Petersburg in the late 18th
century.
Engraving after a painting by Benjamin
Paterssons, 1794

Following page:

70 Anthoni van Leeuwenhoek, a burgher of Delft,
was one of the foremost microscopists of his time.
The Tsar was prompted to make the acquaintance
of the naturalist because of his services to natural
science: he discovered, for instance, the presence
of infusoria in water and of bacteria in dental
plaque. Engraving by Jan Verkolje, 1686.
Staatliche Kunstsammlungen Dresden,
Kupferstichkabinett

ANTONI VAN LEEUWENHOEK,
LID VAN DE KONINGHLYKE SOCIETEIT IN LONDON.
GEBOREN TOT DELFF. A.º 1632.

Daer leeft een aerdigh Man, een vaedigh Man en gauw,   Syn Glase Sleuteltiens en is fer geen ontschoten,
Die nieuwe vonden teelt, en beeft Natuur in't nauw,   Noch kan ontschieten dit s die dappre Man niet maer,
Doorkruypt all haar geheim en opent all haar Sloten   Siet scherp toe, die hem soeckt; t gelyckt hem of hy t
J. Verkolje pinx fec d exc A 1686   CONSTANT.

EDUCATION

CONFLICTS ABOUT the position of religion and the Church in Peter's state made the inadequacies of education in Russia—which had hitherto been the domain of monks and the clergy—all too apparent. Experts and officials were needed for the economic, cultural and political spheres, but the existing educational institutions were unable to meet the challenge of training them. So a completely new system of school education was needed. However, Peter did not sweep aside the system of Church schools and education, but instead placed the existing institutions at the service of the state. At the same time, he increased the demands made on Church schools, as was illustrated by the raising of the Mohyla College to the status of an academy as early as 1701.

In the same year, the Tsar assigned Yavorski the task of reorganizing the Greek School in Moscow, of which the latter was patron. For this purpose, suitable teachers were summoned from Kiev, and Latin exercises in particular were given greater emphasis. The school itself assumed the name of the Slavonic-Latin Academy. Latin became the principal subject, and was the language in which theological training was given. Not until 1738 did Greek and Hebrew reemerge from their relative obscurity, and in 1775 the Moscow Slavonic-Latin Academy was renamed the Greco-Latin Academy.

It is important to point out that the Ecclesiastical Academy in Moscow was attended by children from all classes of Russian society, from young princes to the sons of peasants. In this respect, the institution bore the same social countenance as the secular schools which Peter I was later to found. The Moscow Academy played an important part in Russian education as an institution at which secular scholars, too, could receive an education. Its graduates included prominent figures of Peter's time, such as the translator, printshop director and editor of a trilingual dictionary, Fedor Polikarpovich Polikarpov-Orlov, who also taught at the Academy, the poet Prince Antiokh Kantemir, the first Russian doctor of medicine Petr Vasilievich Postnikov, the mathematician Leonti Filippovich Magnitski, and many others famous scientists.

After Kiev and Moscow, many other cities also received ecclesiastical high schools; thus Chernigov had its Slavonic-Latin Seminary, Tobolsk its Slavonic-Russian school and Novgorod its Slavonic-Greek school. The higher ecclesiastical seminaries and schools were accessible to all classes.

In the eyes of Peter I the application of intellect and reason were prerequisites for the development and dissemination of the arts and sciences, for training and education, teaching and learning, lessons and school. The spiritual revolution sparked off by the secularization of thinking in the 18th century was nowhere more evident in the sphere of Russian cultural life than in teaching and education. Until this point in Russian history, schoolteaching and education had been the sole prerogative of the Church.

Peter I had already been made very much aware during his first foreign tour in 1697/98 that the powers of reason could open up the world. In harmony with the stimuli of the early Enlightenment, the monarch fought stubbornly against all forms of superstition, sorcery and charlatanry in his empire. He was adamant that the people should be educated about natural processes, the true causes of human ailments and freaks, and was most insistent too in stripping of superstition and deceit the explanations proffered by the Church. Peter's entire intellectual activity was permeated by the need to stimulate others to use their minds and to elevate reason to the status of a guiding principle. In so doing, the Tsar was not appealing to a privileged class or estate, but to everyone—to the entire Russian people.

The thirty or so laws on schools and education enacted by the monarch, which brought into being schools of the most varied types, indicate how much importance the Tsar attributed to the power of education and the school system in the development of a modern society. These were mainly specialist schools, for example for artillery training, navigation, engineering and mining, and medical and technical institutes. Peter gave these schools—in which the class system was observed—priority over the structuring of a primary school system and the establishment of higher schools along the lines of Western academic grammar schools, universities and academies.

One of the first of these schools to be built by the Tsar was the school of navigation which

71 *Private lessons.*
Engraving, 18th century, from Makogonenko,
Radishchev, *Leningrad 1961*

72/73 *School lessons in the early 18th century.*
Two pages from Fedor Polikarpov, Dreisprachige
Fibel, *Moscow 1701*

opened in Moscow in April 1698 and moved in the summer of the same year to Azov. At the same time, the monarch opened a military school for the Preobrazhenskoye regiment, and one year later, in 1699, an artillery school opened its doors in Moscow. The main subjects at both schools were elementary and applied mathematics, as well as nautical and military science. On 10th and 14th January 1701 Peter decreed that a new artillery school and a school of mathematics and navigation would be established in Moscow, at which foreign specialists were to teach, including the Dutchman Andrei Andreievich Vinius and the Scot Jacob Wilimovich Bruce.

In 1713 a special school of military engineering took its place alongside the existing artillery academy in Moscow. Here, arithmetic, geometry, trigonometry, hydraulics and fortifications were the principal subjects on the curriculum. This institution was the basis of the later military academy, whose duty was to provide the Russian army with officer cadres who had a military qualification. In 1723 the school of military engineering in Moscow was merged with the corresponding school of engineering which had been founded in St. Petersburg in 1719, and moved to Russia's new capital city. The St. Petersburg school of military engineering had a large school roll, and acquired great significance as a training centre for Russian officers.

Tsar Peter also placed a great emphasis on the school of mathematics and navigation. Even in its first year, it had 180 students on the roll, and by 1715 this figure had increased to 719. The school's syllabus was devised by the Tsar and the Scottish mathematician and astronomer Henry Farquharson, who was himself a teacher at the school. As well as arithmetic, geometry and trigonometry, the course included astronomy, navigation, geodesy and other subjects. The best specialist teachers in Russia taught there. It was no accident that the very first issue of Russia's first newspaper, which appeared in 1703, carried a report on the school of mathematics and navigation. The Russian scholar L. F. Magnitski also counted amongst a teaching staff which included the foreigners Henry Farquharson, Stephen Gwyn and Richard Greis.

Leonti Filippovich Magnitski was the son of a peasant, and came from the *guberniya* of Tver. He was educated at the ecclesiastical Slavonic-Greco-Latin Academy in Moscow, and taught at the school of mathematics and navigation from 1701. As early as 1703 he published his celebrated *Arithmetic*, which was written in Church Slavonic; the work was more or less an encyclopaedia of mathematics, geodesy, astronomy and navigation, and was widely used as a textbook by entire generations of Russians. He was assisted in the writing of his *Mathematics* by Vasili Onofrievich Kiprianov.

Between the years of 1701 and 1716 a total of 1 200 graduates left the Moscow school of mathematics and navigation to serve in the Russian fleet as non-commissioned officers, gunners, helmsmen and other ranks. The naval academy founded in St. Petersburg in 1715 was in effect the successor of the M cow school which, while it existed until 1752, never again achieved its former importance. Even in the first ten years of its existence, the naval academy won great acclaim. Its work during that period was very closely linked to that of Grigori Grigorievich Skornyakov-Pisarev, who was its president from 1719 to 1722.

At the same time as the schools of engineering, mathematics and navigation were being established in Moscow and St. Petersburg, schools of engineering were also opening their doors in other Russian cities such as Voronezh, Kazan, Astrakhan and Nizhni Novgorod. Elsewhere too, schools of shipbuilding were established, and works schools set up in large factories. Other technical schools were also founded by Tsar Peter, including the Moscow "Medical School", which was established as part of the military hospital in the city in 1707. It was here that medical staff were trained, mainly for service as field surgeons in the Russian army, by the Dutch physician Niklaas Bidloo, who had come to Russia in 1703. The Tsar assigned the task of organizing the Russian medical system to the Scot Robert Areskin (Erskine), who had become a fellow of the Royal Society in London in 1703 and had entered Russian service in the following year. As early as 1706 the Tsar appointed him president of the apothecary *prikaz*, and from 1713 he was also the director of the Chamber of Art and the St. Petersburg library, offices which he held until his death in 1718.

As early as 1709 the Tsar sought to establish specialized mining schools. The boom in metallurgical production in the Urals and in Karelia meant that there was a great demand for well-trained smelters and chemists. Georg Wilhelm von Hennin and Vasili Nikitich Tatishchev in particular made a great contribution here.

The specialized schools of artillery, navigation, medicine and mining were secular institutions where students were trained at the expense of the state. They formed the nucleus of the new school system in Russia in the time of Peter I. Another type of school which also owed its existence to the needs of the times showed similar characteristics: this was the language school of the diplomatic *prikaz*, which was opened in 1701 by the translator Nikolaus Schwimmer, whose work was continued by Ernst Glück. Glück was a Livonian provost from Wettin near Halle, Germany, who had come to Moscow as a prisoner of war in 1703. Through the medium of his housekeeper and foster-daughter Marta Skavronskaya, who worked at the parsonage and who was later to become Empress Catherine I, he was introduced to Menshikov, and soon afterwards to the Tsar himself, who entrusted the Livonian teacher and linguist with the directorship of the Moscow language school.

Glück's school was established as an academic grammar school with the approval of the Tsar. The government provided the necessary financial backing. Initially, the students were almost all sons of noblemen who had been exempted from military service specifically for this purpose. The school comprised six classes, and its main objective was to introduce the students to scientific problems and to help them achieve the necessary proficiency in some foreign languages.

Tsar Peter believed that Glück's school should also play a political role. He wanted to let the children of the upper classes of subjected peoples, such as the Tatars, Kalmyks and Bashkirs, have the opportunity to receive the necessary education at this institution. This meant including Arabic, Turkish and Persian in the syllabus. There was only one university at that time in the whole of Europe where students could be trained in these languages, and that was the University of Halle in Germany. Glück was therefore charged by the Tsar to contact August Hermann Francke, which he did on 8th March 1704, with the express request to send "competent Orientalists" to teach at his Moscow school.

The esteem in which the new Russia of Peter I was held by Pietist circles in Halle is apparent in the fact that Francke himself tried to learn Russian under the guidance of Heinrich Wilhelm Ludolf. Russian-language books and works about Russia were systematically acquired for Francke's library, until he had built up the most complete collection of Russian books and works on Russia in the whole of Germany. Similarly, Francke succeeded in his attempt to set up a Russian printshop in Halle, so that he could print books in Russian himself. Even if it did not become as influential as Francke had

hoped, at least important Russian-language works could be printed in Halle, making the city the centre of Russian studies in 18th century Germany.

In all, 240 students passed through Glück's "Gymnasium Academicum" in Moscow, a contingent which made up a particularly important section of the intelligentsia to be educated at Russian institutes of learning. The school register contained names of students from famous families including those of Bestuzhev-Ryumin, Veselovski, Buturlin, Golovkin, Golitsyn, Zotov, Shafirov, and other prominent aristocratic lineages.

The tutor of the Tsarevich Aleksei, Baron Heinrich van Huyssen, also maintained close ties with Glück and his school. Huyssen's syllabus for the Tsarevich, which was authorized and signed by Peter, revealed him to be a proponent of the principles of the early Enlightenment. Special emphasis was placed upon history and geography as well as on all the rudiments of the mathematical sciences, for which Magnitski's textbook had been recommended.

Huyssen's work also demonstrated the close links between Tsar Peter and his associates and German science and pedagogics. As early as 1699, the Tsar had sent Petr Vasilievich Postnikov to Halle to take up direct contact with Francke. After the great Russian victory over Sweden at Poltava in 1709, these links with Halle grew increasingly strong, and by 1716 there were already several young Russians studying at the University of Halle,

where they were under Francke's personal supervision. In 1716 Count Gavriil Ivanovich Golovkin, the Russian resident in Berlin, also spent some time at the University in Halle. Three years later, in 1719, Count Chernyshev, the Tsar's special ambassador and adjutant-general, visited Francke to inquire after the progress of work in the institutes. Francke designed a project for an orphanage in Moscow at Tsar Peter's request.

Despite the successes inspired by the educational policy of Peter I and his aides, one must not overlook the fact that the main problem which emerged, that of creating the foundations for modern universal education in Russia, was by no means solved by the establishment of specialist schools for the upper classes and higher institutes of learning. The Tsar was only too aware of this. His recognition of this situation was matched by his realization that Russia was not ready at the beginning of the 18th century for the introduction of education for all. At the same time, it was quite clear that at least the first steps in this direction

would have to be taken, if necessary by applying state pressure. Tsar Peter, like all other absolute monarchs of modern times, felt such pressure to be not only permissible, but even beneficial to his subjects.

Unlike the specialist schools and humanistic grammar schools, which were designed along western lines, the establishment of so-called mathematical schools ordered by the *ukaz* of 20th January 1714 followed no foreign model. These were a sort of mathematical elementary school, to be opened in all *gubernii* by law.

The sons of noblemen and officials between the ages of ten and fifteen were to attend, and were to be taught arithmetic and geometry. No fee was charged. A supplementary decree put legal pressure on young people to attend.

Despite the obligatory nature of attendance at these schools, they were very slow to establish themselves. Aristocratic families refused to send their children there, and used every possible means in their attempts to free themselves from state coercion. As it transpired, they succeeded in getting their own way. In January 1716 a new statute appeared containing new regulations for those for whom attendance was compulsory. Subsequently, children from all classes of Russian society were entitled to enrol at the mathematical schools without being individually instructed to do so. Compulsory attendance for the sons of noblemen, which had been part of the 1714 *ukaz* passed when the school was founded, was scrapped.

Further laws concerning the mathematical schools appeared in subsequent years. Thus in the *ukaz* of 1719 it was established that the number of students at these schools was far too low. In view of this, the senate felt it would be appropriate to extend the range of those for whom attendance was compulsory and to include the children of suburban dwellers, i.e. the sons of tradesmen and merchants, church and monastery workers, and, indeed, all classes other than the nobility.

One year later, in 1720, parishes in the suburbs submitted complaints about the administration of obligatory schooling and pointed to its negative consequences on the trading and commercial sectors of the population. Clarification of the position in the senate led to the decision to locate the schools near the homes of the students and, in future, to exempt the children of suburban dwellers, like the sons of noblemen before them, from obligatory schooling. The education of children from the tax-paying classes would, in future, proceed on a voluntary basis. The government of Peter I therefore bowed to the pressures to which it was subjected, and satisfied itself with recruiting the sons of secretaries, clerks and others who could not be classed as noblemen or suburban dwellers. The *ukaz* of 20th October 1721 even freed the sons of Church servants from compulsory attendance at the mathematical schools.

This meant that the experiment had failed. Only 302, or a little more than 14 percent, of the total of 2 051 students, graduated from the schools. Almost 20 percent, or 572, did not attend because, as sons of suburban dwellers or servants of the Church, they were not compelled to. Other students had either fled, or had not gone to the schools in the first place. Peasants' sons were not mentioned by name either in the decrees or in the statistical documents, but were included in a quite considerable contingent along with the sons of soldiers, dragoons, gunners and Cossacks. The government was obviously reluctant to force attendance at these schools on the sons of peasant serfs, and thereby to recognize them as having full citizens' rights.

The reasons for the failure of the project were not hard to find. A combination of different elements was in play: the type of education being offered proved to be irrelevant to those concerned; the schools were extremely badly organized, and the state apparatus proved to be unable to enforce the individual provisions of the laws which it passed. But above all, the most important factor—money—was lacking. Furthermore, Peter's government was unsure in its sociological assessment of the classes and strata of Russian society, as is shown by its release in turn of the children of noblemen, urban dwellers and the clergy from compulsory schooling. It was the resistance of the nobility, especially the aristocracy, which caused the project to fail. The nobility, including the Tsar's own family, preferred private instruction by foreign tutors and the Western ideal of the galant courtly man-of-the-world. The majority of them wanted to know nothing or only little about geometry, mathematics and serious study.

Despite the inadequate organization, the inherent contradictions, the limitations and the noticeable haste of Peter's educational policy, it should nonetheless be seen as an admirable attempt to transform cultural and intellectual life in Russia.

The beginnings of a state school and education system in Russia which were created under Peter I gained a definite profile only in the second half of the 18th century. The development of education up until the early 1750s was extremely slow and not without setbacks. This

75 *Jacob Vilimovich Bruce,*
who was of Scottish descent, taught at the School
of Mathematics and Navigation in Moscow.
Portrait by an unknown artist, 19th century

76/77 *Art gallery attached to the*
Academy of Sciences in St. Petersburg. Building
and cross-section. Engraving, 1741

was particularly true of the mathematical schools established by Peter, which fell into decline and collapsed totally in 1744. As early as 1735 the government of Empress Anna (1730—1740) had stated in connection with village schools that it was not appropriate to compel the common people to send their children to school, and thus to deprive their families of breadwinners. This was the reasoning behind Russia's rulers' and ministers' failure to do anything to educate the vast majority of the common people until the middle of the 18th century.

The schools founded from the mid-twenties to the mid-fifties were mainly private schools and colleges for the upper classes. Their main task was to train officers for the army and navy as well as civil servants. There were also ecclesiastical seminaries and a few public elementary and intermediate specialist schools in the cities. The specialist schools for the upper classes included mainly garrison, artillery and cadet schools, medical colleges and mining institutes. The only intermediate school in its more accurate sense in Russia at that time was the academic grammar school in St. Petersburg.

The garrison schools had existed in infantry regiments since 1732. Here the children of officers, sergeants and soldiers between the ages of 7 and 14 were taught drill and artillery and engineering sciences. Such schools existed in St. Petersburg, Kronstadt, Riga, Reval, Narva, Viborg, Kexholm, Moscow, Kazan, Smolensk, Astrakhan, Voronezh, Belgorod, Siberia and elsewhere. They were generally supervised by the respective regimental commander. These schools had been established along the lines of the Prussian institutions. In 1744 the garrison schools merged with Peter I's mathematical schools.

The Noble Cadet Corps was founded in 1731 to raise the level of education of the higher officer corps and top civil servants, and from the outset it was in competition with the academic grammar school in St. Petersburg. The Cadet Corps was attended by pupils between 13 and 18 years old, and was often given preference over the academic grammar school by the sons of noblemen because military ranks were awarded there; this was important when graduates began service. The syllabus of the Cadet Corps was very comprehensive. Arithmetic, religious studies and military drill were compulsory. Rhetoric, ethics, heraldry and Latin were taught along with general subjects and the arts. The cadet school was designed to slip into the gap which would later be filled by the university, and give young noblemen as broad-based an education as possible. Artists and men of letters emerged from the Cadet Corps who were lovers of poetry, and to whom the development of the Russian theatre was later to owe much.

However, not all the sons of the nobility by any means attended the academic grammar school or Cadet Corps. Many preferred private tutors, most of whom, during the reign of Empress Elizabeth (1741—1761), were Frenchmen. But French educational methods were limited all too often to external forms and an elegant command of the French language. In general, education and training by foreign tutors were of little benefit in later professional life. This meant that in the time of Empresses Anna and Elizabeth, young noblemen often entered the senate chambers and the state colleges as candidates, so as better to learn the practical business of administration. As officials these noblemen were also able to obtain a wider acquaintance with subjects such as arithmetic, grammar, geography, geometry and geodesy.

After the death of Peter I, the artillery and engineering schools he had founded went into a rapid decline. In 1730 there were renewed attempts to found an artillery school in St. Petersburg, but its pupils were almost exclusively clerks. In 1735 this was joined by an artillery drawing school which merged with the artillery school and was later called an engineering school. But these specialized schools could only be viable if compulsory attendance at artillery and engineering schools could be imposed on the children of noblemen in the long-term.

Tsar Peter I had also made a start in providing training for doctors and midwives. Initially, almost all the teachers of medicine were foreigners. In 1733 the St. Mary provincial hospital in St. Petersburg set up a medical school which was attended in the main by the sons of foreign craftsmen. In later years the government tried to legislate to force the students of the Slavonic-Greco-Latin Academy in Moscow to enter the medical and pharmaceutical colleges.

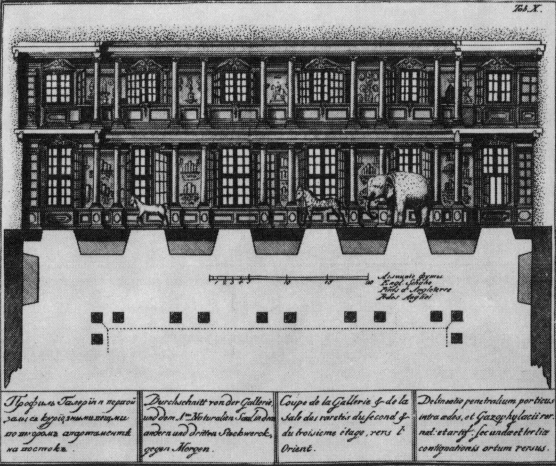

| Профиль Галереи и первой залы съ куріозными вещми по второмъ апортаментѣ на востокъ. | Durchschnitt von der Gallerie und dem 1.ten Naturalien Saal in dem andern und dritten Stockwerck, gegen Morgen. | Coupe de la Gallerie & de la Sale des raretés du second & du troisieme etage, vers t Orient. | Delineatio penetralium porticus intra ædes, et Gazophylacii rer: nal: et artif: secundæ et tertiæ contignationis ortum versus. |

As in the case of the other schools, progress was slow in the medical schools since there was a certain shortage of both students and teachers.

Mining schools also occupied an important place in the intermediate education and training system in Russia during the reign of Peter I. As early as 1724 twenty-two students had been sent to Sweden to work in the mines and improve their technical knowledge. The mining schools put great stress on the close ties between theoretical and practical training of the students.

The concept of the academic grammar school which was established in conjunction with the founding of the Academy of Sciences in St. Petersburg in 1725 was very reminiscent of the earlier humanistic grammar school of Ernst Glück. Its pupils were taught languages, writing, arithmetic and the rudiments of the sciences, together with drawing and dancing. No fees were charged. The pupils in the top classes then "graduated to the higher lessons of the academic colleges as students". During its early years the academic grammar school commanded great respect, and had as many as 112 students in its second year. Subsequently, attendance figures dropped dramatically: this was clearly related to the founding of the Noble Cadet Corps in 1731, to which most of the grammar school pupils transferred. The school did not recover throughout the second half of the 18th century.

Another grammar school was established in conjunction with the founding in 1755 of the University of Moscow. On the initiative of the directors of the University another grammar school was opened in Kazan a few years later, in 1758, bringing the total number in Russia at that time to three. But these intermediate schools were totally inadequate in meeting the educational needs of young people in the Russian Empire. The second half of the 18th century saw a great step forward in the Russian school and education system. A call was made for a basic reform of the existing school system and the introduction of a state system of popular education in the plans made for education. Despite all the half-heartedness and inadequacies of the system, many cultural, scientific, artistic and scholastic institutions were founded which were extremely important for Russia's further development into a modern state. The measures taken by Catherine II and the government in her schools attempted to take account of economic, social and political changes in the country, and made up an element of the reform policies of enlightened Absolutism in Russia.

Empress Catherine II (1762—1796) took a personal part in discussions on questions of education, schooling and training which had been raised in France particularly by Rousseau and in Germany by Basedow, Salzmann, Pestalozzi and others. She often talked about schools and education in her many letters, for example in those she wrote to Friedrich Melchior Grimm and Denis Diderot. She sought contemporary pedagogical theories which she might be able to put into practice in her em-

pire. For this purpose, she assigned the Director of the Academy of Arts, Ivan Ivanovich Betskoi, who was also the director of the Noble Cadet Corps and in charge of the supervision of public buildings, with the task of working out a draft reform for the Russian school system. Betskoi prepared a "General plan for the education of young people of both sexes", which was ratified as the generally binding education plan by the *ukaz* of 12th March 1764.

Betskoi's school project was an important step forward along the difficult path to breaking the nobility's monopoly of education and making it accessible to the entire populace. Completing this work proved to be much more difficult than founding academies, universities and higher institutes of learning. In Betskoi's eyes, the main evil of the status quo lay in the fact that in the past it had not proved possible to provide education for the masses: "Thus Russia has been unable to the present day to create the kind of citizen who is categorized elsewhere as belonging to the middle class." Like all the progressive teachers of his time, Betskoi saw education as the "source of all good and evil", the only means of creating "in a sense, a new generation, or new mothers and fathers". Taking this as his starting point, he called for the establishment of "educational schools for children of both sexes", who were to attend school from the age of five or six until their eighteenth or twentieth year. The main task of Betskoi's schools was to instil discipline, and he placed great importance on the

role of boarding schools: "They (the pupils)
may not have the least association with others
during the entire period (of education), so that
even their closest relations, although they will
be able to visit them on certain days, will do so
only in the school itself and in the presence of
their superiors."

Betskoi felt that "the entire education which
the first new generation" was to receive depended on the "educational institutes", as he
called his proposed schools. As the founder of
these schools, Betskoi himself invested large
sums of money to be made available as grants,
and set up a boarding school at the Academy
of Arts at which foundlings, in particular, were
to be trained as artists. Indeed, Betskoi devoted much attention to the education of foundlings and illegitimate children, of which he
himself was one. For example, in his "General
plan for the Moscow house of education", he
promised that no-one who brought an illegitimate child there would be under any obliga-
tion to disclose his identity or give any details
about the child's background. The children
there were to be fed, educated and trained at
the state's expense. But Betskoi's plans were
realized only in part.

Discussions about the establishment of schools
received a fresh stimulus when Catherine's
"Legislative Commission" was convened and
began work in 1767 and 1768. When she instructed the commission on its work, the Empress stressed the importance of education.
Most of her ideas corresponded with those of
Betskoi. She demanded that three main types

of institution should be established: primary
schools, grammar schools and universities. To
this end, Catherine II set up a "Subcommis-
sion for schools and those in need of welfare"
when the Legislative Commission completed its work. This standing commission was to
be responsible for the detailed preparations
required before the new schools and a
number of welfare institutions could be established.

The schools commission presented several
draft proposals, most of which dealt in detail
with the creation of primary schools, which
were to take the form of village and town
schools open to the public. It was proposed to
make attendance at village schools obligatory
for all male children between eight and twelve
years of age. Girls would only be admitted
with the express approval of their parents.
These schools were to be designed along Prus-

ers were obviously undecided about how to introduce the proposed reforms of school-teaching and education.

This being the case, Empress Catherine II renewed her attempts to communicate with experts from outside, as is demonstrated by her enquiries of the Parisian encyclopedists, in particular Diderot, with whom she entered into correspondence. The Empress succeeded in persuading the famous scholar to travel to Russia in 1773. After his return, in 1775, Diderot sent the Empress of Russia his promised *Plan d'une université pour le gouvernement de Russie* (Project of popular education in all the sciences). When talking of education, the French scholar made a distinction between two types of knowledge; indispensible and conventional. Indispensible knowledge he specified as original knowledge; it concerned all classes. But not all classes "require the same degree of that original or elementary knowledge constituted by the long chain of complete university study. The message-boy or journeyman needs less than the tradesman, who needs less than the merchant, who in turn needs less than the officer, who needs less than the high official or clergyman, and all together need less than the statesman." In Diderot's opinion, the objective of public schools, such as were to be set up in Russia, was not "to train a highly-educated man in one particular subject, but to introduce him to a large number of fields of knowledge."

But despite Diderot's view that children of noblemen and peasants could not be taught in

sian and Austrian lines with the principal objective of teaching reading and writing to the children of peasants. The village clergy were to take charge, and classes were to be taken by deacons or, if there were none, sextons. Only in exceptional cases would laymen be allowed to teach. The landowner of the respective village was responsible for the running of the school, and was also empowered to appoint and dismiss its teachers, who were paid in kind. The town schools were run along similar lines, with the exception that girls of seven and over were also obliged to attend, although they learned only to read. Apart from primary

schools, schools of mathematics were also to be established in towns where there was no other form of higher education.

As well as the schools commission, the Academy of Sciences also had a hand in elaborating these proposals. Demands were already being made for a central state education authority to be created, to which the management and supervision of all school affairs were to be transferred. But progress in realizing the reform drafts and proposals for the establishment of new types of school was very sluggish, and many of the recommendations proved impossible to implement. The Empress and her advis-

the same classes and brought up in the same manner, given the same exercises and made to study the same sciences, the French encyclopedist strove to integrate popular education into the national system of education. No talent was to remain undiscovered or fail to be encouraged, and public institutes of education up to university level should be open to the children of all classes and estates without exception. Diderot hoped that his plan would help Russia to develop into a society of "enlightened and virtuous citizens", and he put forward proposals on "how a people can be guided to a consciousness of freedom and to a civilized condition".

To this end, Diderot directed his attention in the main towards developing a prosperous and confident bourgeois middle class, and towards establishing the intermediate teaching institutions which this required. This is the main reason why Catherine II allowed Diderot's educational project for Russia to sink into oblivion.

At that time in Russia there were several forms of intermediate school, or intermediate and higher teaching institution. New proposals recommended that unification of the various intermediate school establishments be striven after, for example by abolishing the clerical seminaries and, in future, sending laymen as well as clergymen to grammar schools in order to fill the empty classrooms. This proposal came from the schools commission in particular, which also suggested transforming the big monastery rooms into grammar school class-

rooms. The problems which faced Russia's three grammar schools are indicated by the fact that the new grammar school which was opened in Kazan in 1759 proved to be unviable, and had to be closed again in 1785.

The artillery, engineering and military schools also showed few signs of progress. The Cadet Corps experienced a noticeable upsurge from 1765 to 1773 when Betskoi took over the directorship of the institution. Some of the teachers at the mining schools were members of the Academy of Sciences, which allowed the scientific standard of training at these schools to be improved further.

The Smolny Institute, a boarding school for the daughters of the nobility founded on 5th May 1764, was particularly remarkable. Even Peter I had contemplated setting up an educational institution in Russia specifically for women. Catherine II also considered setting up a girls' school along the lines of the Saint Cyr institution near Versailles in France. Betskoi was commissioned to create an institute which would be able to accept 200 girls from the nobility. Four age-groups were to be catered for: six to nine-year-olds, nine to twelve-year-olds, twelve to fifteen-year-olds and fifteen to eighteen-year-olds. Betskoi made it a principle to prohibit girls from leaving the school before they had completed a three-year course. In the first class, the girls learned Russian and foreign languages, as well as arithmetic, in the second geography and history, and in the third literature, architecture and heraldry. The fourth class was devoted to practical exercises. Young

pupils were taught by older girls to prepare the latter for the duties of a mother. Twelve women teachers worked at the institution, most of whom were foreigners. Their main task was to familiarize female pupils with all types of conversation, and to develop their interest in culture and art. Concerts and dramatical events performed by the pupils themselves were also organized with this aim in mind.

Only one year after it had been founded, on 31st January 1765, the Smolny Institute opened a "bourgeois department"; or in other words, it had the right to accept 240 girls of bourgeois origin who had been selected as worthy of an education. The age-groups taught were the same as for the noble girls, but the demands which the curriculum made upon them were somewhat less taxing. The Smolny Institute as a women's educational institution offered Russian girls of noble and bourgeois birth access to higher education for the first time, under the aegis of Empress Catherine II. Many generations of "high-born" and bourgeois girls were educated and given a training at the Smolny Institute, which survived until 1917.

During the first Russo-Turkish War from 1768 to 1774, the Empress had boys recruited in Greece who were educated in Italian schools at the expense of the Russian government. After a peace treaty had been signed with Turkey on 17th April 1775, Catherine ordered the building of a special grammar school in Russia at which Greek pupils between the ages of twelve and sixteen could be educated. At the

Greek Grammar School, as it was called, they learned arithmetic, algebra, geometry, geography, history and drawing, as well as Russian, German, French, Italian, Turkish and Greek. After graduating from the school, the pupils could attend a number of different specialist schools, such as the Naval and Artillery Cadet Corps, or the grammar school attached to the Academy of Sciences. The activities of the Greek Grammar School in Russia formed a coherent part of that aspect of the Empress's Oriental policy known as the "Greek project". This was directed towards the partition of Turkey and the final creation of a separate Daco-Grecian Empire under Russian suzerainty.

In the early eighties, Catherine II and her schools commission were able to take a major step forward on the road to establishing a popular grade-school system in Russia. As the Empress had rejected Diderot's proposals, she now looked to Austria for a lead in creating such schools. Under Maria Theresa and Joseph II the school system there had been re-organized, and a modern school system which extended to the non-German peoples of the monarchy had been structured.

The inspiration to use the Austrian model in reorganizing the Russian school system came from the Academy member, astronomer and physicist Franz Ulrich Theodor Aepinus, who was commissioned by the Empress to write his *Determinations of the points of view from which a national school plan must be regarded.* Aepinus based his ideas around the principle that the prosperity of a nation depends on the quality of its schools, which in turn depends on the quality of the curriculum and teaching methods. He believed that what was taught depended on the objectives of the school, and that methodics belonged in the hands of experts who understood something about the subject. In this respect, Aepinus advised the Russian leader to "demand from His Majesty the Holy Roman Emperor as many teachers and persons as are required for the three or four schools to be established". He also stressed that "only the main principle of the Viennese curriculum should be taken as a basis on which to build, but everything else, if Her Majesty please, should be subjected to careful examination and not accepted blindly", the "main principle" being that the aim of the school system should be to establish a respectable number of good schools, and to keep these in a good condition.

The school order which was in force in Austria at that time had been drafted by the Silesian school reformer Johann Ignaz Felbiger in 1744. It was based upon normal schools in the towns and trivial schools in the country. Aepinus felt that Felbiger's basic principles of a "general school order" were suitable for application in Russia, and wished to use them to improve elementary education in that country. He proposed that an immediate start should be made to setting up normal schools after the Austrian model, perhaps in St. Petersburg, Moscow, Kazan and Kiev. Early in 1782 the Empress made an official request to the Austrian Emperor Joseph II, asking him to send suitable schoolteachers, if possible Serbs, who

would support the Russian school reform. Joseph II asked Felbiger to attend to this matter; he, in turn, recommended the Orthodox Serb Yankovich for the task. Yankovich was considered in Austria to be one of the best teachers of his time. As early as the spring of 1782 he was able to draft a plan for the establishment of popular schools in Russia. The basic principles and finer details of this plan, which ushered in the school reform of 1782, were based upon the Austrian experiences. Immediately after his arrival in St. Petersburg, the Russian Empress issued a decree on 7th September 1782 in which she appointed a commission—the Commission on National Schools—to establish teaching institutes, and explained the fundamental principles behind the imminent school reform. Yankovich was not a member of the commission, having merely an advisory function, but the main burden of work fell on him. Yankovich had proposed three main types of school; lower, intermediate and higher. "A lower school comprises merely the first and second classes; the intermediate school has a third class, and the higher school a fourth. Teaching proceeds identically in the three schools: in the first and second classes one learns the alphabet, spelling, reading of an ABC book, the catechism and a reading book on the duties of a man and citizen, and the rules for learning to write, count and spell. The third class is taught the greater catechism, Biblical history, Christian morals, the Gospel with exegesis of the same, grammar and dictation, continues with the reading book, the rules

of spelling, and arithmetic, and is given a short introduction to history and geography. The syllabus of the fourth class includes fine handwriting, written essays, arithmetic, geometry, architecture, mechanics, physics, natural history, geography, political history, drawing, foreign languages and a continuation of the catechism with proofs from Holy Scripture." The commission summarized the main aims of the new scholastic institutions as follows: "It is the ultimate desire of a human being to be happy. But this requires education and learning."

Even in 1782, Yankovich and the commission were extremely active. The translation into Russian of Austrian textbooks, and the writing and compilation of their own schoolbooks, proved to be very time-consuming. Even the training of suitable teachers proved none too easy.

As the Empress was able to assert in her *ukaz* of 29th August 1783, the schools commission she had appointed had "continued its efforts successfully and established a few Russian public schools as well as an advanced school".

Thus Yankovich's attempts to establish popular schools in Russia were already showing signs of success. But Yankovich's ability and the enthusiasm of those directly concerned in school reform could not overcome the inadequacy of the legal and material base of the new national school system in Russia. For this reason, Catherine II asked the schools commission to draw up a detailed programme with a view to extending normal schools throughout the Empire. Once again, Yankovich applied himself to the task, and on 10th February 1786 he presented the *Statute for National Schools* to the commission. In August of the same year, this programme was ratified by Catherine II.

The Statute of 1786 brought important changes. It departed noticeably from the Austrian model, and attempted to take greater account of the social conditions prevalent in Russia. The nine chapters of the new statute covered the various types of school, the duties of the teachers and pupils, the powers of the curator, headmaster and inspector and the tasks of the directors of the secondary schools. The most important innovation was a restriction to two types of school, higher and lower. Higher schools were to be established in the larger cities of the *gubernii*, and lower schools in the regional and district capitals. This restriction by law to towns and large settlements excluded the village population, to a large extent, from school reform, in that the villages did not generally have their own schools. It was therefore of little benefit to them that the statute of 1786

entitled all subjects of the Russian Empire to send their children to schools in the towns and larger communities. Neither did the statute make education compulsory in the Empire. According to the curriculum, teaching at the higher schools was to be organized in four classes, and in two in the lower schools. The syllabus corresponded to the requirements which had already been stipulated in the primary school law of 1782.

Despite the half-measures of the law of 1786, and the fact that there was a shortage of money, textbooks, teachers and, for a long time, pupils, the new decree nevertheless laid the foundations for a modern school system in Russia. The measures taken by Catherine II proved to be much more far-reaching than those of Peter I with his mathematical school experiment. There was a steady increase in the number of schools in the Russian Empire. According to social statistics from the eighties and nineties, the pupils came from the following classes and social and professional groups: 14 percent from the bourgeoisie, 12 percent from the merchant class, 11 percent from the military, 11 percent from serfs and unfree servants, 8 percent from officials and non-noble civil servants, 5 percent from free farmers and *odnodvortsy*, 4 percent from Cossacks and foreigners and 2 percent from the clergy.

These statistics show that the school reform of 1782—1786 was quite wide-ranging in its effect, and was a first step towards the enlightenment and education of the population of the Russian Empire. One particular characteristic

was the exclusion of the clergy from the organization of school education. The sole concession which was made to the Orthodox Church was to approve the religious books of the Novgorod Metropolitan; but their authors were secular. The schools commission, appointed in 1782, was replaced in 1802 by the secondary school directorate, which was the nucleus of the first Russian Ministry of Education (or Enlightenment). In 1804 this body introduced a new reform of the Russion educational system.

THE ST. PETERSBURG ACADEMY OF SCIENCES AND ITS SCHOLARS

THE 18TH CENTURY saw fundamental changes in most European countries. This was a period when manufacturing production was growing, trade was flourishing and the bourgeoisie was growing in strength. Linked with this were the evolution of a new social philosophy and the laying of the foundations of modern sciences. Rationalism and enlightenment established themselves as the predominant intellectual currents, and gradually undermined the ideological basis of the old society. It was under these conditions too that science was to develop. The Enlightenment saw the development of the natural sciences in particular, which dominated the field of science in general. Many 18th century scholars set an example for this sort of universal conception of the world. They saw medicine and philology, philosophy, physics, mathematics and politics, history, poetry and other natural and intellectual scientific disciplines as highly important elements of a conceptual whole embodied in their activity and work.

In assessing the development of the sciences in Russia before Peter I, one must remember that the tsardom produced no great intellects or representatives of the world sciences of the same calibre as Copernicus, Galilei, Kepler, Newton, Leibniz or others who emerged in Central and Western Europe. Thus, as far as the development of the sciences was concerned, pre-Petrine Russia was regarded by educated contemporaries at home and abroad as a "tabula rasa", as Leibniz put it. Tsar Peter and Feofan Prokopovich were of the same, or al-most the same, opinion, and Lomonosov too made a similar comment some time later.

There was no doubt at all, then, that scientific development in the Russia of Peter I had remained remarkably backward in comparison with the more advanced countries of Central and Western Europe. But contemporary foreign scholars—including Leibniz—were sometimes extremely ignorant about Russia, and thus the image they had of intellectual standards in the tsardom was not always an accurate one. Even Russian contemporaries and their immediate successors felt the Petrine period to be a sharp antithesis to the period which went before, a deep caesura which threw the new Russia of the 18th century into relief against the old Muscovite Empire.

Russia had no academies and universities such as existed in Central and Western Europe until the reign of Peter I. The reunification of the Ukraine with Russia in 1648—1654 meant that the teaching material for the Ukraine was disseminated in Russia. The Latin School founded in Moscow in 1665 was important in this respect; it was established mainly for the purpose of preparing top Russian diplomats for service abroad by furnishing them with the necessary foreign languages. In 1685 the Jesuits in Moscow also established a language school with similar intentions. Its successor was the Slavonic-Greco-Latin Academy, which was set up by the Russian Orthodox Church in 1687 and which was the highest Russian place of learning until the founding of the St. Petersburg Academy of Sciences in 1724/25.

In the face of the setbacks which he had suffered in setting up and running his new schools, the Russian Tsar showed especial care and attention to detail in his preparations for creating an Academy of Sciences, the "source of light" for which he had worked so long. As early as 1697 Peter I had asked Gottfried Wilhelm Leibniz to compose a memorandum on the organization of scientific research, and had considered the idea of setting up a Russian Academy of Sciences. In subsequent years, too, the idea was given repeated consideration. But as long as Russia could not prevail against Sweden in the war between the two countries, there was no question of seriously tackling these plans and making them a reality. It was only after the Russian victory at Poltava on 8th July 1709 that Peter and his advisers were able to devote more energy to the reform work they had initiated.

The details of the drafts and scientific memoranda which Leibniz submitted to the Tsar and his advisers are known to us. The same is true of Peter's correspondence and discussions with Christian Wolff, a pupil of Leibniz, on the same subject. By involving Leibniz and Wolff in the preparatory work for the founding of an Academy of Sciences in Russia, Peter's academy project assumed importance on a European scale.

The philosopher, mathematician, diplomat and polymath Gottfried Wilhelm Leibniz, one of the most prominent representatives of academic thought in Europe, worked to establish scientific academies in St. Petersburg, Vienna,

made every effort to come into personal contact with the Russian ruler, but succeeded only in later years.

Even then, Leibniz was fascinated by the personality of the great Tsar. He described him in letters as a "grand homme" and "héros", and praised him as a monarch who exhibited a rare combination of wisdom and power. Leibniz presented his first great memorandum on Russia in August 1696. Here he put forward basic ideas for a comprehensive plan for developing the arts and sciences in the tsardom. They included the establishment of an institution for the promotion of the arts and sciences, the creation of libraries, printshops, bookshops and natural science collections, the assembling of illustrative material of a technical and artistic nature, the development of an education system, ranging from primary schools to an Academy of Sciences, and research into the geography, history and languages of the peoples of Russia. Leibniz felt that on this basis the standard of agriculture, mining and craft work could be improved, and it would be possible subsequently to build roads and canals and to drain marshes.

In his memoranda on Russia, Leibniz stressed the importance of mathematics for the development of education and the sciences. This was a point to which he returned repeatedly in his later submissions. From 1700 until his death he constantly made fresh proposals on the creation of an education system in Russia. Almost all of his drafts culminated in his recommending the "foundation of a respected, autho-

Dresden and in other European cities, after his involvement in the establishment of the Berlin Academy of Sciences in 1700. As the president of the Berlin Society he knew, like no other, the work which was being carried out by scientific societies in his time. He saw the setting up of a society of scholars on Russian soil as a cornerstone of the world republic of sciences which he envisaged, and which he wished to see extend through Russia to China. Throughout his lifetime, Leibniz was fascinated by Russia. He cherished the idea of using the great potential of the tsardom to reshape European civilization, and of driving the Turks back out of Europe with assistance from the great Empire. Thus he addressed countless letters to important figures of the time in which

he developed proposals for helping the great Eastern European state to develop rapidly in the field of the sciences.

Leibniz saw Russia as being the central empire in a world, some parts of which were better known than others at that time. It was a land where three continents met: Europe, Asia and America. East Asia, i.e. China, with its great ancient culture, was regarded particularly highly by him. As early as the 1690s, he developed seemingly fantastic plans for channels of communication between China and Europe. It was not by chance that the scholar published his *Novissima Sinica* in 1697 to coincide with the first great visit to Europe of the Russian Tsar, in order to stress categorically the importance of Peter's journey to the West. Leibniz

86 *Diploma awarded by St. Petersburg Academy of Sciences to Christian Wolff on the occasion of his election as an honorary member in June 1735*

rized college" in Russia which would take responsibility for the management of schools, arts and sciences in the tsardom. 1711 saw his first encounter with Peter I in Torgau; it was to be followed by two more.

Leibniz did not live to see the founding of the Academy of Sciences and the establishment of schools of higher education in Russia, which he himself had called for; he died in 1716. Right up until the end of his life, Leibniz was utterly fascinated by the young, ascendant Russia and her talented leader, prompting him in his last days to speak enthusiastically, not for the first time, of the Tsar: "I cannot admire enough the vitality and judgement of this great prince. He summons people from all corners, and when he talks with them they are amazed at how knowledgeably he speaks."

From the outset, the Russian ruler had a high opinion of the value of the sciences. He strove tirelessly to promote them, and proved to be extremely versatile, imaginative and full of initiative in this respect. He showed the greatest interest in scientific investigations and experiments throughout his life, as he proved on his educational journeys. There is no doubt that Peter's insight into French culture and science, not least into the work of the Paris Académie des Sciences, was a major stimulus behind his plans to found an Academy of Sciences in Russia. In June 1718 a plan was presented to the Tsar on the education of young people and the training of officials, to which Peter's response was the noteworthy resolution: "Build an academy." In a second directive he added: "Now

those Russians are to be sought out who are educated and have the inclination", i.e. to be appointed members of the academy. The Tsar entrusted the preparations for the founding of the academy to his new personal physician Laurentius Blumentrost, who had succeeded Dr. Areskin after the latter's death in 1719. Blumentrost was assisted by the librarian Johann Daniel Schumacher.

The Blumentrost family originated from Mühlhausen, but had lived in Russia for three generations. Laurentius Blumentrost, a former pupil of Glück at the Moscow grammar school, had studied at the University of Halle. It may have been he who again drew the attention of Tsar Peter to Christian Wolff during the Tsar's search for learned men for the future Russian Academy of Sciences. It was Wolff who had succeeded in developing Blumentrost's interest in mathematics and physics, as a student. Wolff's interest in mathematics was in keeping with the times. Tsar Peter had also been totally receptive to this field. In the foreign quarters of Moscow and even more so in Holland in 1697 and in England in 1698, the Tsar had shown a predilection for the company of mathematicians. Peter I had heard of Professor Wolff of Halle during his travels through Germany. In July 1716 he obtained scientific references about him and asked him to enter Russian service.

Wolff was then at the peak of his career. In his Russian memoranda, Leibniz had highly recommended this scholar from Halle to the Tsar as the editor of the best and most modern text-

book of physics. Peter in fact needed mainly mathematicians and physicists for his academy. In his view, the institution should combine the promotion of the sciences with practice, and serve the exploration of the vast country and the development of the national economy. Leibniz had championed the same view in all of his plans for European academies. The Academy at St. Petersburg was to be not only the focal point for scientific research, but at the same time the centre of education in the tsardom. It paid particular heed to the historical needs of the country and the possibilities at Russia's disposal, taking into account all the stimuli which came from academies in London, Paris and Berlin, as well as the important advice which came from Leibniz, and later also from Wolff. The academy project presented on 22nd January 1724 read: "One cannot follow the pattern accepted by other states, but must consider conditions in this state both in terms of teachers and pupils, and construct an institution which will not only spread the fame of this state as regards the elevation of the sciences in the present day, but will also serve the people in the future through its teaching and influence." On 28th January 1724 Tsar Peter I issued the official founding *ukaz*, to which was appended the approved academy project. These two together constitute the statute for the founding of the St. Petersburg Academy of Sciences.

This new institution was intended to cover for the university which Russia still lacked. The establishment of an academy and a university

87 Laurentius Blumentrost,
personal physician to Peter I, who was
commissioned by the Tsar to found an Academy
of Sciences. Lithograph by Petr Stepanovich
Andreev, ca. 1800

88 Document appointing Laurentius Blumentrost
first president of the St. Petersburg Academy of
Sciences by Empress Catherine I, dated 20th
November 1725

at one and the same time was too daunting a task for the Petrine state. For this reason, the statute prescribed the division of the institution into three stages: an academy along the lines of the Paris Academy, a university with public lectures by academy members and a grammar school where pupils trained by academy members would be able subsequently to teach young people the rudiments of science. The Academy was organized in three classes: one for mathematics, a second for mechanics, physics, anatomy, chemistry and botany and a third for the humanities (rhetoric, antiquities, history, natural law, public law, politics, ethics

and economics). The Academy also had its own library and museum (Kunstkamera) and a printshop. The University had three faculties: Law, Medicine and Arts. Theology was taught neither at the Academy nor at the University, but at the ecclesiastical Slavonic-Greco-Latin Academy in Moscow. This separation of the sciences from theology was a logical consequence of the scientific concepts of Tsar Peter I, and the division predetermined the course of the later development of science in Russia. When the first independent university in Russia was established in Moscow in 1755, it too lacked a theological faculty.

As for the grammar school, which was subordinate to the academy and university, the pupils there were to be taught the rudiments of science, such as geometry, arithmetic, history, geography, logic and rhetoric, as well as languages, writing, drawing and dancing. The most important languages taught were Latin and German. The best pupils of the grammar school were to be admitted as students at other colleges and to be given more intensive training by professors in the relevant subjects. According to the plan made when it was founded, the Academy of Sciences was to be accompanied by an Academy of Arts with the relevant institutions and studios.

Peter the Great died unexpectedly on 28th January 1725, and was never to see the academy which he had founded open its doors. However, his successor Empress Catherine I (1725—1727) was determined to continue Peter's project, and in the summer of 1725 several of the Academy members met in St. Petersburg. They included the mathematician Jakob Hermann, the physicist Georg Bernhard Bülfinger, the mathematicians Christian Goldbach and Friedrich Christoph Meyer, the ecclesiastical historian Johann Kohl and the physicist Christian Martini. They were followed in the autumn of the same year by the brothers Nikolaus and Daniel Bernoulli, both mathematicians, and the historian and geographer Adjutant Gerhard Friedrich Müller. Soon afterwards, on 7th December 1725, Catherine I approved the academy statute issued by her predecessor, and on 20th December she appointed Laurentius Blumentrost as its president. There were then no more obstacles to the opening of the St. Petersburg Academy of Sciences, and on 27th December 1725 the inaugural session was held.

In 1726 the Academy welcomed some new members to complement those already there: the brothers Louis and Joseph Nicolas Delisle, both astronomers, the anatomist, surgeon and zoologist Wolfgang Krafft, the physiologist Josias Weitbrecht, the lawyer Johann Simon Beckenstein and the archaeologist and historian Gottlieb Siegfried Bayer. The professors were able to commence public lectures in the University and were also able to start teaching the classes of the academic grammar school.

The University brought Russians and Ukrainians into contact with representatives of almost every European race, such as Germans, Frenchmen, Italians, Englishmen, Danes and Swedes. They all brought their own concepts of science with them to Russia, and developed them there in their creative work. German scholars were dominant among the first members of the Academy, most of whom supported the doctrines of Leibniz and Wolff.

Reports on the first few years of the St. Petersburg Academy of Sciences reveal that Catherine I put considerable funds at the disposal of the institution, so that teaching and research could continue unhindered. The catalogue of lectures given in 1726 clearly shows the priority given to the natural sciences. As the plans drawn up in Peter's time had stipulated, the teachers at the Academy, who also taught at

the University and the grammar school, tried to be clear and easily comprehensible to all. It was not long before printed introductions to astronomy, geography and physics appeared. Geographical and cartographical works attracted the greatest interest, since it was at this time that Russia began systematically to survey the enormous expanses of the empire.

At the same time, much energy was put into exploring the past, i.e. Russian history. The transition from knowledge to science proceeded in 18th century Russia as it did in historical thinking in other European countries. The changeover from studying history to scientific historical research and representation was one facet of this. One important feature of this process was the gradual improvement in the methods of the scientific source analysis and source criticism. It was only then that historical knowledge became scientific historical awareness, to which Peter I himself had attributed great importance for the education of future generations.

Military successes, the great territorial expansion of the country and the outstanding international position of the tsardom gave rise to patriotic feelings among the populace which were rooted largely in the history of its homeland. Consciousness of the glorious past encouraged efforts to embellish Russian history with heroic deeds and great virtues, and to assign outstanding figures their rightful place in history. There was a desire to give Russia the same place in history as was occupied by ancient Greece and Rome. This con-

centration on the heroic gave historical works a markedly monumental style. Works which examined the languages of the Russian peoples also attracted great interest. The Academy of Sciences sponsored extensive expeditions to Siberia and Kamchatka for these purposes. *Commentarii*, published by the Academy from 1728, played an important role in informing the people about the results of this research. At the same time as the Latin series of writings, the "short descriptions of the commentaries" appeared in Russian. The Academy also published a popular science journal, the *St. Petersburg Gazette.* In the 1730s it also published foreign-language dictionaries and grammar books.

After initial difficulties had been overcome, printshops, letter foundries, drawing schools and workshops for engravers, glass and mirror cutters, wood turners, stone cutters, etc. were set up. Particular importance was placed on printshops which were, nevertheless, poorly equipped initially, so that little printing could be done. Accordingly, printing presses had to be imported from Holland and printers brought from Germany. There were similar difficulties in technical and artistic fields: graphics, architecture, sculpture and painting, metal and stone cutting, and glass cutting. Many experts had to be sought out abroad and trained in Russia for these occupations.

In 1727 the Academy benefitted from the presence of a new member, in the person of the still young mathematician Leonhard Euler (1707—1783), who followed his Swiss countrymen Daniel and Nikolaus Bernoulli to St. Petersburg. Euler worked until 1741, and again from 1766 until his death, at the Russian Academy of Sciences, and greatly enhanced its reputation. The work of the Bernoulli brothers and of Leonhard Euler advanced the cause of one of the most important objectives of the St. Petersburg Academy: to improve mathematical investigations and the technical apparatus of research into the natural sciences.

Georg Wilhelm Richmann (1711—1775) was one of those physicists who had outstanding experimental achievements to offer in the fields of both thermodynamics and electricity. Whilst Euler was particulary interested in perfecting the mathematical apparatus of the natural sciences and a mathematical consideration of physical processes, the empiricist and experimentalist Richmann preferred to come to scientific conclusions by practical means, i. e. by experimentation. Nevertheless, the two worked together fruitfully, as is illustrated by their work to improve the telescope and the microscope. Even when he was active at the Berlin Academy, Euler retained his links with its St. Petersburg counterpart. The great mathematician freely acknowledged how much he owed to his first stay in Russia in a letter written in 1749: "I and all the others who have had the good fortune to spend some time at the Imperial Academy must confess that we owe everything that we are to the exemplary conditions in which we found ourselves there."

Despite the blindness of the great scholar, his second visit to St. Petersburg was marked by unceasing activity. Of his some eight hundred publications on a wide variety of subjects, half date from the period after 1766. Catherine II felt honoured to have won the services of the great scholar a second time for the Imperial Academy of Sciences. Many of the discoveries made in Euler's lifetime in the field of mathematics can be attributed to his genius. The most numerous and comprehensive works by Euler were publications for the St. Petersburg

Academy of Sciences. He did not restrict himself to mathematics, but also wrote about astronomy, mechanics, artillery, shipbuilding, optics and cartography. He compiled handbooks for teaching elementary algebra and arithmetic, which were translated into Russian by the scholar's two Russian pupils, Rumovski and Golovin. Euler insisted that "good communication with foreign scholars is absolutely imperative", since he was convinced that "the usefulness of an academy of sciences is not restricted to the single country where it is founded, but that all other countries always benefit from it too". Euler promoted the development of the sciences in his time not least by his enormous correspondence with scholars from all over Europe. He made a major contribution to laying the foundations of mathematical science in Russia with the help of his pupils and colleagues Semen Kirillovich Kotelnikov, Mikhail Soffronov, Stepan Yakovlevich Rumovski, Mikhail Yevsevevich Golovin and Nikolai Ivanovich Fus.

Even more important for the development of Russian culture, education, science and literature than Euler's work was to be that of Lomonosov, the first great universal genius in Russian history. Mikhail Vasilievich Lomonosov was one of the most creative figures of his time, and his works occupy an outstanding position in the international development of science. The achievements of this great scholar clearly demonstrate the standard which had been reached by Russian science in the mid-18th century. Lomonosov's work made a deci-

92 *Daniel Bernoulli.
Born in Switzerland, he
worked for many years as
a mathematician in
St. Petersburg, and made
important contributions to
the theory of differential
equations, sequence and the
theory of probability.
He also made a name for himself in the field of physics
as the founder of theoretical
hydrodynamics and the
creator of a critical theory
of gases.*

93 *Portrait of the mechanic
Ivan Petrovich Kulibin, a
member of the Academy of
Sciences. Painting by Pavel
Petrovich Vedenetski, 1818.
State Museum of History,
Moscow*

94 *Building of the Imperial Academy of Sciences in St. Petersburg. From Richter,* Ansichten, *Leipzig 1804*

95 *Leonhard Euler.*
This mathematician and natural scientist, born in Basle, worked for many years as a regular member of the St. Petersburg Academy and Director of the Mathematical Class at the Berlin Academy, and made an important contribution to developing relations between the two academies. His scientific achievements did much to promote mathematics and the natural sciences in the 18th century. Painting by Jakob Emanuel Handmann, 1756. Deutsches Museum, Munich

98 *Mikhail Vasilievich Lomonosov. The son of a state peasant, he had to overcome great difficulties before becoming a University scholar. After studying in Moscow, Kiev, St. Petersburg, Marburg and Freiberg, he was appointed professor of chemistry in St. Petersburg in 1745, but also distinguished himself in other fields of the natural sciences, linguistics, art, history and poesy. The University in Moscow which bears his name was founded on his initiative in 1755. Engraving by Nikolai Ivanovich Utkin after a painting by an unknown artist, 18th century. Mikhail Vasilievich Lomonosov Museum, Leningrad*

КРАТКОЙ
РОССІЙСКОЙ
ЛѢТОПИСЕЦЪ
съ
РОДОСЛОВІЕМЪ.

Сочиненіе
МИХАЙЛА ЛОМОНОСОВА.

ВЪ САНКТПЕТЕРБУРГѢ
при Императорской Академіи Наукъ
1760 года

ПЕРВЫЯ ОСНОВАНІЯ
МЕТАЛЛУРГІИ,
ИЛИ
РУДНЫХЪ ДѢЛЪ.

ВЪ САНКТПЕТЕРБУРГѢ
печатаны при Императорской Академіи
Наукъ 1763 года.

99 Title page of Lomonosov's
Concise Yearbook of Russian Regents,
St. Petersburg 1760

*100–102 Title page and drawings
from Lomonosov's* First Rudiments of
Metallurgy and the Metal-Working
Industry, *St. Petersburg 1763*

sive contribution towards strengthening the national independence of Russian science and
combatting alienation in the fields of culture
and literature. His scientific work was notable
for its great diversity, and his passionate thirst
for knowledge drove him to tackle one problem after another. His "dissertations", "meditations", "speeches" and "odes" reflected the
great variety of nature—the perpetual motion
of the earth and the planets, the constant changes on earth, the creation of mountains and
minerals, soil types and animal species, the interaction of chemical materials and so on.

Lomonosov's life was short. When one consid-
ers that it was not until his thirtieth year that
he was able to complete his school education
and his first studies of the rudiments of
science, then one realizes that he was left with
only a little more than twenty years in which to
conduct his own scientific work. And even in
these two decades, conditions were not always
suitable for scientific work. In the face of all
this adversity, in the short time left to him, Lomonosov was able to give impressive justification of his reputation as the greatest Russian
scholar. Apart from chemistry—he established
the first Russian laboratory—he worked particularly in the fields of mathematics, physics,
mineralogy, geology as well as history, linguistics, literature and poesy. He was not only one
of the instigators of the new university which
was set up in Moscow, but also, in his public
lectures and speeches, tried to arouse the interest of broad sections of the population in the
new sciences of his time. In so doing, he fol-

lowed the example of Peter the Great, in trying
to harmonize the tasks facing science with the
practical needs of his homeland. The development of mining in the Urals caused Lomonosov to devote an increasing amount of attention to the mineralogical exploration of Russia.
He completed his life's work by compiling the
Russian Mineralogy, which was to provide the
necessary scientific guidelines for mining.

Mikhail Vasilievich Lomonosov was born in
the village of Mishaninskaya on the island of
Dvina near the town of Kholmogory, the son
of a prosperous landworker, who was also a
merchant and a fisherman. At the age of 19 he
left his childhood home and burned all his
bridges behind him. Almost penniless, he
joined a convoy of fish-sellers taking their
wares to Moscow by sledge. Once he arrived
there, he made a successful application to join
the Slavonic-Greco-Latin Academy in 1731,
where he was taught the rudiments of Latin,
Church Slavonic, Greek, singing, geography,
mathematics, rhetoric and literature. But its
scholastic climate did not appeal to him, and in
1733 he went instead to the Mohyla Academy
in Kiev, where he expected the atmosphere to
be less restrictive, and where he intended studying the natural sciences. But here too his
hopes were dashed, and he soon returned to
the Moscow Academy. Despite his poverty,
Lomonosov continued on his chosen path.
Soon he was to be given an important opportunity: the senate selected twenty of the most
promising pupils of the Slavonic-Greco-Latin
Academy in Moscow who were to be sent for

further training to the academic grammar
school in St. Petersburg in 1736; one of these
was Mikhail Lomonosov. However, this education was to last only ten months.

The Russian Empire was desperately short of
experts in mining and metallurgy. The St. Petersburg Academy of Sciences in particular
needed competent chemists and metallurgists.
For this reason, the new president of the Academy, Johann Albrecht Korff, established contact with Professor Johann Friedrich Henckel,

104 Title page of the collection of speeches
by Academy members at the opening session of
St. Petersburg Academy of Sciences on 27th
December 1725

105 Title page of volume one of the commentaries of the Imperial Academy of Sciences,
St. Petersburg 1728

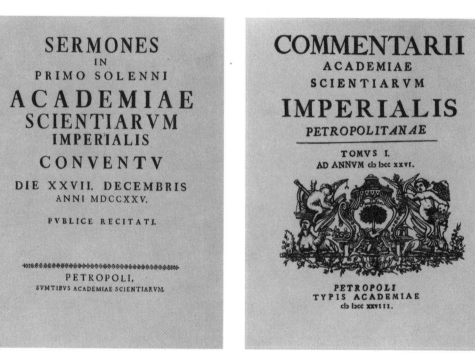

disciplines which Wolff also taught were even more important for the future mining specialists. They included mechanical engineering, instrument manufacture, general constructional engineering, hydraulic engineering, pyrotechnics and others. As Wolff certified, Lomonosov not only worked hard, but proved himself, as the Marburg scholar was to report to St. Petersburg, to be the "most alert of them". On the instructions of the Academy in St. Petersburg, Lomonosov, Raiser and Vinogradov made their way to Freiberg in the summer of 1739. Unfortunately, quarrels soon arose with Professor Henckel, ending in a complete rupture of relations. In 1741 Lomonosov returned to St. Petersburg and became a deputy head of department at the Academy of Sciences. He embarked on a period of creative work, for which his studies in Marburg and Freiberg had provided the foundation.

At the time when Lomonosov was starting work in St. Petersburg, the Academy of Sciences was in something of a predicament, affected by the uncertainties which marked the rule of Catherine I's successors. The resulting social evils had a detrimental effect on teaching both at the university and at the grammar school, whose roll was showing a steady decline. Disputes between the professors and the administrative director encouraged some leading scholars to leave the Academy. Other members died in office. To fill these professorial chairs, several functionaries became members of the Academy and were promoted to the rank of professor.

a mining official from Freiberg in Saxony, who enjoyed an international reputation as a mineralogist and metallurgist, and asked him to recommend a chemist for the St. Petersburg Academy. Henckel answered this Russian request with the proposal that Russian students should be sent to him in Freiberg for training in mining and metallurgy.

The Academy at St. Petersburg agreed to Henckel's proposal, but first the three students selected for study abroad—Gustav Ulrich Raiser, Dmitri Ivanovich Vinogradov and Mikhail Vasilievich Lomonosov—were to finish a foundation course with Christian Wolff, who

was then teaching in Marburg. They were then to be sent to Professor Henckel in Freiberg for specialized studies in mining. Thus the practical training of the three students was to be preceded by a theoretical one.

At that time, Lomonosov was twenty-five years old, and was already well-versed in the natural sciences. Christian Wolff took responsibility for the Russian students, teaching them mathematics, physics, mechanics, hydrostatics, hydraulics, logic and metaphysics. Wolff also introduced Lomonosov and his colleagues to other sciences, such as astronomy, meteorology, geology and palaeontology. The technical

Despite such restrictions and setbacks, great successes were achieved in the Academy's work in the thirties too. In 1732 the Academy continued with the large-scale exploration of Siberia which had been initiated under Peter I, and begun immediately after his reign. Lomonosov showed a very great interest in the development of the Urals and Siberia, which continued in the following decades. This was demonstrated by his treatises on the theory of mining, which he published in the early forties, immediately after his return from Marburg and Freiberg. On 25th July 1745 he was appointed professor of chemistry at the St. Petersburg Academy of Sciences on the strength of his dissertation *On the Lustre of Metals*, and on 12th August of the same year, he was able to attend the Academy conference for the first time as a full member.

The forties heralded a new stage in the history of the Academy of Sciences. In the past, only foreigners had been members—with the exception of Vasili Yevdokimovich Adadurov, who was deputy head of the higher mathematics department from 1733 to 1741—but now Russian scholars too were taking up posts in the Academy; apart from Lomonosov they included the official Grigori Nikolaevich Teplov, the geographer Ivan Fomich Truskott, the philologist and poet Vasili Kirillovich Trediakovski and the naturalist and explorer Stepan Petrovich Krasheninnikov.

The statute of 1747, which introduced a series of new regulations and clarified certain constitutional problems, proved to be very impor-

tant. Lomonosov began work as a member of the Academy of Sciences on the basis of the 1747 regulations. His work brought him into close contact with many Academy members and professors, including the physicist Georg Wolfgang Krafft, Lomonosov's former teacher at the Academy grammar school, as well as Johann Ernst Zeiher, Franz Ulrich Theodor Aepinus, Joseph Adam Braun, who was the first to solidify mercury by mixing and freezing it, and Georg Wilhelm Richmann, who acquired his fame through his experiments on atmospheric electricity, and was killed by lightning.

Lomonosov's work also brought him into contact with the chemists Johann Georg Gmelin and Christlieb Ehregott Gellert, the brother of the famous writer of fables Christian Fürchtegott Gellert, as well as with the astronomer Gottfried Heinsius. Gmelin was Lomonosov's predecessor in the chair of chemistry and became famous through his *Flora Sibirica*, for which he collected material on ambitious expeditions between 1733 and 1743. Lomonosov was not to meet the Swiss mathematicians Daniel Bernoulli and Leonhard Euler at the Academy, as they had already left St. Petersburg. Nonetheless, a lively correspondence between Lomonosov and Euler meant that there was a great exchange of ideas between them. From the outset, Euler, who followed Lomonosov's work at the Academy of Sciences in St. Petersburg with great interest from the Berlin Academy, had recognized the former's genius, and showed great respect for him

in his reactions to his work. Euler's friendly relationship with Lomonosov and his support for the work and opinions of the gifted Russian scholar greatly enhanced the latter's authority at the St. Petersburg Academy of Sciences.

Other eminent chemists worked at the St. Petersburg Academy in Lomonosov's time apart from those who have already been mentioned. These included the metallurgist Johann Schlatter, the president of the mining college and councillor of the St. Petersburg mint, the apothecary Johann Georg Model, Johann Christian Kerstens, who was at the same time professor at Moscow University, and Johann Gottlieb Lehmann. In the second half of the 18th century, too, respected chemists worked at the St. Petersburg Academy: apart from Johann Gottlieb Georgi, they included Nikita Petrovich Sokolov, Yakov Dmitrievich Zakharov, Vasili Mikhailovich Severgin, Ivan Ivanovich Lepekhin, Nikolai Yakovlevich Ozeretskovski, Johann Georg Gmelin, Gerhard Friedrich Müller, Peter Simon Pallas, Johann Anton Güldenstädt, and many others. These scholars, such as the chemist and academic Tobias Johann Lovitz, made considerable advances in the exploration of Russia.

"Professors should not be concerned merely with theoretical knowledge, but just as much with its actual benefit to society, especially with the flourishing of the arts; this is particularly valid for scholars in practical disciplines, such as chemists." Lomonosov wrote these words in 1750 at the height of his career in a report to the Academy's directors. He also

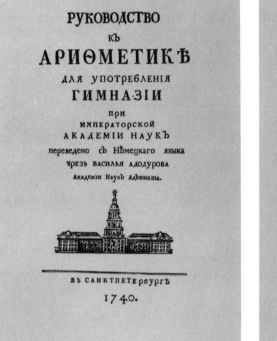

made a programmatic pronouncement on the same question in his speech *Discourse on the Usefulness of Chemistry* which he delivered on 6th September 1751 at the public session of the Academy of Sciences. In this speech, Lomonosov spoke at length of the relationship between the sciences and the arts. He gave metallurgy the leading place among the arts. In his book *First Rudiments of Metallurgy and the Metal-working Industry,* which he wrote in 1742 and which was published in 1763, Lomonosov had laid extensive foundations for his concept of the importance of metallurgy. In other works and projects too, he returned on numerous occasions to the importance for society of mining.

Lomonosov's work as a chemist was closely bound up with his research into the technology of glass and glass production. The Academy of Sciences had opened a chemical laboratory on Vasilevski Island in St. Petersburg in 1748. Lomonosov worked there until his death. He justified his scientific opinions in his now famous *Letter on the Use of Glass,* which he wrote in verse-form. In 1753 he founded his own factory for the production of coloured glass not far from Oranienbaum (now Lomonosov), so that he could work without any interference from others. Here he made perfume containers and tableware, turquoise carafes, jugs with lids and other items. His research and experiments on glass technology aroused admiration in other countries too.

From the late fifties, Lomonosov turned his attention increasingly to economic, social and political matters. He stated quite categorically that the cultural and intellectual educational standard of the Russian Empire has to be raised, and was the author of a large number of projects, plans, commentaries and other writings to this end. These displayed clear tendencies and elements of bourgeois democratism; this was expressed particularly in his assessment of the common people, the peasants and workers.

Lomonosov spared no effort in his impassioned determination to develop a national culture and science in Russia. As a member of the Academy and a professor, the development of a Russian intelligentsia lay particularly close to his heart. To this end, the scholar, whose own roots were among the common people, fought a tough and exhausting battle against all resistance in the path of this objective. In his *Memorandum on the Necessity of Reforming the Academy of Sciences* of 1758/59 he demanded that all gifted children, including the sons of peasant serfs, should be given the opportunity to study at the academic grammar school, the university and the academy regardless of their social background. "Many other European

110 "The electric arrow"
on Lomonosov's house, 1753

111 Experiments with
the electrostatic machine.
Engraving, early 18th century

states", he wrote, "have many academics from all classes; for no man is prevented from studying at a university, no matter who he may be, and the student who earns the greatest respect at university is he who has learnt most—no-one asks who his father is." Lomonosov pointed out the great economic advantages for the Russian state of educating competent Russian scientists, even from the peasant estate, despite its having to pay impoverished students a grant, and remarked sarcastically, "And if the state begrudges them the 40 altyns (= 120 kopecks), then it doesn't resent paying 1800 rubles when it comes to employing foreigners." Lomonosov called on the government to introduce schools, grammar schools, universities and academies where class played no part, in other words, he demanded a democratization of the entire education system. The great scholar's sense of responsibility for the living conditions of the Russian people was also illustrated in other writings, such as a letter he wrote in 1761 to Count Ivan Ivanovich Shuvalov. In this letter he talked in detail about the "maintenance and growth of the Russian population", putting most emphasis on questions of health, the improvement of social mores, and ways of feeding and educating the people, promoting agriculture, crafts, the arts and trading, and achieving a long period of peace for the people of the Russian Empire. This was the first work written in Russia about population policy, and Lomonosov used Pososhkov's *Book On Poverty and Wealth* to help him to write it.

Lomonosov's writings on the economy and economic geography belong in the same context, and had the same basic principle: the need to develop efficient agriculture and industry in Russia itself, abolishing the country's dependence on others. Lomonosov drew particular attention to the importance of the metalworking industry. At the same time, he called for the utilization of the rich mineral resources lying dormant in his own homeland in the north of the Russian Empire. It was important, he said, to link agricultural work and industrial techniques closely together, in other words to mechanize agricultural production. To this end he drew up several plans and projects, such as one for the publication of a Russian economic lexicon and an atlas of economic geography, and even in the year of his death he drafted a plan to establish a "Class for agriculture and agronomy" at the Free Economic Society in St. Petersburg.

Lomonosov's activities at the St. Petersburg Academy of Sciences were also monitored with interest in other countries, and in Germany, of course, more than anywhere else. As early as 1746, the *Göttingische Zeitungen von Gelehrten Sachen* and the *Erlangische Gelehrte Nachrichten* were reporting that Lomonosov was lecturing in Russian on Wolff's *Physics*, which he was also translating into Russian. Thus Wolff contributed to Lomonosov's work in developing a Russian scientific terminology.

In thought and action, Lomonosov showed himself to be an uncompromising fighter for justice and progress, and an enthusiastic scientist right up until the end of his life. He died on 4th April 1765. It was he who once said: "I would be only too happy to be silent and to live in peace, but I fear the chastisement of Justice and Almighty Providence, which have left me not without the talent and an eagerness to learn, and which have given me the opportunity, patience, stamina and boldness to overcome all of the obstacles to the dissemination of the sciences in my fatherland, which is the dearest thing in my life."

The outstanding discoveries made by Lomonosov enriched the scientific and cultural life of Russia. For the first time, Russia boasted a world-famous scholar who was keen to place within the broad framework of collaboration between all the sciences the latest findings of experience and research in the natural sciences in particular. It was through his own efforts that Lomonosov rose from the people to become Russia's leading scientist. As Aleksandr Pushkin rightly observed, he not only created "the first university, but it would be truer to say that he was our first university."

THE MOSCOW UNIVERSITY AS THE LEADING INSTITUTE OF HIGHER EDUCATION

THE UNIVERSITY of Moscow, which was founded on 12th January 1755 at Lomonosov's instigation, assumed central significance in the Russian educational and scientific system. Lomonosov's basic concept, which he developed in his brief plan for the university, centred around the idea that "the university must serve all future generations". Together with the Academy of Sciences in St. Petersburg, the University of Moscow became the leading centre of science and culture in Russia. Even after the construction of the new metropolis of St. Petersburg, Moscow had remained the largest city of the Russian Empire and had in no way lost its former importance. Moscow boasted numerous manufactories, factories and craft enterprises, and the city was the centre of trade and commerce, the representatives of which made an important contribution to the foundation of schools and other centres of learning.

Given that the university attached to the St. Petersburg Academy of Sciences had proved not to be viable, the University in Moscow, which opened its doors for the first time on 16th April 1755, was from the outset the first real university in Russia. Following Lomonosov's proposals it consisted of faculties of Arts, Law and Medicine, with a total of ten professorial chairs, those of philosophy, rhetoric, history, physics, general law, Russian law, politics, chemistry and natural history. The faculty of Arts was best endowed; it boasted four chairs alone, and, following the example of the older European universities, was also responsible for the basic training of students of the other faculties of the university.

The grammar school demanded by Lomonosov was established at the University at the same time. It was organized in two sections, a grammar school for the nobility, and one for other estates. The noble grammar school taught primarily the classical subjects, whilst the other concentrated on the arts and technical disciplines. In 1758 another grammar school was established on the same dualistic lines in Kazan. According to its syllabus, the subjects taught at the Moscow University grammar school were humanities, philosophy, Latin, Greek, Russian, German, French, Italian and Tatar, history, geography, mathematics, architecture, fortifications, artillery, algebra, drawing and painting, music, fencing, dancing, reading and writing. The 1777/78 syllabus lists 35 teachers; this had risen to 41 by 1782/83. Some of these teachers also worked at the University. The same subjects were taught at the noble school, which also belonged to the University. This school was a university institute separate from the grammar school, although grammar school teachers also taught there. The noble school had fewer staff than the grammar school; there was a core of sixteen teachers.

The fact that the University of Moscow, and the other Russian universities which followed it, had no theological faculty demonstrates the continuing development of the secular education system and the increasing divide between secular and religious education. It can also be explained in part by the fact that theological higher education was already being provided by the two theological academies in Kiev and Moscow. In addition, the theological colleges and their directors sternly resisted any connection with the secular sciences in a state university. Scholastic thinking still dominated to a large extent in the clerical academies. Not infrequently they regarded the new spirit of science as a dangerous rival and often opposed scientific progress. Thus any significant link between the old religious colleges and the new University of Moscow was unthinkable.

As Lomonosov had predicted, the work of the University was fraught at the outset with difficulties in filling the chairs with suitable Russian professors. For this reason it was primarily German scholars, obtained through the agency of the famous Leipzig man of letters, Johann Christoph Gottsched, and the Academy member Gerhard Friedrich Müller, who worked at the University in the early years of its existence. On the recommendation of Gottsched, his pupils Johann Gottfried Reichel and Christian Gottfried Köllner also took up professorial appointments.

As well as Germans, French, Italian and Greek scholars also answered the call to the new University of Moscow. Following the accession to the throne of Catherine II in 1762, the number of Russian professors at the University increased rapidly. Some of these had been trained at the new institute. Its graduates included the jurist Semen Yefimovich Deznitski, the writer and translator Vladimir Trofimovich

Solotnitski, the economist and jurist Ivan Andreevich Tretyakov, the mathematician and philosopher Dmitri Sergeevich Anichkov, the director of the Academy of Sciences, Sergei Gerasimovich Domashnev, the naturalist and agronomist Matvei Ivanovich Afonin, the translator and Rector of the University, Khariton Andreevich Chebotarev, the author and judge of the criminal court, Ivan Vladimirovich Lopukhin, as well as the writer Denis Ivanovich Fonvizin, the architects Vasili Ivanovich Bazhenov and Ivan Yegorovich Starov, the historian, writer and folklorist Mikhail Dmitrievich Chulkov and others.

The size of the teaching staff at the University in the seventies and early eighties may be deduced from the lecture programmes of the period. Nikolai Nikitich Popovski and Semen Gerasimovich Zybelin were also among those scholars who, in addition to the aforementioned, sought to equip the young academics of Russia with progressive scientific knowledge in the lecture-rooms of Moscow University. Deznitski and Tretyakov were particularly important as representatives of law and economics; they had studied at the University of Glasgow and had attended lectures by Adam Smith.

The first professors of jurisprudence to teach at the University of Moscow were scholars who had come from Germany. In the main they were proponents of the theory of natural law. Thus when Semen Yefimovich Deznitski took up his appointment at the University, the dominant doctrines in his field were those of

Samuel Pufendorf and Christian Wolff. Deznitski himself was none too impressed by the theory of natural law, and was fond of polemicizing against Pufendorf in his lectures. Deznitski's ideal jurist was a scholar who was a lawyer, historian and sociologist in one. Deznitski's social philosophy is expressed particularly clearly in his *Project for the Establishment of a Legislative, Judicial and Executive Power in the Russian Empire*, which he presented in 1768. This was the first ever scheme for a bourgeois constitution in Russian history.

If Deznitski had remained silent in his memorandum on the survival of serfdom in Russia, in works he produced in the eighties he clearly advocated the abolition of peasant servitude, invoking agrarian advances in England as an example. Deznitski's views were by no means free of contradictions. In this he was at one with those thinkers who put all their hopes of an improvement in the social conditions in the enlightened monarchy of Catherine II. Thus Deznitski gives equal prominence to a theoretical justification of imperial autocracy and to

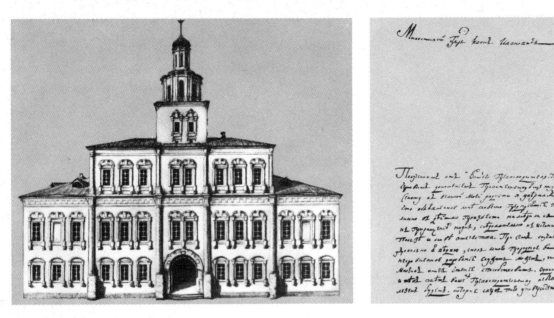

113 *The first building of Moscow University on Red Square*

114 *Letter from Mikhail Vasilievich Lomonosov to Count Ivan Ivanovich Shuvalov about the founding of the University of Moscow, June/July 1754. Archive of the Academy of Sciences of the USSR, Leningrad*

115 *The new, larger building of the University of Moscow was built between 1786 and 1796 by the architect Matvei Fedorovich Kazakov. It was rebuilt by Domenico Giovanni Gilardi between 1817 and 1839. Watercolour by Fedor Yakoblevich Alekseev, late 18th century*

the propagation of possibilities for a constitutional regime in Russia.

As a bourgeois humanist thinker, Deznitski demanded equality for all the peoples of the Russian Empire, and the social equality of men and women. These were certainly far-reaching ideas at that time, and had they been realized, they would have opened up the way to rapid progress in Russia.

Deznitki's colleague, the sociologist, economist and jurist Professor Ivan Andreevich Tretyakov, expounded similar ideas. Inspired by Adam Smith's lectures in Glasgow, Tretyakov had published his *Meditations on the Causes of Superfluity and the Gradual Enrichment of the State in Both Ancient and Modern Nations* in 1772, i.e. four years before Smith's epoch-making *Inquiry into the Nature and Causes of the Wealth of Nations*. Like Smith, the Russian university professor Tretyakov recognized labour as the basis and source of all social goods and of the wealth of nations.

The work of Deznitski and Tretyakov at the University of Moscow in the field of economics was synonymous with the emergence of the first outlines of modern bourgeois political economy in Russia. This process certainly did not take place without struggles and resistance. The foreign, and predominantly German, economists who taught at the University of Moscow were mainly representatives of cameralism. Deep divisions opened up between them and the Russian scholars, Deznitski and Tretyakov, regarding the further development of economics at the University.

According to the minutes of the university conference held on 22nd March 1768, Tretyakov was preparing a second dissertation in which it appears he intended to deal with the abolition of serfdom in Russia. In the theses he drew up for this work, he posed the question: "From which does the state receive the greater benefit, from the slave or from the free man and the abolition of slavery?" Only after great hesitation did Tretyakov opt, on the advice of the assembled members of the university conference, for another, less politically charged topic for his dissertation: *On the Origins and Establishment of Universities in Europe.*

Tretyakov, however, did not admit defeat. He merely awaited another opportunity to re-state his opinions publicly and vehemently. This chance came on 25th August 1769, in connection with the disputation on the dissertation by Dmitri Sergeevich Anichkov. The first copies of Anichkov's doctoral dissertation were publicly burned by his opponents in the course of the incipient controversy. The historian Professor Johann Gottfried Reichel proved himself the most energetic of Anichkov's adversaries. In his report on the disputation on Anichkov's dissertation, the Metropolitan informed the Synod that this work, entitled *Conclusions Drawn from Natural Theology about the Origins and Character of Natural Worship* was extremely dangerous and subversive. In the opinion of the Metropolitan, Anichkov had cast doubt on the moral origins of Christianity and had denied the authenticity of the Scriptures. The Metropolitan took the opportunity

to draw attention to the merits of Professor Reichel, who had taken an "intelligent and pious" stance in his Latin refutation of Professor Anichkov.

Neither could the thinkers of the time avoid discussing such a cardinal question as the problem of serfdom. This caused deep divisions and a sharp interchange of opinions. As far as Moscow University was concerned, the question of what path the new university should follow in the future was the subject of increasingly animated debate from the sixties onwards. The works of Deznitski, Tretyakov and other professors inspired new hope in the Russian people of an improvement in social conditions in the tsardom. Those who made particularly valuable contributions to this debate as scientists at the university included Bryantsev, Zybelin, Veniaminov, Politkovski, Keresturi, Afonin, Strakhov, Arshenevski. Andrei Mikhailovich Bryantsev, a pupil of Anichkov, was particularly prominent in the field of atomic and molecular research. The development of medical science at the University of Moscow was championed emphatically by the first Russian professor of chemistry and practical pharmacology there, Semen Gerasimovich Zybelin. S. G. Zybelin, who taught in Russian, worked at the University for a total of forty years. He was not only popular with the students, but was highly regarded in the poor quarters of Moscow, where he treated the sick free of charge. Petr Dmitrievich Veniaminov was the first Russian professor of botany to teach at the University of Moscow. Fedor Gerasimovich

Politkovski, a pupil of Zybelin, made an important contribution as a natural historian to the establishment of the university museums and the mineralogical collection. The work of Professor Frants Frantsevich Keresturi was connected mainly with the development of anatomy. Matvei Ivanovich Afonin was an important soil scientist. He was a disciple of Linnaeus and had been trained in Switzerland. In his work with students, Afonin regarded a close link between theory and practice as very important. This scholar made a particularly valuable contribution to the development of the science of forestry in Russia. Another very popular teacher was the Russian physicist, Professor Petr Ivanovich Strakhov, who took up his appointment at the University in 1789. Strakhov was mainly interested in meteorology, but he also held the office of Rector. As a corresponding member of the Academy of Sciences, he co-operated closely with scholars in St. Petersburg. Vasili Kondratevich Arshenevski took up his post as professor of mathematics at the University in 1788. He combined his classes on higher mathematics with expositions on navigation, astronomy, military engineering and other technological sciences. Arshenevski's work in the field of integral and differential calculus was also of significance; here he relied heavily on Leonhard Euler, Abraham Gotthelf Kästner and Anton Alekseevich Barsov, publishing an edition of Barsov's *New Algebra* in 1797.

In the first few decades of its existence, the new University of Moscow constituted a first-class centre of science and education. Even at this time the number of students from non-noble backgrounds was increasing significantly. Thus in 1764, of a total of 48 students, only 8 were noblemen. Of the other 40 students, 19 were the sons of soldiers, 6 of low-ranking clerics, 3 of civil servants, 2 of teachers and 1 the son of a serf. In 1765, only 10 of the 55 students belonged to the nobility, and in succeeding years more and more non-noble students filled the lecture-halls.

The number of students at the University of Moscow—about three hundred between 1765 and 1775—outstripped that of St. Petersburg University from the earliest years of its existence. In contrast with St. Petersburg, the new university proved to be much more open. This meant that in isolated cases even serfs and other representatives of the poll-tax paying population could receive an academic training. The foundation statute of the University of Moscow differed from the constitution of the St. Petersburg Academic University in admitting this possibility, even if it was hedged around with conditions. This was obviously the legacy of the spiritual father of Moscow University, Mikhail Vasilievich Lomonosov.

Translations of English, French and German writings carried out by students and staff at the University of Moscow and printed by the University Press were especially important in spreading progressive ideas and social theories. Translations of English works, e.g. those of Thomas Hobbes, a thinker who had made a thorough analysis of the questions of society and the state as early as the 17th century, were important for the spread of knowledge of the natural sciences. A Moscow student, Semen Nikiforovich Venitseev, assisted by some of his fellow-students, undertook a translation of Hobbes. Venitseev was the son of an impecunious artillery officer. He enrolled in the university grammar school in 1756 and matriculated as a student in 1762. By 1767 he was already working in Catherine II's Legislative Commission. According to Novikov, Venitseev was also active as a poet in his student days, composing many poems which were never, however, printed. Nevertheless, his trans-

lation of Hobbes's *De Cive*, which appeared in Moscow and St. Petersburg in 1756, was an important event in Russian intellectual life.

Also of particular significance were the efforts to translate parts of the great *Encyclopédie* into Russian. This work was begun at Moscow University in 1767, at a time when Catherine II's Legislative Commission was sitting in the city with the task of drawing up a new legal code. The man charged with organizing the translation was the writer and director of the University, Mikhail Matveevich Kherashkov. He was assisted by respected representatives of the nobility such as Count Andrei Petrovich Shuvalov, the future president of the College of Mines, Count Apollos Apollossovich Musin-Pushkin, the Marshal of the Legislative Commission Aleksandr Ilyich Bibikov, the son of the poet and Procurator of the Holy Synod Prince Fedor Alekseevich Kozlovski, Novikov's future ally in Moscow and his adviser in

matters of publishing, Prince Nikolai Nikitich Trubetskoi, the Naryshkin brothers, Professors Barsov, Veniaminov and Zybelin, and others.

This team of scientists and patrons of the sciences prepared a Russian edition of twenty-seven articles from the *Encyclopédie* in three volumes. The majority of these dealt with general terms such as the entries under "Geography", "Mineralogy", "Ethics" and so on. Voltaire's article on "History" was also translated, in which the author disputed the validity of historical reports insofar as these were based on Biblical sources. Other terms, such as "Sorcery", were found worthy of translation. However, work on the Russian edition of articles from the *Encyclopédie* did not make any great progress and finally had to be abandoned.

One factor which attained especial significance for the training of students at Moscow University was that they became acquainted with the works of Rousseau; Russian editions had been

published from the sixties onwards by the University Press. In Russia too, Rousseau made inroads at this time into the dominant influence exercised by Voltaire.

The major translator of Rousseau's writings was Pavel Sergeevich Potemkin, who was probably trained at the University of Moscow. Potemkin came from a noble family of restricted means whose position had changed considerably for the better thanks to the career of one member of the family, Grigori Aleksandrovich Potemkin, who rose to be the all-powerful favourite of Catherine II and *de facto* joint ruler of the Russian Empire. In 1768, Rousseau's entry for the competition organized by the Dijon Academy, which he entitled *Discours sur les sciences et les arts*, appeared in Russian; it was followed in 1769 by *La nouvelle Héloïse* and in 1770 by the *Discours sur l'origine et les fondements de l'inegalité parmi les hommes*.

The publication of Russian editions of Rousseau's works from the end of the sixties was a sensation in Catherine II's empire; after all, the Empress and her advisers knew that the works of Jean-Jacques Rousseau took a much more radical stance than those of Voltaire and the *encyclopédistes*. Rousseau not only pilloried the oppressive practices of the *ancien régime*, but demanded equality for all men on Earth. In this respect it was particularly significant that Rousseau's works appeared in the tsardom at a time when social unrest was increasing in both city and country; this was to culminate in the great Peasants' Revolt led by Pugachev (1773—1775). In the summer of 1771, the spread of the plague had already led to an uprising of the poor in Moscow.

The majority of the students at Moscow University who came from the lower classes and distinguished themselves as translators of foreign works cherished the hope that further scientific progress would of necessity lead to socio-political changes in the country. It is therefore understandable that translators of foreign writings came in particular from among the non-noble students and graduates who were interested in problems of history and philosophy as well as in political education. Some of these translations remained unprinted and were circulated without information as to the identity of author or translator.

Thus among others we know of a student of the faculty of Law who graduated in 1770. Aleksei Artemevich Artemev, the son of a village priest, is regarded as the first Russian ju-

rist to produce a textbook of Russian law; it was printed in 1777. A whole generation of law students at Moscow University used this book in their work. Another Moscow student, Vasili Petrovich Ivanov, translated Ludwig Adolf Baumann's textbook of geography from German into Russian; this appeared in several editions in 1775, 1781 and 1788.

Manuals of mining and metallurgical engineering were of particular importance. Textbooks of this kind were not only of scientific significance, but were very important for the economy, since the first great smelting-works were being built in Russia at this time. Thus it was no accident that students and scientists from Moscow University in particular were delegated by the government to work in factories, enterprises and administrative departments. The career of Aleksei Nikitich Gladkoi, a soldier's son, was to become famous. Immediately after leaving university he was charged with working in Catherine II's legislative commission in 1767/68, following which he was appointed to the College of Mines. Finally he was given a managerial post in the Perm gold mines. In 1775 he published a Russian translation of the essay on metallurgical engineering by Johann Friedrich Henckel, the metallurgist and "phlogiston" chemist, from Freiberg in Saxony.

Nikolai Ivanovich Danilovski, who also came from a humble background, translated works from French in the most varied fields of knowledge, ranging from light-hearted genres to scholarly treatises. He showed a preference for political, philosophical and sociological lit-

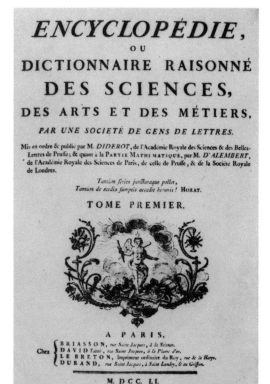

erature. Thus he translated passages from the works of Montaigne, Shaftesbury, Rousseau, Helvétius and other foreign writers. He paid particular attention to the problem of man's legal position in society.

This wide range of translations carried out by students and scholars of the University of Moscow from English, French and German gives us an impressive idea of the various directions taken by social thought in Russian society in the second half of the 18th century.

SCIENTIFIC INSTITUTIONS AND LEARNED SOCIETIES

THE FOUNDATION of the St. Petersburg Academy of Arts in 1757, following upon the opening of the University of Moscow, was an important event for Russia in the mid-18th century. It was the result of an initiative from the University of Moscow inspired principally by Count Ivan Ivanovich Shuvalov. He secured the co-operation of French artists in the project through the agency of Diderot and Voltaire. The model for the Russian Academy of Arts was the French École des Beaux-Arts. This new artistic institution was inaugurated in 1758, and in 1764 Catherine II re-endowed the "Academy of the Three Finest Arts, Painting, Sculpture and Architecture, and also the training-school associated with them".

According to the Statutes of the Academy, its main objective in training artists was to educate not "crawling slaves" but "free men". To this end, Catherine II issued a proclamation which expressly stated: "We hereby most graciously declare that all those born in our Empire who are at present Members, Adjuncts, Academicians and Apprentices at the Academy or who will in future graduate from the training-school established at the Academy, if by their laudable conduct and their good manners (to which attention shall be paid above all) they excel and also gain excellent skill in the arts and crafts, and have obtained a certificate to that effect from the Academic Assembly, shall be completely free for their own persons and for their children and descendants in perpetuity ... In consequence of this we hereby forbid one and all, no matter their estate,

most gravely, from enslaving such masters and artists, or their children and descendants, in any way ... The artists and masters proceeding from this Academy shall be free throughout the Empire and shall be admitted and accepted without let or hindrance to all royal and public works for which they possess the skill, and to any employment they seek and at which they can be used."

During the thirty-year presidency of Ivan Ivanovich Betskoi, who was firmly rooted in the pedagogical ideals of the *encyclopédistes*, the Imperial Academy of Arts achieved notable success despite all the hindrances and adversity it faced. The attainment of artistic excellence demanded technical skills which had to be practised in workshops. Thus there were special schools of steel and copper engraving and stone-cutting. A studio for the production of bronze figures was set up in 1786. The Academy's success in creating the basis for the development of a national artist class was particularly important. The significance of the institution was demonstrated not least by the names of those who graduated from the St. Petersburg Academy of Arts in the 18th century and were famous in later life. These included the architects Vasili Ivanovich Bazhenov, Ivan Yegorovich Starov and Adrian Dmitrievich Zakharov, the sculptor Fedot Ivanovich Shubin and the painter Anton Pavlovich Losenko, who later returned to the Academy as teacher and Rector. The famous portrait-painter Fedor Stepanovich Rokotov also spent some time as a student at the Academy.

During the second half of the 18th century, science made increasing inroads into the area of production. Numerous economic societies came into being which dealt primarily with questions of agricultural development. Based on precise observations, measurements, experimentation and systematization they made a practical contribution to the gradual development of agricultural science. The extensive expansion of agricultural production, as in the reclamation of marsh and swampland for agricultural utilization, was accompanied by the major issue of intensifying existing agricultural production.

The Free Economic Society was founded in St. Petersburg in 1765. It was one of the oldest economic societies in Europe, and survived until 1919. Many outstanding figures from the fields of science and practical economics were active in the Society, including economic theorists, agriculturalists, industrialists, physicians, naturalists, technologists, and representatives of other sciences and spheres of practical economics, but also merchants, entrepreneurs and peasants. The main function of the Society in the 18th century was primarily to contribute to the all-round development of estate management. The Free Economic Society published most of its studies in the main series of publications of the Society, *Trudy* (Works), in which the most disparate areas, such as agronomy, cattle-breeding, agricultural technology, industry, medicine, education and others were discussed. At the same time the Society organized essay competitions in which the

119 Petr Ivanovich Rychkov.
In his great work, the Orenburg Topography,
he dealt with problems regarding the archaeology,
ethnography, geography, orography and
hydrography of Russia, with particular regard to
the Volga region and the area around the Caspian
Sea.

120 Princess Yekaterina Romanovna Dashkova.
She was director of the Academy from 1783 to
1796, and was at the same time president of the
Russian Academy. This institution dedicated itself
to research into the Russian language, and it
counted famous Russian writers and scholars
amongst its members. Engraving by Gavriil
Ivanovich Skorodumov

topics set dealt with agriculture, the breeding of plants, the keeping of cattle, veterinary medicine, the health service, housing, the production of agricultural machinery and other matters.

In the entries submitted to the Society some very tricky problems were addressed: whether the peasant should have proprietorial rights over the land, the question of whether the labour of free wage-labourers was more useful to society than that of serfs, and whether serfdom should be abolished in Russia. The dominant theme, however, was the dissemination of agronomic and economic knowledge in all areas of Russian economics.

The foundation of the Free Economic Society was a clear expression of Catherine II's policy of enlightened absolutism. Persons of great merit were active members of the Society in the 18th century, including scholars such as Euler, Bolotov and Rychkov. All of them made some sort of pronouncement on the state of agriculture in the Russian Empire.

The works of Andrei Timofeevich Bolotov were of particular significance among this agrarian literature. Bolotov was an active member of the Free Economic Society for fifty years, and is regarded as the first Russian agronomist. The geographer, economist, historian and naturalist Petr Ivanovich Rychkov also achieved much; he was the founder of economic geography in Russia. Rychkov's works are important contributions to the archaeology, ethnography, orography and hydrography of the Russian Empire, and in particular of

the Volga region, the areas around the Caspian Sea and the East. Rychkov's *magnum opus*, the *Orenburg Topography*, became particularly well known.

As well as agronomic theorists and practical agriculturalists, work in the areas of the natural science and agricultural technology was performed by such eminent scholars as Afanasi Avvakumovich Kaverznev, Peter Simon Pallas, Ivan Ivanovich Lepekhin, Kaspar Friedrich Wolff, Nikolai Yakovlevich Ozeretskovski, Martyn Matveevich Terekhovski, Aleksandr Mikhailovich Shumlyanski, Matvei Ivanovich Afonin, Ivan Mikhailovich Komov, and many more.

The competition essays submitted by scholars to the Free Economic Society occupied an important place in the discussion of agricultural questions. This was particularly true of the dissertation by the jurist and historian Aleksei Yakovlevich Polenov and the work submitted under the name of S. Aleksandrov. Both essays contained a swingeing critique of the Russian system of serfdom. Voltaire was among the entrants from abroad. Similarly, another member of the Free Economic Society, the scholar, diplomat and writer Dmitri Alekseevich Golitsyn, gave a detailed exposition of his views regarding agricultural development in Russia in his major work *On the Spirit of the Economists*, which appeared in 1796.

From the time of its foundation in 1765 the Free Economic Society in St. Petersburg provided an intellectual centre from which important impulses for the development of the

Russian economy emanated. What it lacked was a subsidiary institute for the training of the necessary economic experts. The School of Commerce which was established in 1772 was unable to fulfil this function.

The higher and intermediate colleges, and the specialized academies and learned societies, including the Free Russian Society at Moscow University which was founded in June 1771, provided a kind of substitute for the other universities which failed to materialize after the foundation of the University of Moscow. The aim of the Society was to collect historical material about the Russian Empire in general and about specific events in particular, to assess it and to assist in promoting the development of the Russian language. One specific task in this respect was the compilation of a major dictionary of the Russian language. All members were called upon to participate in this project. At the same time, an appeal was made to all friends of Russian history and antiquities to seek out the history of their districts and regions, to record any important events and to communicate them to the Free Russian Society at the University of Moscow.

Work progressed well until 1774, and a large body of preparatory work had already been done on the projected dictionary of the Russian language. In addition, material had been prepared for a revised ecclesiastical lexicon, and new data were available on the topography of Astrakhan. The questionnaires which were sent out to all parts of the Russian Empire, in imitation of the St. Petersburg Free

121 *Catherine II.*
Influenced by the thinking of the French
Enlightenment, it was Montesquieu's writings in
particular that the Empress consulted when she
wished to give the Empire a new code of laws.
Engraving by Young after Fedot Ivanovich Shubin

122 *Imperial instruction to the Commission*
for the elaboration of a new civil code.
St. Petersburg 1770

Economic Society, to ask for cooperation and information, were already beginning to bear fruit. It was therefore possible to proceed to the organization of an annual essay competition.

On the whole, the Free Russian Society at the University of Moscow could not in any way be compared with the Free Economic Society in St. Petersburg. Indeed, the Free Russian Society went into liquidation in 1784 without having achieved the aims it strove for. The work it had begun could only be resumed and brought to a successful conclusion by its successors at the end of the 18th and beginning of the 19th century. These included the Russian Academy, which was founded in 1783 and continued until 1841, becoming a centre for research into the Russian language. It counted famous writers and scholars among its members even in the 18th century, including Denis Ivanovich Fonvizin, Gavriil Romanovich Derzhain, Yakov Borisovich Knyazhnin, Vasili Vasilievich Kapnist, Stepan Yakovlevich Rumovski, Aleksei Protasevich Protasov, Semen Kirillovich Kotelnikov and Ivan Ivanovich Lepekhin, who held the office of academic secretary from 1783 to 1802. From 1783 until 1796, the President of the Academy was Princess Yekaterina Romanovna Dashkova. The first major publication of the Academy was a monumental dictionary of the Russian language, which appeared between 1789 and 1794 and was reprinted between 1806 and 1822.

The theological academies, colleges and seminaries which existed in several cities of the Empire were not unaffected by the intensified process of secularization which took place in Russia during the first half of the 18th century. The policy of enlightened absolutism was particularly important in this respect; it found its most cogent expression here in the secularization of church and monastic estates decreed by Peter III and Catherine II. This measure largely deprived the Orthodox Church of its economic power. Catherine II was eager to continue the work begun by Peter I. The French *encyclopédistes*, Pierre Bayle, Voltaire and Montesquieu, exerted a marked influence on the Empress. Inspired by Voltaire's deism, and whilst not denying the existence of God, the Russian monarch nevertheless regarded the historical process as independent of divine influence. Thus for Catherine II, the state required no religious rites but a legal order enacted by the monarch. She renewed Peter I's demand that the Church as an institution should subordinate itself to this order, i.e. yield to the state and to the will of the sovereign.

The outcome of all this was that enlightened thought increasingly found its way even into the theological academies in Moscow and Kiev. Thus the Archbishop of Moscow, Platon Levshin, studied the writings of Voltaire, Helvétius and Rousseau and saw to it that students of theology too became acquainted with the works of these thinkers. In his function as religious tutor to the future Tsar Paul, the archbishop continued his work to this end. Along with other high prelates, Platon was assigned the task of reforming the ecclesiastical schools by Catherine II in 1763. In the reorganization of the two theological academies, great attention was paid to the plans of Feofan Prokopovich, whose sermons and speeches appeared in three volumes between 1760 and 1765. An apparent revival of interest in Prokopovich was thus taking place. In the curriculum of the theological institutes, the previously dominant studies of scholasticism were increasingly replaced by the philosophy of Wolff as propagated in the textbooks of Friedrich Christian Baumeister, which were published in Russian in Moscow.

Given the inroads made by the enlightened streams of thought into the theological institutes, it is little wonder that the Moscow Academy should produce such a freethinker as the future Professor Anichkov, who was nonetheless fiercely opposed by the Orthodox Church and the Metropolitan. However, men like Prince Aleksei Semenovich Kozlovski, who was Procurator of the Holy Synod from 1758 to 1763, energetically championed the dissemination of enlightened and libertarian thought even in the ecclesiastical colleges, seminaries and institutes of the Russian Empire.

EXPEDITIONS AND VOYAGES OF DISCOVERY

THE IMPORTANCE of Russia for the development of scientific research in Europe was apparent even in Siegmund von Herberstein's *Rerum Moscoviticarum comentarii* of 1549, and in Adam Olearius' *Ausführliche Beschreibung der kundbaren Reisen nach Moskau und Persien* (Detailed description of all travels to Moscow and Persia) of 1646. The aforementioned works were read by many learned people in the 16th and 17th centuries. Laurentius Rinhuber's *Wahrhafte Relation von der Moskowitischen Reise* (Truthful relation of a journey to Muscovy) of 1690 and Georg Adam Schleissing's *Neuentdecktes Sibirien* (Recently discovered Siberia) of the same year caused an awakening of interest in the great Russian Empire with its vast Eastern expanses between Europe and Asia. Naturally enough, particular interest was excited by mysterious Siberia, which connected Russia and China. Thus, even in the 17th century there were several voyages of discovery, reaping a rich harvest of scientific data, especially in the fields of botany, zoology and archaeology.

By the 1670s the Russian colonists had already established firm footholds in the regions around Tobolsk, Verkhoturye, Tura, Tyumen and Tara, where they ruled over a population of almost 17,000 tax-payers. Russian penetration of the region was initially hindered by the fact that no-one had yet established sovereignty there, as was demonstrated by the warlike behaviour of the Kirghiz people. The Cossack Semen Ivanovich Dezhnev undertook his now famous voyage of discovery, accompanied by Fedot Alekseevich Popov, as early as 1648, in the course of which the party under his command sailed round Kamchatka in simple boats. In the second half of the 17th century, this same peninsula was opened up from the base at Okhotsk, in 1697 Verkhne-Kamchatsk, and in 1700 the port of Bolsheretsk, were founded on the west coast of Kamchatka.

As well as being an expedition base, the Siberian capital of Tobolsk was also a centre for the gathering of information. News which was collected there was then sent on to the diplomatic *prikaz* in Moscow. Although the results of scientific exploration were kept secret to a large extent, intellectual circles soon knew all about them. The writings of a Dutchman, Witsen, contributed greatly to the spread of information about Siberia. Nicolaas Witsen, born the son of a patrician in Amsterdam, travelled through Russia in the 1660s, accompanied by a delegation from the Netherlands which had been assigned the task of promoting trade links between Holland and the tsardom. The Witsen family had been trading with Russia for more than fifty years. As well as his work as a merchant and his scientific activity, Witsen was also active as an intermediary with reformed parishes in Russia. In 1692 he published his work *Noord en Oost Tartaryen* (Northern and eastern Tartary), which included a description of Siberia and a map which was of great importance for the later development of Siberian cartography, as was the map of Siberia prepared in 1701 by the geographer and historian Semen Ulyanovich Remezov. Witsen's book, which was reprinted in 1698 and 1705, was a reliable reference work for many years, and even today it is an indispensable source document of Russian history, not least because of its many illustrations.

Missions to China which traversed Siberia also produced a significant amount of new material about the enormous land-mass. Particular note should be made of that which travelled to Peking in 1692 to 1694 on the instructions of the tsarist government, and which was led by Eberhard Isbrand-Ides and Adam Brand. They returned in 1695, and in the following year Brand and Isbrand both published a detailed travelogue in German. In 1704 Isbrand followed his up with a Dutch version. Both works, which were also translated into other languages and were reprinted several times, contain valuable material and vivid illustrations on the lifestyle of the Siberian peoples.

The general interest felt in China at the end of the 17th century greatly consolidated knowledge about Russia and the Russian language. Hinrich Wilhelm Ludolf's *Russische Grammatik mit Sprachbuch* (Russian grammar with dictionary) went a long way towards meeting this new interest. It was printed in Oxford in 1696 with the cooperation of Witsen. This book gave, for the first time, a scientific analysis of the Russian language as it was spoken by the people. The work was of great importance for the foreign merchants and manufacturers who came to Russia at the end of the 17th and beginning of the 18th century, as they were in continual contact with the Rus-

sian people. Ludolf compiled a wordlist for Peter I to accompany his grammar, which gave the most important military expressions in Russian and German.

But it was not only scholars such as Leibniz and Ludolf who were attracted by the idea of exploring Siberia. August Hermann Francke also realized the global importance of Siberia after the publication of Leibniz's *Novissima Sinica* in 1697, even if he did so principally in the context of Christian-Pietist mission. The efforts of the two scholars to promote Oriental languages, in particular Sinology, should be seen in this light. In Germany, the Berlin Academy of Sciences and the University of Halle soon became centres of such studies.

It is clear that in the late 17th and early 18th century, the exploration of Siberia had already begun, even if no major expeditions had yet been organized. In 1697 Cossacks led by Vladimir Vasilievich Atlasov had undertaken a new exploratory expedition to Kamchatka, and in 1711 Danila Yakovlevich Antsiferov and Ivan Petrovich Kozyrevski travelled to the Kuril Islands. The Cossack expeditions were as much forays as voyages of discovery. In 1715, an expedition led by Lieutenant-Colonel Ivan Dmitrievich Buchholtz set off to Central Asia in search of gold, but returned unsuccessful at the end of 1716. Nevertheless, the reports which he made were considered so important that the Senate sent a new, larger expedition to Turkestan under Major-General Ivan Likharev, but it also failed due to illness. In 1722 to 1724 the artillery captain Ivan Unkovski

followed the same route. The scientific results of all these voyages of discovery, including those led by Count Aleksandr Bekovich Cherkasski and Captain Fedor Ivanovich Soimonov, were the first informative maps of Kamchatka, the Caspian Sea and the Aral Sea.

Extensive geological explorations, too, were already being made. The exploitation of hard coal began in the Donets Basin. Russian seamen and cartographers also drew maps of the Black Sea, the Baltic and the White Sea. Indeed, the atlas of Siberia compiled by Semen Ulyanovich Remezov contained 24 sheets. In 1716 the seaman and topographer Aleksandr Ivanovich Kozhin was ordered to explore the sea route to India, and to present all important data in map-form. Two years later, Urusov was given the task of surveying the Caspian Sea. He was to be accompanied by Kozhin and Travin, and was to check the accuracy of the information already provided by Kozhin. "During your observations", read the imperial *ukaz*, "keep a diligent watch for ports and rivers, in particular the River Kura, and ascertain what ships can land. Also find out whether there is somewhere where one can make for shelter in stormy weather, and also where there are sandbanks and rocks and the like under the surface. If there is sufficient time left this summer, cruise on the sea and enter on the map any islands and shallows which you discover, and also how wide the sea is at all points." In 1719 the surveyors Ivan Mikhailovich Yevreinov and Fedor Luzhin finally received their instructions to travel to Kamchatka and to ascer-

tain where Asia and America met. The expedition reached the Kuril Islands, and these were entered on the map.

The Swedish and German prisoners-of-war, who had been brought to Tobolsk, the administrative centre of Siberia, in 1711 and soon afterwards founded an important school there, also played a part in the exploration of Siberia. Francke's envoy Christoph Eberhard also worked in the capital as a Pietist preacher and minister as well as promoting native languages. A book in several parts entitled *Über den inneren Zustand der schwedischen Kriegsgefangenen in Russland* (On the mental state of the Swedish prisoners-of-war in Russia), which appeared in Halle between 1718 and 1721 under the pseudonym Alethophilus, and the work published by Kurt Friedrich von Wreech in 1728, *Wahrhafte und umständliche Historie von den schwedischen Kriegsgefangenen in Russland und Sibirien* (Genuine and intricate history of the Swedish prisoners-of-war in Russia and Siberia), give important indications of the scholastic activity and efforts to explore Siberia made by these Swedish and German prisoners. Christoph Eberhard also drew the attention of Tsar Peter to the physician Dr. Daniel Gottlieb Messerschmidt. The doctor, who was born in Danzig, had studied at the University of Halle, where he had received an excellent education. In September 1717 the Tsar's personal physician, Areskin, persuaded him to carry out voyages of discovery on behalf of Peter I, and Messerschmidt entered Russian service early in 1718.

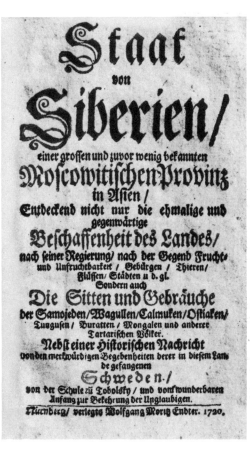

From 1720 to 1727 Messerschmidt travelled through Siberia, the first learned man to do so officially on the orders of Peter I. Although the St. Petersburg Academy of Sciences had not yet been founded, this trip to Siberia can be regarded as its first project. The eight-year expedition resulted in a wealth of new scientific, archeological and linguistic knowledge. In March 1727 Messerschmidt returned to St. Peters-burg, which he had left in 1719. Much had changed during his absence. The great Tsar was no longer living, and Empress Catherine I was already on her deathbed. Messerschmidt had to surrender the research material he had brought back from Siberia to the Academy of Sciences and to promise to keep silent about it. But as early as 1730 Messerschmidt's companion during the first year of the expedition, Philipp Johann Tabbert von Strahlenberg, published his sensational work *Der nord- und östliche Teil von Europa und Asien* (The northern and eastern parts of Europe and Asia) in Stockholm and Leipzig, which was soon translated into French and English. Naturally enough, it found a particularly receptive audience in Russia, especially in the great scholar and organizer of Russian mining and metallurgy, Vasili Nikitich Tatishchev, who was in personal contact with Strahlenberg and made numerous comments on the work. Thus there was obviously intense interest in Messerschmidt and his journey of exploration in St. Petersburg around 1732, although Strahlenberg had revealed only fragments of the material gathered in Siberia.

After Messerschmidt's sudden death in March 1735, however, it seemed more improbable than ever that the scientific facts and documents from his expedition would ever appear in print. However, he had ordered the collection very carefully, so that it could already be put to good use. The historian Gerhard Friedrich Müller and the naturalists Johann Amman, Johann Georg Gmelin, Samuel Gottlieb Gmelin and Peter Simon Pallas made the most of this opportunity. But only Pallas published a few details from Messerschmidt's expedition journal in 1782, which related to regions which he himself had not visited on his travels. It was not until 1962 to 1977 that the results of Messerschmidt's expedition to Siberia were published in five parts. Even today, these journals are an excellent, largely untapped source of information on the natural history, society and culture of 18th century Siberia.

Shortly before his death, Tsar Peter had assigned the Dane Vitus Bering, who entered Russian service as a naval officer in 1703, the task of exploring the straits which separated Asia and America, and recording them on maps. As a young sailor, Bering had served on Dutch ships and travelled to the East Indies. He had quickly made a name for himself during the Northern War. The knowledge he had acquired during his voyage to the East was the deciding factor appointment to lead the 1st Kamchatka Expedition (1st Bering Expedition). He was accompanied and assisted by the Dane Martin Petersohn Spanberg and by Russian seamen such as the naval second lieutenant Aleksei Ilyich Chirikov and the mate Petr Chaplin. Bering's expedition had a large back-up team of 158, including carpenters, smiths and soldiers.

On 24th January 1724, four days before the death of Peter I, the advance party of the expedition left St. Petersburg by land. So considerable were the difficulties that had to be overcome that the journey to Okhotsk took nearly

127 *Link to the west coast of America, map ca. 1800*

128 *Map of the Sea of Kamchatka from Billings, Reisen, Weimar 1803. Fred Götze entered the routes followed by the explorer.*

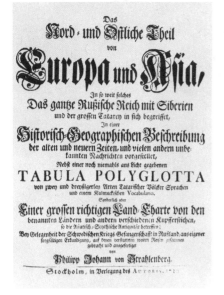

two years. It was not until the summer of 1727 that Bering was able to cross to the peninsula of Kamchatka, which is 1200 km long and 450 km wide, in his sloop "Fortuna", which had been built in Okhotsk. He landed at Bolsheretsk on the west coast. At the beginning of July the second and larger ship, the schooner "St. Gabriel", was launched in Okhotsk. The great journey into the unknown began a few days later. Bering sailed round the southern tip of Kamchatka and then northwards up the coast past the Chukotski peninsula without sighting land. As autumn was approaching and he was convinced that America and Asia did not meet in the north, he ordered his crew to return to Kamchatka.

Bering had not, then, caught sight of the west coast of Alaska. In early September 1728 the "St. Gabriel" dropped anchor in Nizhne-Kamchatsk, where the expedition spent the winter months. The following year Bering made a second attempt to find the west coast of North America, but again without success. In March 1729 he returned to St. Petersburg, his mission still unaccomplished, and reported on the progress of the expedition. Although his account was suitably well-received in the capital, it left important questions unanswered. The west coast of North America was still uncharted, and no more was known about the possibilities of sailing on the northern seas than before. Thus the results of the Bering expedition were unsatisfactory, and new voyages had to be undertaken to ascertain the necessary information. The next expedition to Kamchatka

therefore had to be prepared much more extensively and meticulously than the first. Its assignment was to map the entire northern and eastern coasts of Siberia. Once again, Vitus Bering was the overall leader of the expedition, with another Dane, Sven Waxell, as his deputy and first officer.

The 2nd Kamchatka Expedition (2nd Bering Expedition) of 1733 to 1743 was one of the greatest events of its kind in 18th century Russia. It had been superbly equipped by the Academy of Sciences. Some idea of the scale of the undertaking is indicated by the fact that it took all of eight years to transport the expedition force of six hundred men under Bering's immediate command with their equipment from Tobolsk to Okhotsk. On the 2nd Kamchatka Expedition there were also several scholars, such as the historians Gerhard Friedrich Müller and Johann Eberhard Fischer, who were concerned with the history of Siberia, the astronomer Joseph Nicolas Delisle, the naturalist Johann Georg Gmelin and the physician Georg Wilhelm Steller, the botanist Stepan Petrovich Krasheninnikov and students.

The task of the 2nd Kamchatka Expedition was not only to answer the question about the link between Asia and America, but also to explore Siberia comprehensively. For the sake of better organization, the participants were assigned to small groups led by Vasili Pronchishchev, Khariton Prokopevich Laptev, Semen Chelyuskin and others. The Arctic Ocean was to be penetrated from West to East starting from the mouths of four rivers: the Dvina,

the Ob, the Yenisei and the Lena. The expedition which was to travel from Arkhangelsk to the mouth of the Ob, and then to the mouth of the Yenisei, accomplished its task by mapping the northern coast of Siberia from Arkhangelsk to the Kolyma. However, it was not possible to circumnavigate the Chukotski peninsula as enormous ice masses barred the way. In 1739 Laptev only got as far as the Kolyma, and went from there to Anadyr overland. He explored Tamir Bay with his helmsman Chelyuskin. In 1742 Chelyuskin completed his work of mapping the eastern coastal region of the Tamir peninsula, whose tip was named in his honour. Laptev explored the mouths of the Indigirka and the Kolyma from 1734 to 1741.

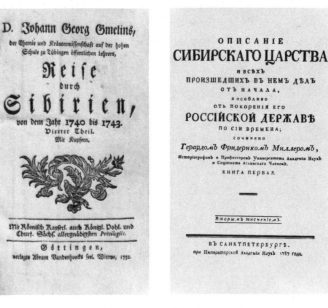

At the same time, attempts were being made to map the mouths of the Yana and Olenek, as well as Khatanga Bay.

The party working under Bering, Spanberg and Chirikov also achieved important results. Spanberg ordered several ships to be built in Okhotsk which he used on his voyages to the Japanese islands from 1737 on, from where he reached Nippon. Bering was still seeking the North American coast, and indeed eventually found it. He was accompanied by Delisle, a member of the Academy. On the return journey from the American continent, where Chirikov had landed at the 56th and Bering at the 58th parallel, Bering's ship ran aground off a rocky coastline in 1741. Bering and Delisle were both to die on the island, which was later named Bering Island. The survivors were led back to Russia by Sven Waxell in 1742. In a detailed account, Waxell vividly described the eventful 2nd Kamchatka Expedition and what befell it.

Of the Academy scholars who accompanied the expedition, only Delisle and Steller had undertaken a sea voyage; the others had remained on dry land. The historian and geographer Müller collected a considerable amount of material which proved to be an inexhaustible source of information on the history, ethnography and geography of Siberia. Gmelin's travels in Siberia reaped valuable results. The natural science collections which he amassed were highly valued, even by contemporary experts, and his book on the Siberian flora was highly regarded everywhere as a classic work.

Krasheninnikov, who acted as an academic assistant during the expedition, made a great name for himself in the scientific world in consequence of his description of Kamchatka. Steller's natural science studies of Kamchatka were also very highly regarded. Steller was the academic member of the expedition who set foot on America. Finally, Delisle's work added quite dramatically to contemporary knowledge about the geography of Siberia.

The Academy scholars who participated in the second large-scale expedition to Kamchatka gathered important material on the flora and fauna, geography, ethnography and history of Siberia. Particular importance was attached to the maps and atlases which were compiled on the basis of data obtained during the expedition. Several years' work had already been devoted to the *Atlas of the Russian Empire*, principally by Ivan Kirillovich Kirilov, the head of the Orenburg Commission. Kirilov worked as a chief secretary in the senate, and was responsible for drawing maps of the country from 1720. His position at the centre of things enabled him to collect extensive material, which he first prepared for publication in 1727 and revised in 1736. As the head of the Orenburg Commission, he had to ensure that the Yaïk region of the Urals was scientifically surveyed. Accordingly, Kirilov helped both to prepare and to execute the two Bering Expeditions.

In 1745 the great cartographic work commissioned by the Academy of Sciences, the *Atlas of the Russian Empire*, appeared. The best

cartographers and mathematicians in the tsardom, including Leonhard Euler, had collaborated on the project. It also embraced the information which Kirilov had gleaned from his many years of work as a cartographer. The atlas comprised a general map and nineteen specialized maps on which the "entire Russian Empire and its neighbouring countries are depicted in accordance with the rules of geography and the latest observations". These latter were the results of the 2nd Kamchatka Expedition, which visibly advanced the development of cartography in Russia.

The great voyages of discovery gave a major boost to the sciences in Russia in general. This led not only to a reassessment of the disciplines taught at the St. Petersburg Academy, but also resulted in the creation of new branches of science. It became increasingly obvious

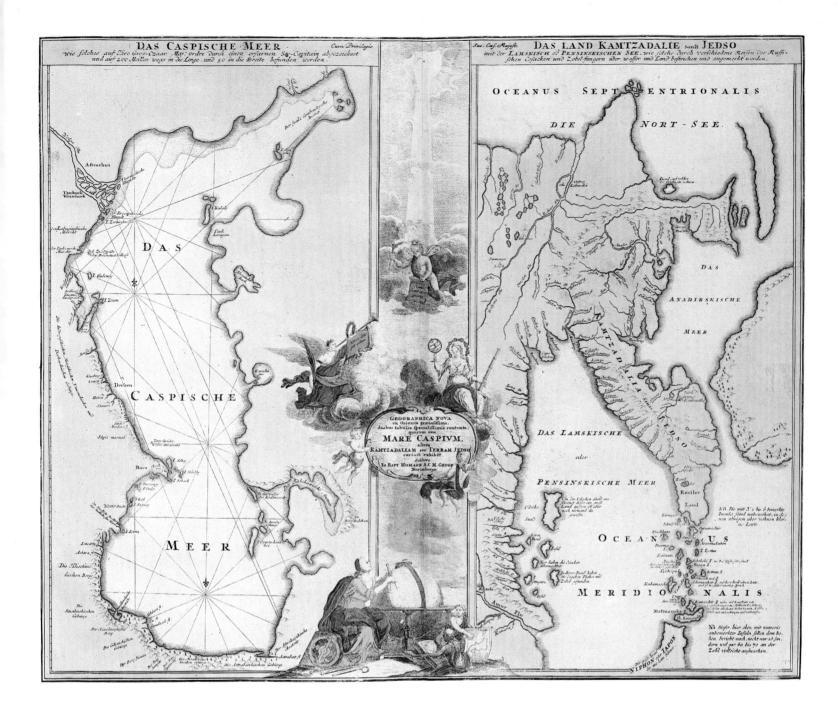

DAS CASPISCHE MEER. *Cum Privilegio*

wie solches auf Ihro Groß-Czaar. Maj: ordre durch einen erfarnen See-Capitain abgezeichnet und auf 200 Meilen wegs in die Länge, und 50 in die Breite befunden worden.

Sac. Cæs. Majest. DAS LAND KAMTZADALIE sonst JEDSO

mit der LAMSKISCH & PENSINSKISCHEN SEE, wie solche durch verschiedene Reisen der Russischen Cosacken und Zobel-fangern über wasser und Land bestrichen und angemerkt worden.

DAS CASPISCHE MEER

OCEANUS SEPTENTRIONALIS

DIE NORT-SEE.

GEOGRAPHICA NOVA
ex Oriente gratissima,
duabus tabulis specialissimis contenta,
quarum una
MARE CASPIVM,
altera
KAMTZADALIAM sive TERRAM JEDSO
curiose exhibet
editore
Io. Bapt. Homann S.C.M. Geogr.
Norimbergæ.

OCEANUS

MERIDIONALIS.

Steur vangst inde Rivier de WOSGA

136 Tatar woman.
From Bruyn, Reisen,
Amsterdam 1714

137 View of the harbour
in Petropavlovsk.
From Steller, Kamtschatka,
Frankfurt and Leipzig 1774

138 The mouth of the Volga.
From Stryuss, Reysen,
Amsterdam 1678

139 Laplanders.

140 Bashkir woman.

141 Yakut girl.

142 Kuril man.

143 Kirghiz man
on horseback.
From Georgi, Beschreibung,
St. Petersburg 1776

144 *Tunguzy men building a yurta.*
From Steller, Kamtschatka, *Frankfurt and Leipzig*
1774

145 *Samoyed man.*
From Bruyn, Reisen, *Amsterdam 1714*

146 *An Ostyak ermine-trapper. From Georgi,* Beschreibung, St. Petersburg *1776*

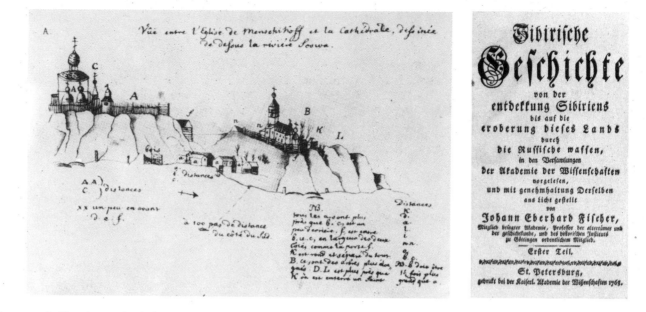

147 Sketch of the settlement of Berezov. Drawn by Joseph Nicolas Delisle during the expedition to Siberia, 1740

148 Title page of Johann Eberhard Fischer's Sibirische Geschichte. St. Petersburg 1768

how important the tsardom and Russian science were for scientific development in Europe as a whole. The peoples of the Russian Empire with their numerous languages were just as interesting for comparative philology as the countless species of plants and animals were for zoology and botany. The *Flora Sibirica* published in three volumes by Johann Georg Gmelin in 1747–1749 (the fourth did not appear until 1770), and the four-volume *Reise durch Sibirien von dem Jahr 1733 bis 1744* (Voyage through Siberia in the years 1733–1744), which the same author published in 1751 and 1752, indicate what was to be expected of Russian science in the field of botany in later years.

The scientific land surveying expeditions had a multi-faceted character. One of their purposes was to discover deposits of valuable raw materials, such as ores and coal. Leibniz' principle, *"theoria cum praxi"*, lay at the root of all scientific explorations in 18th century Russia. The same was true of the scientific works which appeared in ever increasing numbers. One example was Stepan Petrovich Krasheninnikov's two-volume *Description of the Land of Kamchatka*, which was published in Russian in 1755, in English translation in 1763 and 1764, and in a German edition in 1766. Gerhard Friedrich Müller published his history of Siberia in five parts in his journal *Sammlung russischer Geschichte* (Collection of Russian history), the last part appearing in 1764. Georg Wilhelm Steller's *Beschreibung des Landes Kamtschatka* (Description of the land of Kam-

chatka) was not published in Leipzig until thirty years after the completion of the expedition, i.e. in 1774, and not until 1783 in St. Petersburg. Steller's *Topographische und physikalische Beschreibung der Beringinsel* (Topographical and physical description of Bering Island) appeared in 1781, the St. Petersburg edition following in the wake of James Cook's expedition across the world.

The reforms introduced principally by Lomonosov and Johann Albrecht Euler, the eldest son of Leonhard Euler, in the mid-1760s provided good conditions at the St. Petersburg Academy of Sciences for the further development of the sciences in Russia. Johann Albrecht Euler acted as a scientific organizer on a large scale, and held the post of secretary of the Academy from 1769 until 1800. The Geographical Department, presided over by Lomonosov from 1758 until his death in 1765, was a centre for the promotion of scientific research. Here the Russian research expeditions, which provided an important stimulus for scientific advances throughout Europe, were prepared and assessed. The Chamber of Art, which enjoyed close links with the St. Petersburg Academy of Sciences, obtained important collections from the expeditions which were vitally important for several of the sciences, such as botany, zoology and linguistics. Kaspar Friedrich Wolff was able to add considerably to the theory of evolution in 1759 by evaluating the wealth of material at the Chamber of Arts with the assistance of his pupil, Peter Simon Pallas.

Lomonosov's memorandum of 1763 reveals how much he supported a continuation of research expeditions; it contained an assessment of the benefits gained to date from such projects and what could be expected from future ones. The *Concise Description of Various Voyages of Discovery on the Northern Oceans and Details of a Possible Passage from the Siberian Ocean to East India* played a part in inspiring an expedition in his own lifetime to confirm that it was possible to sail north-east across the Arctic Ocean. The project was led by the captain and later admiral Vasili Yakovlevich Chichagov, who, in 1765–66, made two unsuccessful attempts to penetrate this area from a base in Kola.

There were other expeditions too. Individual sailors made several attempts at their own expense between 1760 and 1770 to penetrate northern waters and lands, sailed through the Vaygach Straits and the Kara Sea, circumnavigated Novaya Zemlya and pushed further east. In 1768 Matoshkin Shar was discovered. A merchant called Lyakhov found fossilized ivory and masses of cow, sheep and horse bones on an island in the New Siberians, and discovered the islands of Mali and Kotelni.

Research work at the St. Petersburg Academy of Sciences was greatly encouraged by Empress Catherine II. Mathematical research at the Academy received a new stimulus with the return to St. Petersburg in 1766 of Leonhard Euler. Furthermore, Russian scholars won increasing influence at the Academy after the death of Lomonosov; these included the natu-

149 *Winter quarters on Kamchatka. From Steller,* Kamtschatka, *Frankfurt and Leipzig 1774*

150 *Title page of Georg Wilhelm Steller's* Beschreibung von dem Lande Kamtschatka, *Frankfurt and Leipzig 1774. Steller joined Bering's Second Kamchatka Expedition in 1737, and was one of the first Europeans to set foot in Alaska.*

151 *Stepan Petrovich Krasheninnikov, a member of St. Petersburg Academy of Sciences, took part in the Second Kamchatka Expedition and explored the peninsula between 1737 and 1741. Engraving by Aleksei Agapyevich Ossipov, late 18th century. Hermitage Museum, Leningrad*

152 *Title page of Krasheninnikov's* Beschreibung des Landes Kamtschatka, *St. Petersburg 1755*

ral scientist Ivan Ivanovich Lepekhin, who won international recognition as the author of a four-volume travelogue on the Volga region, the Urals and the north of European Russia, the astronomer Petr Borisovich Onokhodtsev, who made his name by his observation of the transit of Venus, Euler's pupils Semen Kirillovich Kotelnikov and Stepan Yakovlevich Rumovski, the anatomist Aleksei Protasevich Protasov, the naturalist Vasili Fedorovich Zuyev and others.

From 1768 to 1774 major new expeditions were organized in the tsardom, which have en-

tered the annals of Russian scientific history as the "Academic Expeditions". These aroused considerable interest throughout the scientific world. The attempts at reform sought by the government of Catherine II were behind the expeditions of these years, but the final impulse was given by the observation of the transit of Venus which had been made in Tobolsk in 1761 by the French astronomer Jean Chappe d'Auteroche on the instructions of King Louis XV of France. Doubts were cast on the validity of the information given by the scholar, not only by the St. Petersburg Acad-

emy of Sciences, but also by its Parisian counterpart.

The anticipated transit of Venus in 1769 gave the St. Petersburg Academy of Sciences the opportunity to demonstrate the high standards which had been achieved by Russian astronomy, while for Empress Catherine II the participation of the Academy in the observations was also a matter of prestige. The Empress commanded the Academy to make a further exploration of the Russian Empire. The transit of Venus was indeed successfully observed by several scholars in Kola, Yakutsk, Guryev, Orenburg and Orsk, but this original objective was now put in the shade by the major project of an academic expedition ordered by the Empress. The main purpose of the new expeditions was to survey the country further and to increase the economic exploitation of Russia.

The main efforts to achieve an overall expansion of the planned expeditions came from the Free Economic Society in St. Petersburg. In the course of preparations, the explorers were assigned to three main groups: the Orenburg Expedition, with detachments led by Pallas, Lepekhin and Falck, the Astrakhan Expedition with parties led by Güldenstädt and Gmelin, and the Astronomical Expedition. Each individual group was prescribed a route and given its own instructions for the observations it was to make. These stated that the regions to be explored were to be described geographically, and a record made of any observations on mineralogy, botany, zoology, history, ethnology, agriculture, animal husbandry, fur-

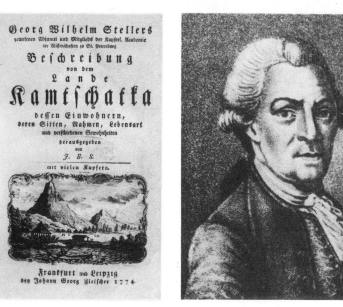

trading, fishing, crafts, industry, commerce, the customs and traditions of the inhabitants, prehistoric phenomena, illnesses suffered by humans and animals and much more. The most important expedition was that led by Peter Simon Pallas, which began in 1768 and ended in 1774. Pallas was accompanied on his journey by Vasili Fedorovich Zuyev and Nikita Petrovich Sokolov, the artist Dmitriev and the dissector Yakov Danilovich Shumski. He was later joined by Captain Nikolai Petrovich Rychkov, Georgi Bykov, Gerasim Stepanovich Lebedev, Johann Jaehrig, and others.

Pallas reached the Urals in the first year. In the second he advanced as far as the Caspian Sea, and in the third he reached the Altai Mountains. In the fifth year he explored the Baikal region, returning to St. Petersburg via Lake Elton in 1774. Pallas had sent his travel reports at intervals to St. Petersburg where they were immediately translated into German, French, Russian and English and published under the title *Journey through Various Provinces of the Russian Empire* (three parts, St. Petersburg 1771—1776). Once he had returned to the capital, Pallas made a further analysis of the results of his travels, and published his *Flora Rossica* between 1784 and 1788, which was to make him a central figure in the Russian scientific world. Empress Catherine II, who had a very high opinion of him, commissioned him to compile a comparative dictionary of all languages, and herself contributed material for it. This unique work compared 47 European and 153 Asian languages and dialects with

each other on the basis of 273 selected words. After an extended sojourn in the Crimea from 1793 to 1810, Pallas returned to Berlin, where he died in 1811. After his death, Pallas's extremely valuable herbaria were acquired by his travelling companion, the Englishman Cripps, and are now in the Botanical Department of the British Museum in London.

The expedition led by Samuel Gottlieb Gmelin, nephew of the botanist Johann Georg Gmelin, explored the Caspian Sea and the Caucasus, and also achieved important results. Many other explorers were also successful, for instance Johann Anton Güldenstädt, who also travelled in the Caucasus, although by a different route; Johann Peter Falck, a pupil of Linnaeus who explored the area around Orenburg and western Siberia; Johann Gottlieb Georgi, who accompanied first Falck and then Pallas, and Ivan Ivanovich Lepekhin, who crossed the Volga region and the European north of the Russian Empire with Nikolai Yakovlevich Ozeretskovski. The reports and journals of most of the explorers were quickly published, so that many new scientific data were available at the end of the "academic expedition" for the further exploration of the Russian Empire.

But the expeditions also claimed their victims. In 1773 Falck, completely exhausted, committed suicide, while Samuel Gottlieb Gmelin was captured in the Caucasus and died in prison in Ak-Mechet. Güldenstädt only narrowly escaped the same fate as Gmelin. The explorer Georg Moritz Lowitz, who found himself caught up in the conflict between Tsarist forc-

es and Pugachev's insurgents in the Volga region, met his death there. The Pugachev uprising was eventually to lead to the premature termination of the expeditions to regions under the control of the rebels.

Nevertheless, Pallas proposed seven new expedition routes in 1776, and the other members, too, made their own suggestions. But none of these proposals was to be realized in the 1770s; it was not until the eighties and nineties that such projects were resumed. Thus Vasili Fedorovich Zuyev traversed the Crimea in 1781/2, Karl Sievers went to the Irkutsk region, where he remained from 1790 until 1794, and Marshal von Bieberstein made another exploration of the Crimea and the Caucasus in 1795—1798. There were also less extensive land explorations and sea-voyages in the Pacific Ocean. Jakob Reinegg's voyage of adventure to the Caucasus in 1778—1781 was of a completely different kind to the expeditions ordered by the Russian government, but despite their unreliability, Reinegg's travelogues contain material and observations which provide important information about the history of the Caucasus.

The voyages of merchants and fishermen were instrumental in establishing links with the American continent. Such voyages gradually opened up the entire chain of islands between Russia and northwest America from the middle of the 18th century. Russian seal-hunters had been hunting there for over forty years, unbeknown to the rest of Europe. It was only after James Cook's third voyage around

the world, in about 1780, that this fact became known, and the area was immediately flooded with seamen from all corners of the globe. At that time, the Russian seamen, fishermen and merchants had already built up a flourishing fur-trade with the Chinese. After the opening-up of Siberia, this trade was an important asset to the economy of the tsardom. Since the Chinese market was like a bottomless pit, fur-trading experienced a considerable boom with the discovery of the chain of islands in the North Pacific. The major expeditions organized by the Academy of Sciences became combined increasingly towards the end of the 1760s with voyages to Alaska. Records show that these expeditions were extremely perilous and ended not infrequently in catastrophe. The maps and drawings made on these voyages proved extremely useful, making it possible for new expeditions to be undertaken and brought to a successful conclusion.

The most famous Russian trader in the northern Pacific was Grigori Ivanovich Shelikhov, who was dubbed the "Russian Columbus" by some of his contemporaries. He created the basis for the activities of the Russian-American Company, which operated under the auspices of the state. The numerous independent expeditions of earlier times were undertaken by only a few merchants and entrepreneurs from Central Russia during the seventies and eighties because of the high costs of shipbuilding. These included the arms manufacturer Orekhov from Tula and the merchant family of Golikov from Kursk, as well as Grigori Sheli-

khov from Rylsk. Shelikhov eventually succeeded in gaining control of the entire Pacific trade by means of treaties, arranged marriages and presentations at court.

Shelikhov's ships were fitted out in Okhotsk, which had had its own shipyard since 1714. Despite the light construction of the ships, most of which were two-masted galliots, they proved to be extremely seaworthy, and could hold a crew of fifty men each. A hunting voyage would last four to six years, until the ships were able to begin the return voyage full of pelts. The profit realized was many times the cost of fitting out the ships. Shelikhov created a permanent settlement on the island of Kadiak, which had been sighted by Bering, as the main base for his trading company. This is the largest of the islands off the American mainland, and even today the straits there are known as the "Shelikhov Straits". When Shelikhov died in 1795, his company merged with the Irkutsk trading company.

In the subsequent period, the Tsars Paul and Alexander I, as well as many other aristocrats, involved themselves and their capital in this company, which was now given the right to occupy land for the Empire and to found Russian settlements. The company eventually controlled the Kuril Islands, the Aleutian Islands with the base at Kadiak and Russian possessions in Alaska. Aleksandr Andreevich Baranov, whose work for the development of Russian-American relations was no less important than that of Shelikhov, became the new director of the company.

When England lost part of North America in 1783, she sought new possibilities for expansion in the northern Pacific. Merchant ships belonging to the Americans, Portuguese, Spanish and French also hurried to these waters. Catherine II's government was extremely perturbed at this maritime acitivity by foreign ships in the Pacific. For this reason, plans were made in 1785 for a major new expedition to the North Pacific. The project was to have two main objectives: to clarify Russian possessory interests in the Pacific Ocean and to annex unoccupied territory as part of the Russian Empire. Scholars were assigned the task of further exploring these areas geographically and scientifically. The extreme north of these shores had not been explored since Bering, and the question still remained unanswered of whether there might not be a land bridge between Siberia and America.

This time, the Englishman Joseph Billings led the expedition. He had taken part in Cook's third circumnavigation of the world as his astronomical assistant. Billings had entered Russian service in 1783 as a helmsman, and was appointed leader of the North Pacific Expedition by the government in St. Petersburg on account of his knowledge and experience of the Pacific Ocean. Robert Hall acted as Billings' assistant adjutant, and the ship's papers and log were kept by Martin Sauer, who, like Billings and Hall, was an Englishman. Sauer was also the author of one of the accounts of the expedition, which was published in 1803. Christian Bering, a grandson of the famous

155 Routes of the Academic Expeditions
of the 1760s and 1770s.

156 Ivan Ivanovich Lepekhin,
explorer and member of St. Petersburg Academy of
Sciences. Drawing by M. Kashentsov after a
lithograph by M. Mosharski, early 19th century.
Hermitage Museum, Leningrad

157 Title page of Lepekhin's report
on his travels through the Russian Empire.
Altenburg 1774

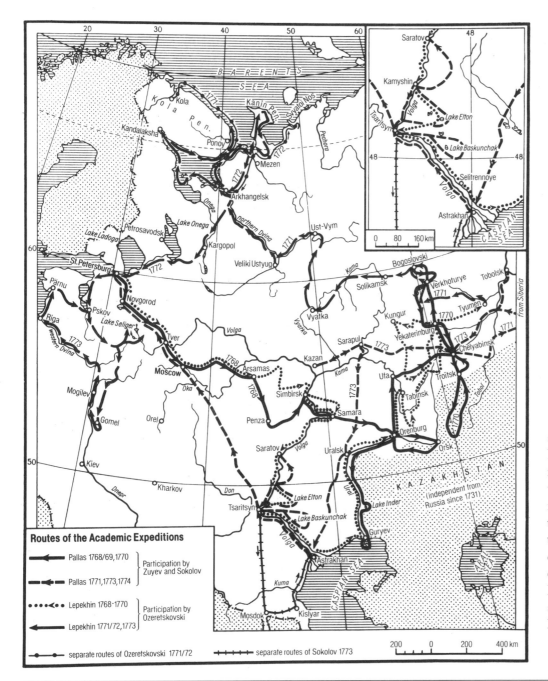

Routes of the Academic Expeditions

←	Pallas 1768/69, 1770	Participation by Zuyev and Sokolov
◄--	Pallas 1771, 1773, 1774	
•••◄	Lepekhin 1768–1770	Participation by Ozeretskovski
←	Lepekhin 1771/72, 1773	
•—•—	separate routes of Ozeretskovski 1771/72	+++++ separate routes of Sokolov 1773

seafarer, also joined the expedition. While Billings commanded the lead ship "Pallas", Gavriil Andreevich Sarychev acted as captain of the second ship, the "Slava Rossii". He was the most competent member of the entire expedition, as is clear from his travelogue, which was translated into several languages. The physician Karl Heinrich Merck also took part in the expedition in his capacity as a naturalist.

Preparations for the expedition were the responsibility of the Admiralty college, and were kept strictly secret. The ships had a total crew of 150 men. A detailed set of instructions specified what had to be observed during the

158 Peter Simon Pallas was commissioned by St. Petersburg Academy of Sciences to publish the travelogues of Johann Anton Güldenstädt. St. Petersburg 1787

159 Adam Johann Krusenstiern, a Russian naval officer, led the first Russian circumnavigation of the earth, together with Lissyanski, between 1803 and 1806.

voyage. The expedition ships left Okhotsk at the end of May 1787. They tried to penetrate the Bering Straits as far as the River Kolyma, but failed. In 1790 and 1792 the two ships set sail for America. Subsequent land expeditions were made on the Chukotski peninsula. In 1794 they returned to St. Petersburg.

The objects and materials brought back by Dr. Merck were of great importance. He had sent his travel reports to Pallas who did not, however, publish them. Nonetheless, they have been kept until the present day, which is also the case with the journal of Pallas himself, who died in St. Petersburg in 1799. To date, the hand-written legacy of Merck on the Billings Expedition of 1787—1794 has scarcely been evaluated. The zoological, botanical, geographical and ethnological information contained in the records on the regions occupied by the North American tribes is far greater than that which is to be found in the accounts of Sauer and Sarychev, and represents, even today, a gold-mine for research.

Billings' expedition was the last great venture to be based in Okhotsk. It was very expensive and time-consuming to equip expeditions from there, since most materials had to be transported overland through Siberia. For this reason, subsequent expeditions at the beginning of the 19th century used St. Petersburg as a starting point, for example the voyage of Admiral Johann Krusenstiern and Yuri Fedorovich Lisyanski in 1803.

Although Russia's possession of the Kuril Islands made her a next-door neighbour of the Japanese islands, there were no official economic, political or diplomatic ties between the Russian Empire and Japan until the mid-19th century. Attempts to establish relations were made by the Russians as early as 1711. In 1720 two surveyors explored some of the Kuril Islands on the orders of Tsar Peter. In 1739 and 1742 Spanberg also visited the Kuril Islands, twenty-one of which recognized Russian sovereignty and were prepared to pay taxes in the form of sea otter, fox pelts and other furs.

The trading ventures and voyages of discovery made in the sixties and seventies by private merchants and entrepreneurs added considerably to Russia's knowledge about the island regions. This was particularly true of the voyages of Pavel Sergeevich Lebedev-Lastoshchotkin and Grigori Shelikhov. In June 1779 a Russian ship dropped anchor in the harbour of the island of Matmai. A remarkable painting exists of this landing, showing the encounter between the Russian crew and the Japanese inhabitants of the island. The Russians, who had landed in leather boats, are shown with their caps doffed in greeting, while the Japanese are depicted bearing weapons. The leader of the Russian crew was the merchant Dmitri Shebalin from Irkutsk. In later years, too, there were meetings between Russian fishermen and fur-trappers and the Japanese. In 1792 an expedition set off for Japan from Irkutsk under the command of Adam Laxmann, the eldest son of the Academy member Erik Laxmann, with the objective of gaining further advantages for Russia in her trade with Japan.

The scientific expeditions undertaken in Russia during the 18th century were, in the main, ventures organized by the state. In the second half of the century, land surveys were also made, and were directed by people who had only loose ties with science. The most famous of these were undertaken by Aleksandr Ivanovich Fomin and Vasili Vasilievich Krestinin in the *guberniya* of Arkhangelsk. In 1755 they both founded a society in Arkhangelsk to examine the antiquities of that region. Fomin was encouraged by Lepekhin to submit his *Description of Arctic Sea Creatures* to the Academy of Sciences in St. Petersburg.

The example of Fomin and Krestinin inspired others, too, to explore particular localities. The material gathered by the physician Dr. Jakob Fries, a native of Switzerland, during his journey through Russia, was particular important.

Fries' accounts include important observations on climate, natural phenomena, plants, bird species, sowing, harvesting, and more. Fries also described the town of Veliki Ustyug with the assistance of the primary teacher Stepan Rychkov, one of Petr Rychkov's sons.

Science and technology made rapid advances in Russia in the wake of the academic expeditions and other voyages of discovery made in the 18th century. The wealth of geographical, mineralogical, botanical, zoological and other material gathered by a large number of scholars, and new findings in many fields, created a powerful scientific potential which was of great significance for the economic, social and cultural development of the Russian Empire.

PUBLISHING
AND THE PRESS

BOOK PRODUCTION, as the basis for the publication of the necessary textbooks, newspapers, journals and scientific works, was closely tied up with the development of the education system, popular enlightenment and science in Petrine Russia. The history of Russian books in the 18th century is characterized by the struggle waged by progressive forces in society for a specifically Russian culture, education and science and for freedom of thought, and by the struggles against the ignorance and spiritual oppression of the people. Books, newspapers and journals helped to open up the cultural treasures of the past and present, and to make them accessible to readers.

The first printed book in Russia appeared in 1554, and about twenty works of various kinds had been printed by the end of the 16th century. In the second half of the 17th century the number of books published rose to 382, and in the 18th century Nikolai Ivanovich Novikov alone published nearly 1 000 books. Immediately after 1554, it appears that there was only one print-shop in Russia. In the 16th century, the books printed in Russia were exclusively ecclesiastical works, secular works beginning to appear only in the 17th century. Yepifani Slavinetski and Simeon Polotski in particular distinguished themselves as translators of secular scientific literature into Russian in the 17th century. Nevertheless, despite the secular works produced by the court print-shop in Moscow under Simeon's direction, ecclesiastical writings dominated the scene. The secular works included scientific works and belles-let-

tres, and above all Simeon's own treatises; Simeon was also active as a playwright. However, there was no decisive breakthrough in the printing of secular literature in Russia during the 17th century. This break through was to happen only at the beginning of the 18th century.

As early as 1698, Peter I brought in Dutch printers to set up the first engraving workshop at the armoury in Moscow. At the same time he succeeded in founding a Russian printshop in Amsterdam by granting extraordinary privileges. By the same token, the Tsar and all his associates supported the creation of a secular Russian alphabet to stand alongside the Church Slavonic; this project was roundly condemned by senior churchmen. As a result, the desired series of characters was not achieved immediately; a few letters which had been removed during drafting had to be re-instated. These were only to disappear finally from the Russian alphabet in the 1730s.

The new alphabet, or "civil script", of 1707/08 facilitated the rapid spread of printed books. The new type initially came from Holland. In 1710 Peter's *ukaz* officially decreeing the introduction of the new alphabet was published. This reform thus drew a distinction even in the script between both secular and ecclesiastical works. This externally visible difference also had the effect of a linguistic emancipation from ecclesiastical tradition. The characters of the civil script were simpler and easier than the old letters, and several letters of Greek origin had been expunged.

The reform of the alphabet, which took several years, was not merely a technical change in the position occupied by books in Russian society up to that point. The new measure led to a change in the intellectual attitudes of Russians. The new content of Russian books during Peter's reign was reflected in a change in their external appearance. Publications now contained a frontispiece, and a title page with a picture intended to give the reader as much information as possible about the content of the book. In 1708, a total of ten books was published. The main theme was war, i. e. the defence of fortresses; this is hardly surprising, given the military defeats incurred by the Tsar's troops at the hands of the Swedes, who had invaded Russia from the north.

The book production of 1708 was largely inspired by Peter himself. The Tsar examined each single work personally before it went to press. These publications were both original works and translations. As well as books on military science dealing mainly with technical questions of war on land and at sea, philosophical and historical works were published. There is no doubt that translations represented a tried and tested method of disseminating knowledge. Peter was constantly pressing translators for haste and made repeated attempts to find suitable translators. He even encouraged those of his closest associates who were of foreign origin and had the requisite linguistic knowledge at their disposal to take part in the work of translation. The Tsar was at particular pains to ensure that translations were

adequately revised, corrected and edited, in order to increase their usefulness and a great effectiveness.

Peter and his associates paid great attention to the production of school text-books. The most important of these was a school reader which appeared in 1717 under the title *A Mirror of Honour for Young People*; four editions were published up to 1723. In 1720, Feofan Prokopovich published his *Primer*. Peter also ordered the re-publication of important Ukrainian works of the 17th century such as the famous *Grammar* by Meleti Smotrytski (1619, new edition 1721), which had been in circulation in many editions since its first publication. The editor and proof-reader was Fedor Polikarpovich Polikarpov-Orlov, who had brought out a primer entitled *Bukvar* in 1701, which he followed in 1704 with a *Slavonic-Greco-Latin Dictionary*, i. e. a trilingual lexicon for use in the teaching of language and reading. Two new editions were printed of the popular *Synopsis* of 1674, a survey of Russian history.

The Russian translations of Wilhelm Stratemann's *Theatrum historicum*, and of the works of Samuel Pufendorf, are particularly eloquent testimony to the Tsar's interest in history and historiography. Polikarpov, Huyssen and Prokopovich were commissioned by the Tsar to write a contemporary history of Russia. Only fragments of this work were completed, primarily by Huyssen. Russian historiographers were evidently overawed by the colossal figure of the Tsar during his lifetime. What did materialize was Petr Pavlovich Shafirov's *Treatise on the Origins of the Swedish War*. The author, Peter's Vice-Chancellor, published his work in 1717. Shafirov's disquisition is the first official justification of Russia's historical claim to have access to the Baltic, to the "land of our fathers and grandfathers", if one disregards the demands already made previously by Ivan III and Ivan IV.

After the building of St. Petersburg, several printing-presses were established in the new city; these made a vital contribution to the realization of Peter's publishing programme. As before, the main emphasis was on translations, including works from the field of the "Arts", i. e. applied science, especially mathematics, physics, anatomy and botany. Numerous translations were successfully completed, but others were not; this was largely due to the translators, who did not have a sufficient degree of proficiency for the work. In particular, Russian scientific terminology still left much to be desired. Later scholars such as Lomonosov were also to bemoan this fact.

Tsar Peter not only urged writers, translators and printers to publish new books in Russian, but also initiated publications in other languages. The main task of these works was the propagation of the domestic and foreign policies of the Tsar. Readers abroad were also to be informed of the changes taking place in Russia. Thus contemporary works in foreign languages on Petrine Russia were also an important source of information.

Pamphlets, newspapers and periodicals appeared for the first time in the tsardom under Peter I, and occupied an important position in the system of publications initiated at this time. The Tsar played an even bigger part in the compilation of the first Russian newspapers than he did in the publication of books. One can justifiably assert that he wrote much of the copy for the first issues of newspapers himself.

Weekly newspapers had been appearing in Central and Western Europe since the 17th century, and the *Leipziger Zeitung* was published daily as early as 1660. A kind of forerunner of newspapers existed in 17th century Russia. These were the so-called corantos, which contained extracts from foreign news reports. It is true that these were not newspapers in any real sense, and in no way satisfied the growing needs of the Russian people regarding information. Here too the change came only with Peter I. On 16th December 1702 he issued an order that all important news from Russia and the surrounding countries was to be collected. The first Russian newspaper appeared in Moscow on 3rd January 1703 under the title *Vedomosti* (News). The full title was "News of military and other matters which have come to pass in Muscovy and in the neighbouring states and which should be known and remembered". The content of the *Vedomosti* was extremely diverse. As well as military and political news, there were reports on enterprises, new discoveries of ore deposits, oilfields, foreign cities, currencies, and titles of nobility.

It was not very long before that Tsar Aleksei Mikhailovich had had all the foreign newspa-

161 Alphabet of the "civil script" introduced
by Peter I, with corrections in the monarch's own
hand, 1710. Central State Archive of Old
Documents, Moscow

162 Letter from Peter I to Frederick I
dated 8th July 1709. In it, the Tsar tells the
Prussian king of his "marvellous victory" over the
Swedes at Poltava. The letter is also an example of
the chancery hand adapted by Peter I under the
influence of the new alphabet, which had just been
introduced. Zentrales Staatsarchiv, Merseburg

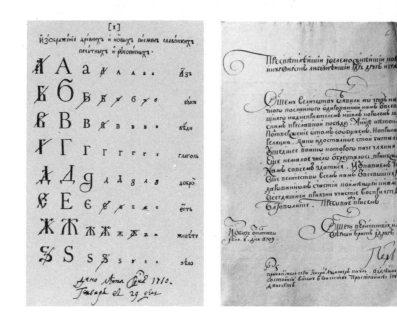

pers and journals circulating in Russia withdrawn and placed under restricted access. Even his associates required special permission to use the foreign periodicals, which were kept under close guard in the diplomatic *prikaz*. Peter's *Vedomosti* were on a small scale, and the size of the print-run varied greatly, from 30, 150 or 400 copies up to 1 000 or 2 500. The establishment of libraries and of book and art collections was very closely bound up with the spread of books. Public libraries set up by Peter already existed alongside private ones. In the course of his conquest of Livonia, the Tsar gained possession of large stocks of books. In addition he gave orders for the purchase of the stocks of the Ducal Library of Courland in Mitau. Books in Latin, French, German and English were imported to Russia from Königsberg and other foreign cities.

Peter himself evidently owned the largest collection of books, as we can see from the catalogue of the Russian Tsar's library. These included text-books of military science, fortress construction and artillery and many other works. A large part of Peter's library was taken up by atlases, maps, descriptions of parts of Russia, calendars, and reference works. Peter brought back some of these works from his travels in Germany, Holland, England and France. The Tsar's associates also owned large book collections. Peter I's collection formed the basic stock of the library of the St. Petersburg Academy of Sciences.

Despite the indisputable contribution made by Peter I to publishing and the press, these only really prospered in the mid-18th century. Whereas in the first twenty years of the 18th century the number of published works barely exceeded one hundred, in the last twenty years of the same century there were no fewer than five and a half thousand, including countless scientific works. Russia's westward advance, following the expulsion of Sweden and the initiation of lasting economic, cultural and political links with the other countries of Europe, resulted in a lively interchange between the peoples of East and West, North and South. Associated with this there was an increase in the knowledge of languages, combined with extensive travels and not least the readership of books, pamphlets, periodicals, newspapers, encyclopaedias, grammars, almanacs and many other printed works.

During the reign of Peter I and his immediate successors, Russian publishing was kept under close observation by the government and by Church leaders. There were only a few state and church-owned printing-presses in the whole tsardom, and none at all in private hands. It was important that the printshop at the newly-founded St. Petersburg Academy of Sciences was removed from the control of the Synod in 1727 and taken over by the Academy itself. Even in the first half of the 18th century, attention was drawn to the fact that the state monopoly of printing, publishing and the press was seriously inhibiting the development of the book industry and that this must of necessity lead to a noticeable shortage of the books required. The exercise of state and ec-clesiastical control over printed products was linked to the close control of the distribution of books, periodicals, almanacs and so on. Many of these went straight from the bookshops in Moscow and St. Petersburg to the authorities. However, it was also possible to buy books at the Moscow market-stalls, including publications in foreign languages which were offered for sale by merchants from abroad. It was also possible to order books here. In 1728 the Academy of Sciences in St. Petersburg opened its own bookshop; its manager was Gottlieb Clanner, who held the post from 1731 until 1739. Thereafter he was active as the agent of the St. Petersburg Academy at the trade-fair in Leipzig. Clanner's successors as manager of the bookshop were Siegmund Preisser and Franz Hirt. The St. Petersburg Academy of Sciences also operated a bookshop in Moscow from 1767 onwards.

The number of bookshops in Russia increased rapidly from the mid-18th century. In 1747 the Academic Press in St. Petersburg was split up into two parts, a Russian and a foreign section. In 1753 the printshop at the Naval Academy, which had been opened in 1722, was transferred to the newly-founded Naval Cadet Corps. The printing-press of the new University of Moscow began its work in 1756, to be followed in 1757 by the press at the Army Cadet Corps and in 1759 by the printshop of the Chancellery for Artillery and Fortification. After the accession to the throne of Catherine II, several printing-presses were established at the College of War (1763), the Holy Synod (1764) and the Artillery and Engineering Cadet Corps (1765).

At the same time as new state printshops and bookshops were being opened in the two major cities of Russia in the fifties and sixties, printing-presses and bookshops were being leased to private businessmen for the first time. Thus the Moscow University Press and its attached bookshop were operated by the merchant and court messenger Christian Ludwig Weber. The bookshop was taken over by the bookbinder Christian Rüdiger in 1777; he also had the printing press, albeit briefly, in 1779; this then came into the hands of Nikolai Ivanovich Novikov, who managed it until the measures taken against him in 1789. The firm of Rüdiger & Claudy was engaged by the University to run the printshop and bookshop from 1794 until 1800.

Private printers, publishers and booksellers were also coming to the fore in St. Petersburg from the mid-18th century. Thus Johann Jakob Weitbrecht operated the press at the Land Cadet Corps around 1770; his counterpart at the Artillery and Engineering Cadet Corps from 1773 was Johann Karl Schnoor. The two men founded the printing firm of Weitbrecht & Schnoor in 1776, but they remained together only until 1781, and thereafter went their separate ways. Schnoor received a further concession for the establishment of a press in Tver in 1779, and in 1784, Weitbrecht was awarded a contract to print books and documents for the College of Foreign Affairs and the Imperial Cabinet. His enterprise traded under the name

of the "Imperial Press". Christian Friedrich Kleen succeeded Schnoor at the Artillery and Engineering Cadet Corps from 1776 to 1784, initially in partnership with Bernhard Hecke. The newly-formed St. Petersburg *guberniya* administration was supposed to receive its own press in 1783, but this did not come into service until 1797, under the supervision of Petr Alekseevich Plavilshchikov. In addition to the aforementioned printshops, the typefounder Johann Michael Hartung had received permis-

sion in 1771 to set up a private printing-press and type-foundry, but he seems to have produced very little.

Printing and publishing received an added impulse as a result of the work of the Schools Commission in the early eighties. The Commission hired Bernhard Christoph Breitkopf, a member of the famous Leipzig publishing family, who was living in St. Petersburg as the tenant of the Senate Press, to print the documents concerning the compilation and publication of

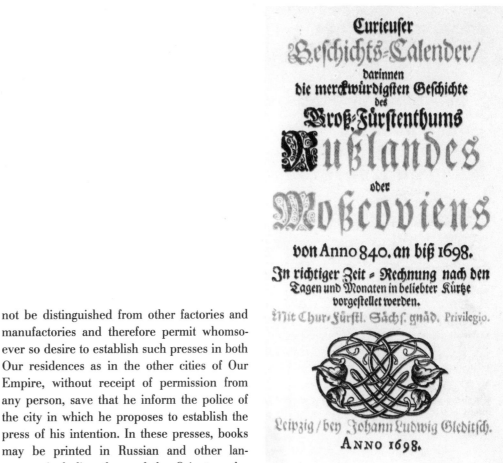

school textbooks. The huge volume of manuscripts to be printed forced the Schools Commission to engage Yemelyan Vilkovski's press in addition. Breitkopf printed the *Orbis pictus* of Comenius for the Schools Commission in Latin-Russian-German and French-Russian-German versions, as well as a Russian translation of Felbiger's manual for teachers, three geographical textbooks by the St. Petersburg headmaster Johann Friedrich Hackmann, an outline of natural history by Vasili Fedorovich Zuyev, a physics book by Johann Ebert, the *History of the World* by Yankovich and Yakovkin, a Russian primer by Yankovich and a Biblical history by the same author. Schnoor published all Betskoi's statutes and regulations. The *Comparative Dictionary of all the Languages*, which was inaugurated by Catherine II, was published twice, in 1787 by Schnoor and in 1790 by Breitkopf. Breitkopf was succeeded by Friedrich Brunkow in 1796. There was also a printing-press at the School of Mines which was opened in 1776, and which was later to become the Mining Academy. Printing work was also carried on in 1784—1787 on the presses run by Christoph Hennig, Pavel Ovshchinnikov and Petr Ivanovich Bogdanovich. The bookseller Friedrich Meyer also did occasional printing work.

The publication of Catherine II's *ukaz* on the establishment of private printing-presses on 15th January 1783 was an important event in the history of Russian publishing in the 18th century. This proclaimed: "We hereby most graciously command that printing-presses shall not be distinguished from other factories and manufactories and therefore permit whomsoever so desire to establish such presses in both Our residences as in the other cities of Our Empire, without receipt of permission from any person, save that he inform the police of the city in which he proposes to establish the press of his intention. In these presses, books may be printed in Russian and other languages, including those of the Orient, under the condition that nothing in them shall run counter to divine or civil law or shall be designed to cause public offence; the books to be printed shall be given a certificate to this effect by the police, who shall refuse to grant such a certificate should there be found anything which infringes against this Our command. Should books giving rise to such offence nevertheless be printed, not only shall they be confiscated, but the utterers of such a publication shall be summoned that they might be punished for infringement of the Law."

The admission of private printing-presses enabled the development of a multi-faceted printing industry. Printing-presses were set up in many towns and cities throughout the tsardom, for example in Kiev, Riga, Reval and even in places like Oberpahlen, a small town near Dorpat. As early as 1765—1766, the Riga *guberniya* administration allowed a physician, Peter Ernst Wilde, to set up a press, under the condition that he should print only his own works, and that these contain "nothing counter to religion, the state or the law of the land". Wilde began printing in Oberpahlen in October

1766. He published books and essays in German, Estonian and Lettish, including his own comprehensive work *Livländische Abhandlungen von der Arzneiwissenschaft* (Livonian studies in pharmacology) in 1770.

The firm of Johann Friedrich Hartknoch, which opened a bookshop and printing-press in Riga in 1765, attained an outstanding position in Russian publishing. As well as Hartknoch, there were other publishers and booksellers, including Johann Zacharias Logan, who operated his business in St. Petersburg. He became known as the publisher of the periodical *The Observer*, of which only a few issues appeared in 1781. The pedagogue August Witzmann was in an exceptional position; from 1776 he was the proprietor of an educational institute in St. Petersburg with its own small bookshop and lending-library. He wrote some of the textbooks for his institute himself and had them printed by Breitkopf and Plavilshchikov. In 1778, Witzmann also published the short-lived periodical, the *St. Petersburg Weekly*. The poet Johann Gottlieb Villa-

166 *New St. Petersburg Journal, 1783*

167 *Essays on the history of Peter the Great by Hartwig Ludwig Christian Bacmeister, Riga 1774*

168 *Title page of the first volume of Hartwig Ludwig Christian Bacmeister's* Russische Bibliothek, *St. Petersburg, Riga and Leipzig 1772. This important bibliographical handbook appeared between 1772 and 1789.*

mov fared better with his moralistic weekly *Promenades*, first published in 1772 and running to 26 issues with a total of four hundred pages. The *Russische Bibliothek* (Russian library), an organ of news and commentary in eleven volumes edited by Hartwig Ludwig Christian Bacmeister between 1772 and 1787, achieved outstanding significance and remains today an indispensible source-work and aid to research. Here we must also mention the *St. Petersburg Journal* directed by Christian Gottlieb Arndt and its continuation, the *New St. Petersburg Journal*, the two running from 1776 until 1784, and the *Nordic Miscellanies*, which were edited by August Wilhelm Hupel between 1781 and 1791, followed by the *New Nordic Miscellanies* from 1792 to 1797. Friedrich Konrad Gadebusch's *Livonian Library* (3 volumes, 1777) was also an important work of reference.

The St. Petersburg Academy of Science also played a particularly important role in the production of newspapers, journals and periodicals in Russia. As early as 1727, the Academic Press was merged with other presses to create the major printing works in Russia. In 1747 many documents were destroyed by a fire which broke out in the Academy building; these contained important information about the beginnings of the Academic Press, so a complete reconstruction of the first steps taken by the printshop is no longer possible. One of the first publications produced by the Academic Press was the *St. Petersburgische Zeitung* which appeared in German without a

break from 1727 until 1915. From 1831 it appeared daily, and from 1859 its management was taken over by a lessee. From 1874, publication passed to a private firm under direct contract to the Ministry of Popular Enlightenment. The *St. Petersburgische Zeitung* was published simultaneously in a Russian edition in 1727, under the title *St. Peterburgskiye Vedomosti*. It was an official publication, and was full of materials from the various fields of the economy, society, culture and politics. Thus even the first issues of the paper carried announcements about the sale of foreign and Russian books in the Academy bookshop, advertisements of puppeteers' performances and much more, including the sale of exotic birds and animals and offers of serfs for sale. The first editors were Christoph Friedrich Gross, Johann Simon Beckenstein and Gerhard Friedrich Müller.

From March 1728 the Russian edition appeared with a supplement, which subsequently appeared independently from 1729 until 1742 under the title *Historical, Genealogical and Geographical Footnotes to the Gazette*. These "Footnotes" were articles written in a popular style in which particular problems mentioned in the *Gazette* were examined more closely. They were widely read and had to be reprinted on several occasions during the sixties. The authors included well-known figures such as Tatishchev, Kantemir, Lomonosov, Trediakovski and Sumarokov.

Journal publication in Russia experienced a remarkable upsurge during the fifties and six-

ties. The Academy of Sciences published the *Monthly Essays for Edification and Entertainment*, edited by Gerhard Friedrich Müller, from 1755 to 1764 in Russian. In the foundation of this cultural and political monthly, the influence of Gottsched played a part; he was editing the journal *Das Neueste aus der anmutigen Gesellschaft* (Latest news from polite society) in Leipzig, which contained contributions about Russian history, literature and art. The *Monthly Essays* carried not only original contributions, but also translations of works on history, language and literature. Disquisitions on economic topics and on industrial production were also included. A further addition in 1763 was the inclusion of announcements of new publications. In general, the Academy's *Monthly Essays* made clear the close links which existed between science abroad and science in Russia. Though the St. Petersburg *Monthly Essays* published more and more Russian translations of English, French and German studies, then foreign cultural journals were at the same time including essays by Russian authors increasingly frequently.

The publications of the St. Petersburg Academy reached a wide readership as soon as they appeared. The Leipzig book market, and the agencies of Schuster and Breitkopf there, who made Russian publications available to scholars abroad, were important in this respect. As well as dispatching publications arriving from the St. Petersburg Academy to individual scholars, Jakob Schuster also offered Russian books for sale direct in his bookshop in Leip-

169 Vasili Nikitich Tatishchev.
He was one of the authors, along with Kantemir, Lomonosov, Sumarokov and others, of the Historical, Genealogical and Geographical Footnotes to the Gazette, *which were published between 1729 and 1742 as a supplement to the* St. Peterburgskiye Vedomosti.

zig. In addition, Schuster's bookshop offered aids to the learning of Russian. Thus Weismann's famous *Dictionary*, a German-Latin-Russian lexicon which also included an elementary Russian grammar, which had appeared in a revised version by Vasili Yevdokimovich Adadurov in St. Petersburg in 1731, was on sale as early as 1732. Schuster also displayed works by members of the St. Petersburg Academy and other Russian authors in the windows of his shop.

In Moscow, the activity of the new university led to an upsurge in press and publishing. Lomonosov and other scholars campaigned energetically for the expansion of the University Press so that it might meet the increased demand. It was not simply a question of education and training, but at the same time also of developing the University as a major centre of culture and research in Russia.

In 1756 the University was already publishing its own newspaper, the *Moskovskiye Vedomosti* (Moscow News), which appeared until 1800. A few years later numerous other newspapers, journals and textbooks were being published, along with an abundance of scientific and popular-scientific works which exerted a decisive influence on national consciousness and the formation of public opinion among the Russian population. The works published by members of the University also included numerous accounts of life in other countries.

Of this mass of translations, it was primarily geographical writings, travelogues and ac-

counts of the history of other peoples which interested Russian readers. Philosophical writings created similar interest. Entertaining literature was also well represented. Thus in the list of translated works published by the University Press we find the Berlin *Vade mecum for merry people*, published in 1773, the two-volume *Amsterdam Market, or Everything the Merchant and Banker Needs to Know* of 1762/63, books on the history of music and many others. In 1771, a catalogue of books was published in Russian, Latin, German and French, which could be purchased from the bookbinder Christian Rüdiger. The *Moskovskiye Vedomosti*, which continually reported on new publications, took care of the advertising.

The reception of the impulses and the insights gained from reading foreign literature was understandably different amongst the members of the various Russian social classes, strata and groups. The aristocratic upper classes not infrequently were most attracted by foreign fashions and manners, but many readers strove to learn from other nations and individuals and to put this knowledge to some use. In 1779, Novikov took over the Moscow University Press. His work in Moscow lasted ten years, and this period constituted one of the most outstanding chapters in the history of Russian culture in the 18th century.

After leaving military service, and following a short period spent practising as a lawyer, Nikolai Ivanovich Novikov, the son of a landowner, began working as a journalist. He used the medium of satire to take up the struggle against

the injustices he saw around him. He set himself the task of advancing the cause of human dignity by popular enlightenment and of making a contribution to the moral education of mankind. To this end he pilloried the despotism of the landowners, the ignorance, coarseness, extravagance and moral turpitude of the aristocracy and their blind adoration of French culture with unsurpassed trenchancy in the satirical journals which he published in St. Petersburg in the late sixties and early seventies: *The Drone* (1769/70), *The Painter* (1773/74), *The Bag* (1774) and others. Novikov paid particular attention to the dreadful excesses of the system of serfdom. In a fictitious correspondence between a country nobleman and his son, who lives in town, he depicted the miserable lot of the peasants under the lash, the mental cruelty of the rough, uneducated landowners and the untrammelled coarseness and licence of the rural aristocracy with deliberate naivety and vivid realism. Novikov's writings described the terrible poverty of the peasant serfs living in hovels unfit for human habitation, the hopeless fate of their children and their terror and helplessness in the face of their masters, with frightening urgency and realistic precision. In the struggle for the creation of proper living conditions for the Russian people, Novikov was joined by Denis Ivanovich Fonvizin, Luka Ivanovich Sichkarev, Vasili Grigorievich Ruban, Vasili Ivanovich Maikov and others.

Following her seizure of power in 1762, Empress Catherine II did all she could to win public support for her policies, both in Russia and abroad. She was very conscious of the importance of the literary and cultural journals of Russia in this respect, a long series of which had begun with the publication, by the St. Petersburg Academy of Sciences, of the *Monthly Essays for Edification and Entertainment* in 1755. She therefore founded her own satirical magazine in 1769, entitling it *All Sorts* and writing most of the articles for it herself. At this time, the Empress was unaware that she was to unleash with her magazine an avalanche of unprecedented breadth and perilousness, thus making possible the first flowering of Russian satirical magazines between 1769 and 1774. Eight such journals appeared in 1769 alone, including Novikov's celebrated *Drone*, which

took up the cudgels with Catherine's *All Sorts*. In the same way as Novikov, other thinkers, such as sociologists, constitutional lawyers, philosophers, historians and poets, used the exchange of opinions officially proclaimed by the Empress as an opportunity to attack the evils of the world around them. The upshot was that Catherine II banned any further publication of Novikov's magazines in the early 1770.

Novikov saw himself forced to shift his field of activity. As early as 1772 he had founded the "Society for the Promotion of Book Publishing" and had obtained the collaboration of a number of scholars. In 1779 he moved from St. Petersburg to Moscow, where he took over the management of the University Press as a tenant. In the space of a few years, Novikov had worked himself up to become the largest and most important publisher in Russia, a position which he defended until the end of the eighties. At times he employed more than a hundred workers at his presses, and within ten years he brought out more than a thousand volumes of scientific, pedagogical, cultural and popular scientific literature. At the same time he established an extensive network of bookshops and public libraries in Moscow and in the neighbouring cities.

From the beginning of the eighties, Novikov and his friends also began a comprehensive programme of charitable works. They opened a pharmacy and gave free medicines to the poor and needy. It was Novikov who pointed out that it was not only necessary to be concerned with research into Russian history

and with the preservation of historic monuments, but that one must also meet the immediate needs of the mass of the population. As a publisher and bookseller, Novikov developed his activities on the grand scale. At his instigation and under his supervision, countless classics of world literature were printed and thus came to the attention of the Russian readers for the first time. He also published many works by Russian scholars and authors. Textbooks were an important element of Novikov's publishing programme. Of the four thousand or so titles which appeared in Russia between 1771 and 1790, about one thousand were published by Novikov in Moscow. In 1768 there was one bookshop in St. Petersburg and one in Moscow; by the end of the century, there were thirty in St. Petersburg and twenty in Moscow. The newspapers and journals which appeared in St. Petersburg and Moscow at this time regularly carried advertisements for new publications, both for works published in Russia and for works published abroad. In the second half of the 18th century there were even some writers in Russia who made their living from the publication of literary articles, essays and books.

By taking over the University Press, Novikov also became the publisher of the *Moskovskiye Vedomosti*; he broadened its scope considerably in the following period. As Karamzin remarked, he strove to stimulate the public to read by all the means at his disposal. He dealt with books as a rich Dutch or English merchant dealt with products from all over the world, in-

telligently, imaginatively and far-sightedly. Thus Novikov succeeded in rapidly increasing the number of subscribers to the *Moskovskiye Vedomosti* from six hundred to four thousand. Less well-off subscribers not infrequently shared the cost of a copy. The income from this business was largely used for the benefit of schools and pharmacies. Novikov was constantly expanding his printshop to increase his printed output. When Catherine II's *ukaz* of 1783 permitted the establishment of private printing-presses, Novikov founded two more presses with the help of friends from the freemasons' lodges.

Problems of education and the school were prominent in the journals and other publications brought out by Novikov. His publications on the education of children were particularly important, as was the children's literature he produced, such as the first Russian magazine for children, the *Child's Reading for Heart and Mind*, which appeared as a supplement to the *Moskovskiye Vedomosti* between 1785

and 1789. The pedagogical ideas of John Locke and Jean-Jacques Rousseau were central to Novikov's children's literature. At the same time, Novikov put his philanthropy into action by creating asylums for the poor and the sick and collecting money for the needy. Novikov's activities in Moscow were supported by many progressives.

In October 1782, the Moscow University Press published an 11-page brochure addressed to "all lovers of science and patrons of learning" and inviting them to attend the inauguration of the "Friendly Learned Society"; the aims of the Society were set out in the enclosed programme, which was published in Latin and Russian. The founders of the Friendly Learned Society were Nikolai Ivanovich Novikov and Johann Georg Schwarz, a professor at the University. The Society aimed to develop its activities in accordance with philanthropic ideas. The founders of the Society saw this as the best means of ensuring that more students were trained and thus made into useful mem-

bers of society. The primary tasks were to be the dissemination of appropriate educational principles, the publication of textbooks and the provision of new institutes of learning. Furthermore, the "most celebrated foreign scholars" should be recruited and "a scientific correspondence begun with some of them". Particular importance was assigned to the training of Russian teachers.

The Moscow Friendly Learned Society was a unique private organization of persons who sought to influence the cultural development, moral renewal and improvement of Russian society. The Society owed its origin not simply to an idea of Novikov's or Schwarz's; the idea had been maturing for a decade in the minds of several figures who became members of this scholarly society. As well as Novikov's circle, there were other rallying points of progressive intellectuals pursuing other ends. The most important of these circles consisted of Nikolai Aleksandrovich Lvov, Gavriil Romanovich Derzhavin, Vasili Vasilievich Kapnist and Ivan

172 Title page of the satirical journal
The Drone *(1769/70). Novikov used his journals to
attack the excesses of the feudal-absolutist system.*

Ivanovich Chemnitzer, who gathered around the *St. Petersburg Messenger* between 1778 and 1781. Contact with the Novikov circle was provided by Mikhail Nikitich Muravev.

The members of the Friendly Learned Society were not revolutionaries seeking political struggle; they campaigned for the self-realization of the personality, for the spread of "true enlightenment", for self-knowledge, knowledge of God, and the moral education of man. These ideas were greatly imbued with the spirit of utopianism and rooted in mystical questing and meditation. As an 18th century rationalist, Novikov and those who shared his views did not reject the institution of imperial autocracy *per se*, but merely the form it had taken under Catherine II. Novikov saw in Paul, the heir to the throne and the true enlightened monarch.

Novikov's thought was not free of contradictions. According to his own testimony, he sought the truth again and again. In doing so he vacillated between Voltaire and religion, but found nothing which could grant him spiritual peace. As a result, Novikov's spiritual quest led him to freemasonry around the mid-seventies, and to initiation in the lodge. There is no doubt that the Pugachev uprising, which deeply affected Novikov, played a part in this. His religious sensibilities rejected any use of violence in the struggle against evil, but his sincerity of character, his philanthropy and his thirst for action urged him to find a way which offered a chance of opposing the unfettered tyranny of despotism. Novikov had heard of a book which provided satisfactory answers to all the great questions of society, life and the soul. The author of this book was the French theosophist and philosopher Louis Claude de Saint-Martin, whose mystic doctrines saw man as a spiritual being in the image of God.

Saint-Martin's work was to play a significant role for the Russian "Martinists". Its title was *Des Erreurs et de la Vérité* (Of errors and truth). This new version of the theory of freemasonry freed the individual from responsibility for not participating in resolute resistance to evil in those cases where it was demanded by conscience and reason; at the same time it offered an idiosyncratic moral system based on pseudo-scientific principles.

Freemasonry, which had penetrated the tsardom as early as the 1730s, began to spread rapidly through educated Russian society in the seventies and eighties. Ivan Perfilevich Yelagin, the Imperial Cabinet Secretary, became Grand Master of the Russian Lodges. The Director of Moscow University, the poet Mikhail Matveevich Kheraskov, was an enthusiastic member of an order of freemasonry. The most prominent men of the Russian Empire obtained admittance to Lodges. Freemasonry developed with bourgeois society and the Enlightenment as the first organizational union of the educated classes of Europe to transcend class barriers and international boundaries. Even if it was more or less incapable of offering any solutions, it did succeed in making its members aware of the problems which dominated the whole century, and in making gradual preparations for reform. The philosophy of the freemasons was based on pantheism and the idea of tolerance: everything in the world formed a unity, and this unity was found in all things. This "all in all" was God, an eternal, immeasurable and supremely wise being.

The Russian centres of masonic thought were in St. Petersburg and Moscow. In Moscow, freemasonry received noticeable stimuli from the work of Novikov and his supporters. The powerful patron of culture, Prince Nikolai Nikitich Trubetskoi, played an important part in promoting freemasonry. With his active participation, an administrative centre, the Supreme Directorate, was formed among the Moscow freemasons; this undertook a re-structuring of the system of lodges, based on the teaching of the German Rosicrucians.

The Moscow freemasons initiated closer contacts with the Rosicrucians in 1781 and 1782. The intermediary was Johann Georg Schwarz, a professor at Moscow University. Schwarz and Novikov worked closely together. Schwarz was working as deputy director at the Pedagogical Seminar which had been established in November 1779. There were some thirty pupils at this institution, including the future Metropolitans Mikhail and Serafim. With support from his friend Novikov, Schwarz founded a society of university scholarship-holders in 1781. A translation seminar was also set up at his instigation. Moreover, Schwarz edited a newsletter at the University in which he reported on various fields of scholarship.

According to those who heard them, Schwarz' university lectures were extremely effective. He lectured on philosophy several times in 1782 and 1783. His ideas were based on German mysticism, on Thomas a Kempis, Johann Arndt, Angelus Silesius and above all on Jakob Böhme. The Rosicrucians and Saint-Martin may also have influenced his intellectual stance to a greater or lesser degree. Starting from this spiritualist basis, Schwarz delivered vehement polemics against the French *encyclopédistes* and materialists, and in particular against Lamettrie, Helvétius and other philosophers. Of his contemporaries, Schwarz paid tribute to Johann Kaspar Lavater and Johann Georg Hamann, who was praised by the Moscow professor as a "new Böhme". Schwarz's guiding principle was that there did not have to be any conflict between faith and reason or between philosophy and theology.

Schwarz died near Moscow, at the age of only 33, in February 1784. A few months after his death, on 1st September 1784, Novikov and fifteen of his masonic friends founded the "Typographical Company", a limited company with two printshops and twenty presses and boasting a large staff of authors, translators, editors and printers. The Typographical Company immediately began to prosper, printing many books and opening several new bookshops. The results of his work with the company clearly put Novikov in competition with the cultural and political ambitions of Catherine II; the Empress had already initiated the publication of a *Collection for the Advancement of the Translation of Foreign Books into the Russian Language.*

There was an unusual complement of men of letters, philosophers and historians among the Russian freemasons. The Empress cynically referred to the freemasons as "monkeys" and composed a number of pieces attacking them, including the comedies *The Deceiver, The Deceived* and *The Siberian Shaman.* In her letters to Friedrich Melchior Grimm she referred to freemasonry as one of the "greatest idiocies" in the history of mankind. Yet Catherine's attitude to the Russian freemasons was not without its contradictions. Thus on the one hand, she saw them as agents of obscurantism, whilst on the other she suspected them of revolutionary and subversive machinations. In 1784, the Empress began to take repressive measures against freemasonry, which became enormously more powerful under the influence of the French Revolution of 1789. The conflict between the Empress and the heir to the throne, Paul, also intensified during these years. The Empress had long regarded Paul's court at Gatchina with a suspicious eye as a hotbed of palace conspiracies.

After the French Revolution had proved to her the malign influence the Russian "Martinists" could exert, Catherine II moved on to the offensive against the freemasons. In her opinion, the Martinists in the tsardom included primarily people like Novikov, whose activities were now brought to an abrupt end. The monarch accused the Friendly Learned Society and the Typographical Company, which were directed by Novikov, of activities likely to endanger the state. Novikov was arrested in April 1792 and imprisoned in the Schlüsselburg. Four years later, in 1796, and following Catherine's death, he was freed on the orders of Tsar Paul. He spent the last years of his life in retreat on the family estate at Avdotino, near Moscow. In 1812 he is said to have offered succour to Napoleon's exhausted troops. He died on 31st July 1818.

THE ORIGINS OF A
NATIONAL RUSSIAN LITERATURE

AS IN THE COUNTRIES of Western Europe, the emergence of the Russian nation brought with it the development of a national consciousness and, associated with this, of a national Russian literature. The fruits of these developments were an awareness of, and concern for, the national language, the creation of standards of style and expression in the Russian literary language and the cultivation of that language in belles lettres and scientific prose. At the same time, national history was examined from a didactic and educational standpoint. The development of the Russian nation and of Russian national consciousness was based on the increasing emergence of bourgeois social relations; thus the basic character of Russian literature in the 18th century was that of a bourgeois national literature. Its central theme was social and cultural advance in Russia.

The idea of progress was a crucial element in the intellectual attitudes of Peter and his associates. In order to popularize his plans for reform, and to acquaint the broad mass of the people with the cultural achievements of the time, Peter had a public theatre established in 1702. The scant literature of Peter I's time reflects the struggle for hegemony which was taking place in Russia between theological and secular literature. In this struggle, progressive clerics took the side of the enlightened Tsar, supporting Peter's work of reform in their writings. Thus the Archbishop of Novgorod, Feofan Prokopovich, came out in favour of social and cultural progress in his school dramas.

The Petrine reforms and the new lifestyle of the time opened up a broad range of activity to literature. However, Russian poets and authors in that period had neither the requisite linguistic preconditions at their disposal, nor did they have the necessary artistic experience to capture the ever-increasing sophistication of social life fully in literature. For this reason, the first works to appear were occasional poems and stories in which an attempt was made to create a new image of man. Thus in the story of the Russian sailor Vasili Koriotski, in the story of the Russian merchant Ivan and in the tale of the Russian nobleman Aleksandr we encounter typical figures of the Petrine epoch. Diligence, studiousness, humility, many-faceted erudition, courage and enterprise, inventiveness, but also cosmopolitan culture and patriotism: those were the qualities of the new generation of Russians to whom the literature of the Petrine period turned its attention. They were also the qualities required to make a career in the new Russia.

If Peter I's reign was primarily a period of seeking after new subjects in Russian literature, then the second third of the 18th century brought the first noticeable steps towards the development of a national literature characterized by the early Enlightenment. The main literary form was a very strongly national classicism. Russian classicism clearly reflected the systematization of old and new elements which had become necessary in poetry. The predominant theme during the reigns of the great Tsar's immediate successors continued to be a

firm belief in the inexorable advance of society and culture in the Russian Empire. Taking this as their starting-point, poets invoked Peter the Great in their works and called on his successors to continue the work he had begun. They recognized possibilities for development, particularly in the sciences, which had hitherto been inconceivable.

The economic and social rise of Russia, and the advance of the Empire to the forefront of the European powers filled Russian *literati* with a sense of national pride. Thus their poetic image of the world around the middle of the 18th century rested on the unshakeable conviction of Russia's increasing greatness. The successful campaigns and victories of the Russian armed forces were lauded in high-flown odes, tragedies and heroic epics. Satire, comedy and lampoon were directed against customs and prejudices which stood in the way of general progress, against the gallomania and extravagance of the nobility, the ignorance of the clergy and the heartless treatment of serfs by the landowners.

The first Russian writer to concern himself more intensively with the artistic method of classicism was the satirist Prince Antiokh Dmitrievich Kantemir (1709—1744), the youngest son of the Moldavian hospodar Demetrius Kantemir. As a writer and poet, Antiokh Kantemir was an important pioneer of modern Russian literature. In his works he presented the Petrine statesmen and dignitaries who had been honoured for their services to the state and the Russian nation as models to his aristo-

cratic equals. At the same time, however, the poet's satires pointed to incipient changes in the class structure and to the advance of bourgeois social forces. He made an impassioned appeal to the noble landowners to rouse themselves from their idleness and lethargy, their moral decadence and egoistic isolation. Kantemir was particularly explicit in his satire *On the Malevolence and Pride of the Corrupt Aristocracy*, in which he recognized true nobility as residing in the citizen who worked for the common good, irrespective of his social background. Kantemir's ideal Russian nobleman and citizen was possessed of an all-round education, a critical intelligence and an openness to new ideas; he was free of all class prejudice,

took an interest in science and literature, and renounced all extravagance. He regarded the basic demands on the aristocracy as being the duty to serve one's country in the armed forces, justice and humanity towards other classes and active commitment to the general welfare of the state. Kantemir took the view that the aristocrat was bound in duty to set an example to other citizens and to inspire his fellow-citizens to good deeds, as Tsar Peter had done. Honesty, decency, sympathy for those in need, bravery, and a willingness to make personal sacrifices should mark out the nobleman, otherwise he was not deserving of his rank and title.

The problem of a modern Russian verse-form occupied above all the philosopher and literary theorist Vasili Kirillovich Trediakovski during the thirties. His greatest work, the *Tilimakhida*, is a less than successful translation of Fénelon's *Télémaque* into Russian hexameters, and it incurred the scorn of literary scholars. Yet it is Trediakovski's achievement to have introduced the syllabotonic line of verse into Russian poetry. In his theoretical treatise, *A New and Brief Method for the Composition of Russian Verse* of 1735, he recommended the use of accentual cadences. Trediakovski's attempts at reform formed the basis for discussion of further proposals for the creation of harmonic Russian verse.

Mikhail Vasilievich Lomonosov also occupies a special place among the Russian poets of the mid-18th century. Indeed, this versatile scholar was celebrated by his contemporaries as an

important legislator on the Russian literary language and as a lyric poet embodying a new aesthetic awareness. Lomonosov understood poetry as "the oracle of a higher, exalted life, as the herald of all which is sublime and great". Literary activities were for him an inseparable component of his multi-faceted scholarly work. In a progress report to the directors of the Academy, Lomonosov listed twenty-two odes, thirteen lyrics, two poems and two tragedies alongside research into the vacuum, the lustre of metals, quicksilver, the telescope and the Russian chronicles. By prescribing norms of rhetoric and grammar and devising prosodic rules for Russian verse and literary style, he provided Russian poesy with a firm foundation. He also created the preconditions for the development of a modern Russian scientific and technological terminology.

Aleksandr Petrovich Sumarokov occupied one of the leading positions as a Russian classicist playwright. He was concerned to serve the welfare of the Russian nation, the keystone of which he regarded as the nobility, with the aid of the civilizing and educative function of literature. He nailed his colours to the mast of enlightened absolutism and rejected the abolition of serfdom. At the same time, however, he inveighed against the vices and licence of his class, which he saw as damaging the common good, in works such as his satire *On the Nobility* of 1771/72, and in his *Chorus on the Decadent World* the poet gave expression to the yearning of the common people for a country in which there were no corrupt, unjust or ava-

ricious officials or judges, no tax-collectors, lickspittles or slave-drivers, a land in which peasants, bourgeoisie and aristocracy worked equally for the welfare of the land of their birth.

As Trediakovski had done, Sumarokov sought in his theoretical studies to comprehend Russian literature as part of the wider process of world literature and to assign it to its proper place within it. To this end he took a great interest in the role of French literature as a model. The latter had, according to Sumarokov, indisputably set the necessary standards for modern literature. At the same time, he saw French classicism as the legitimate heir to the best traditions of antiquity and the Middle Ages, but he avoided the pitfall of primitive gallomania. The transition to classicism in Russian literature was accomplished in the work of Lomonosov and Sumarokov. In their works, these two poets made an important contribution to the development of national consciousness in Russia.

A new generation of writers began to emerge in Russia during the 1760s, a generation which had gained its education in the grammar schools and technical colleges and at the University of Moscow. A receptive and discriminating reading public developed simultaneously; this consisted largely of merchants, officials, teachers and students. Associated with this was a sudden upsurge in book production. The deficiencies in the knowledge of foreign languages which were prevalent amongst this new readership as opposed to the much more culti-

vated aristocracy meant that from this point on, translations of the most important writings of contemporary foreign authors became a lucrative business. In Russia too, literature, and in particular trivial literature for the mass market which dealt with themes of everyday life, began increasingly to assume the characteristics of a commodity. In the tsardom as elsewhere, writing which sought to satisfy the growing reading requirements of broad circles of the community, in particular the urban population, became a means of earning a living.

During the reign of Catherine II, which extended over three decades, Russian literature developed into a force in society, acting as the conscience of the nation, and assuming a leading intellectual and political role. In his authors' lexicon of 1772, Novikov listed two hundred authors along with their works, but the number of poets, playwrights and translators of foreign literature proliferated within a very short time. The number of theatre performances also reached previously unprecedented levels in the last third of the 18th century.

Catherine II was a ruler who was receptive to culture, literature and art. Her contemporaries at home and abroad were quick to praise her and spoke of her in terms of the highest regard. She maintained a lively correspondence with many cultured figures. Lastly, she herself tried her hand at writing and attracted talented poets to her court who, dazzled by its glamour and pompous magnificence or won over by Catherine's lavish generosity, sang the praises of the great Empress in fulsome eulogies.

Despite the efforts made by Catherine II to direct the development of Russian literature into the channels prescribed by her and her spokesmen, the emergence of a new generation of writers, and changes in the social structure of the reading public, brought with them the emergence of a new type of figure in Russian literature: the hero from the middle and lower classes, craftsman, carter, vendor, soldier's widow, lackey and peasant serf. The fate of the common man began to take up more room in literature. New heroes and new themes demanded new literary stylistic means and methods. As a result, tales, novels, sketches, travelogues, reportages, magazine articles and many other literary genres became increasingly widespread, since they offered the possibility of an adequate and accurate depiction of the social conditions, joys and sorrows, feelings and emotions of the lower classes. This meant that Russian classicism with its rigid canon gradually lost ground. Realistic genre pictures and scenes of everyday life began to take the place of the pompous panegyrics which had previously held sway. The transition from enlightened aristocratic classicism to enlightened democratic realism was already making its presence felt in Russian literature.

This process was accompanied by a significant intensification of the critique of the aristocracy. Here the Russian literature of the second half of the 18th century was able to continue a national tradition. Completely new topical questions were now raised, such as the responsibility of the sovereign before the law, the ideal of

175 *Russians in national costume.*
From Breton, La Russie, *vol. 1, Paris 1813*

176 *Genteel people on a sleigh ride.*
From Breton, La Russie, *vol. 1, Paris 1813*

177 *Denis Ivanovich Fonvizin.*
His comedy The Squire *was regarded as a social*
critique, and brought him into conflict with
Catherine II. Painting by Armand Charles Caraffe,
1784. Institute of Russian Literature, Leningrad

178 *Gavriil Romanovich Derzhavin,*
a Russian lyricist, wrote among other things his
Ode to Felitsia, *in which he glorified Catherine II.*

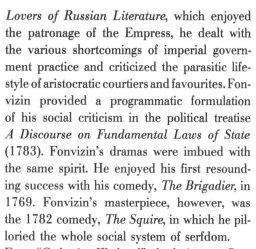

constitutional monarchy, and the position of the bourgeoisie, and in particular of the merchant class, in society. The major issue in Russian literature in the second half of the 18th century, however, was the question of the peasants and of serfdom.

Progressive Russian writers protested passionately against serfdom. Not only journals proved to be effective weapons in this respect, but all forms of literary production, such as travelogues, fictitious correspondences, fairy-tales, exotic tales, fables, fantasies and many more. Some Russian authors did not even shirk a public controversy with the crowned head of state. They deliberately used the far-reaching emotional, didactic and informative function of literature, and its broad, public character, to exert an active influence on the social development of the tsardom. Russian authors and poets championed the interests of the people, criticized existing evils and outlined their images of a better, indeed ideal, society in impressive sketches. They no longer addressed their appeals to single persons, as had been the case in the missives and odes of classicism; the authors of this period laid their concerns expressly before the public, before all literate, responsible citizens.

Literature and journalism therefore soon came to be a force to be feared by Catherine II. Those who, like Novikov, carried on public polemics against the authoress Empress, included the writer of comedies Denis Ivanovich Fonvizin. In the twenty questions which he submitted in 1783 to the journal *The Companion of Lovers of Russian Literature*, which enjoyed the patronage of the Empress, he dealt with the various shortcomings of imperial government practice and criticized the parasitic lifestyle of aristocratic courtiers and favourites. Fonvizin provided a programmatic formulation of his social criticism in the political treatise *A Discourse on Fundamental Laws of State* (1783). Fonvizin's dramas were imbued with the same spirit. He enjoyed his first resounding success with his comedy, *The Brigadier*, in 1769. Fonvizin's masterpiece, however, was the 1782 comedy, *The Squire*, in which he pilloried the whole social system of serfdom.

Even "Catherine II's bard", the lyric poet Gavriil Romanovich Derzhavin, took up the theme of the ideal nobleman, and in doing so he struck a distinctly critical note. As a supporter of the regime of enlightened absolutism, Derzhavin "smilingly told our rulers the truth" and called on these rulers to respect the law, to care for the poor and the bereft and to administer justice to all. He hoped for a moral purification of the aristocracy and that it would take to heart its civic duties, and he hoped that the "philosopher on the throne" would create better conditions for all in Russia. At the same time, Derzhavin sang the praises of Russian military victories in the struggle against the Turks and called on enlightened Europe to fight shoulder to shoulder under the leadership of the Russian Empress against the common enemy of Christendom.

Classicism, which was the literary movement governing the process of artistic creation in Russia around the middle of the century, underwent a number of transformations in the last third of the century. Russian literature had its Horace (Kantemir) and its Racine and Molière (Sumarokov). Sumarokov's pupil, Mikhail Matveevich Kheraskov, was to become the Russian Homer. He composed the first great artistic epic, and at the same time represented Russian tragedy in the second half of the 18th century. Kheraskov laid the foundations of his fame with the epic *Rossiyada* in 1779.

Vasili Ivanovich Maikov, who belonged to the group around Kheraskov and was regarded as

a pupil of Sumarokov, contributed several poems to the classicistic genre of the comic-heroic poem. The colourful, knockabout burlesque *Elisei, or Bacchus Enraged* of 1771 is regarded as Maikov's masterpiece. In it the poet, parodying Virgil's *Aeneid*, describes in the epic style the grotesque experiences and adventures of a Russian coachman in the taverns, brothels and shops of St. Petersburg, taking satirical swipes at contemporary social conditions in the tsardom.

The stories of Ippolit Fedorovich Bogdanovich, especially the poem *Dushenka* (1783), were written in a "light" style. Yakov Borisovich Knyazhnin was a direct successor to Sumarokov. He criticized the imperial bureaucracy in his comedies and comic operas *Misfortune from a Carriage* (1779), *The Braggart* (1786) and *Foolish Fellows* (1790), whilst in his tragedies, such as *Vadim of Novgorod*, he eulogized the renowned city republic of Old Russia.

Sumarokov's school also included Aleksei Andreevich Rzhevski, who came from an old noble family. He published primarily smaller works between 1760 and 1763; these included elegies, stanzas, songs, sonnets and idylls, and appeared principally in journals edited by Kheraskov. Between 1765 and 1769 he wrote a few odes and a number of tragedies, of which *Prelesta* (ca. 1765) and *The Alleged Peasant* (before 1769) became more widely known.

Authors from the most diverse intellectual and political camps intervened in the literary discussion which resumed with renewed vehemence at the beginning of the 1780s. Unmistakably critical tones were to be heard in the works of the classicist playwright Vasili Vasilievich Kapnist, such as the *Ode on Slavery* (1783), and several satires in which the aristocrat and poet opposed the extension of serfdom to the Ukraine.

This theme was addressed from the sixties and seventies onwards by writers from the peasantry itself. Despite the enlightened and philanthropic slogans which the Empress proclaimed during the first decade of her reign, she issued an *ukaz* in 1765 permitting landowners to condemn their serfs to forced labour. This was followed in the same year by an order forbidding serfs on pain of punishment to appeal direct to the crown with complaints against their landowners. This *ukaz* removed the peasant's last legal defence against the despotism of his master.

The first literary products of peasant writers took the form of "complaints". The *Servants' Complaint* was typical of the new peasant literature. Other small-scale manuscript novellas, satires and songs about serfdom contained descriptions of peasant slavery and poverty filled with hopelessness; but at the same time, they railed against the stupidity of officials, who allowed themselves to be outwitted by crafty peasants.

The most devastating critique of the existing order, culminating in a call for the revolutionary destruction of aristocratic society and the emancipation of the serfs, was delivered at the end of the 18th century by the aristocratic writer Aleksandr Nikolaevich Radishchev, whose ideas continued to inspire Russian revolutionaries throughout the 19th and at the beginning of the 20th century.

In literary terms, Radishchev's novel *Journey from St. Petersburg to Moscow* (1790), with its predominantly realistic content, is a work of the early realism, which had not yet fully developed, of the age of Enlightenment. The close interaction of early realism and enlightenment, and the simultaneous debate with the rigid forms of predominantly aristocratic classicism, produced the literary current of sentimentalism, which corresponded more closely to the interests

and ideas of the non-aristocratic middle classes. Writers no longer looked for their material among kings and generals, but in everyday life, in the sufferings of the people and in the spiritual conflicts of the peasants and the bourgeoisie, portraying them in dramas, novels, poems and other forms. In this process the previous hierarchical distinctions between literary genres and the rigid rules of the various linguistic styles were swept away. The intermingling of various genres, the introduction of bourgeois tragedy, the merging of high and low levels of language and the extensive use of prose brought literature much closer to social reality. Although Radishchev acknowledged his debt to sentimentalism in many aspects of his writings, he rejected, as Fonvizin had done before him, the stylized treatment of history and folklore which was its hallmark.

Radishchev's literary oeuvre betrays the influence and inspiration of various Russian and foreign writers. His relationship to representatives of German intellectual life such as Herder and Mendelssohn has long been known, but the author of the *Journey from St. Petersburg to Moscow* was just as well acquainted with the works of Albrecht von Haller, Friedrich Gottlieb Klopstock, Christian Fürchtegott Gellert, Salomon Gessner, Christian Ewald von Kleist, and others. By the same token, Radishchev's contacts with German lyric poetry were not restricted to the early Enlightenment and Lessing periods, but also took in the *Sturm und Drang* (Storm and Stress) movement of 1770—1790. At this time German and

Russian writers saw themselves faced with similar tasks: to create a national literature, liberate poetic creation from the domination of crowned heads, and support democratic ambitions among the broad mass of the people. Radishchev's poems contain very clear analogies to the poets of the *Göttinger Hainbund* and writers close to them, such as Johann Heinrich Voss, Georg August Bürger and Christian Friedrich Daniel Schubart. The German writers shared with Radishchev the deep desire to transform the ideas of the Enlightenment into social action, and resolutely to take up the struggle for the liberation of the enslaved peasants.

Radishchev's treatment of the theme of freedom in his *Ode to Liberty* offers eloquent examples of these correspondences with the work of German poets. The relationship becomes quite clear if we compare *Ode to Liberty* with some of Klopstock's odes, with the lyric poetry by Voss, with Schubart's *Oh Liberty, Liberty!*, Bürger's *Incitement to Liberty* and Haller's didactic poem *The Alps*. These correspondences in the treatment of the theme of freedom demonstrate that Radishchev's poetry, and in particular his great *Ode to Liberty*, saw the concerns of the nation in a wider, world-historical context; in this it exhibits many points of contact with the progressive lyric poetry of 18th century Germany.

A new literary theme, which was dealt with primarily by non-aristocratic writers, was that of unhappy love affairs across class barriers. The works which took this as their theme in-

cluded two novels by Nikolai Fedorovich Emin, *Rosa* (1786) and *The Play of Fate* (1789). These works were intended to awaken the sympathy of the reader. Mikhail Dmitrievich Chulkov, the son of a merchant and a talented writer, described *The Pretty Cook, or The Adventures of a Dissolute Woman* (1770), and also published a four-part collection of songs (1770—1774). The heroine of Chulkov's *Dissolute Woman* was a soldier's widow who had sunk to the level of a prostitute. Mikhail Ivanovich Popov's musical-literary opera *Anyuta* was a love-story centred around a peasant-girl, using popular motifs and scenes. Aleksandr Onisimovich Ablesimov's story of the *Miller, Wizard, Quack and Matchmaker* (1779), and the *St. Petersburg Market* (1779) by Mikhail Alekseevich Matinski belong to this same group. Fedor Aleksandrovich Emin depicted the emotions of two lovers in *The Letters of Ernest and Doravra* (1766), which were written in the style of sentimentalism. The life of a poor peasant-girl was the subject of Pavel Yurievich Lvov's sentimental novel *The Russian Pamela*.

Nikolai Mikhailovich Karamzin is regarded as the theoretician, perfecter and at the same time leading representative of Russian literary sentimentalism. In 1792 he published his famous short story *Poor Liza*, in which he relates the unhappy love of a poor peasant girl for a frivolous young aristocrat who seduces the girl he loves but marries a rich aristocrat. Karamzin's sentimental tales were followed by a flood of emotional love stories which had the same ef-

The origins of a national Russian literature

183 Ivan Andreevich Krylov chose fables as a medium to criticize social wrongs in Russia without fear of censorship. Engraving by Orest Adamovich Kiprenski. State Tretyakov Gallery, Moscow

184 Nikolai Mikhailovich Karamzin. Painting by Damon. State Tretyakov Gallery, Moscow

185 Aleksandr Petrovich Sumarokov was not only a writer, but also the director of the first Russian theatre in St. Petersburg. Portrait by Fedor Stepanovich Rokotov. State Museum of History, Moscow

fect in Russia as Goethe's *Sorrows of Young Werther* had in Germany.

A few of Karamzin's tales already contained a strong streak of romanticism; these were set in Scandinavia (*Bornholm Island*, 1793) and in Spain (*Sierra Morena*, 1795). Karamzin's passionate interest in the history of his own country found expression in *Natalya, the Boyar's Daughter* (1792) and in *Governor Marfa* (1803). His ballads, *Count Guarinos* (1789) and *Raissa* (1791), and the poem *Ilya Muromets* (1794), which had its roots in folklore, were pure Romanticism.

After being appointed Court Historiographer to Tsar Alexander I, Karamzin devoted the last two decades of his life almost exclusively to the study of Russian history. His twelve-volume *History of the Russian Empire* (1816—1824), which is imbued with great patriotism, is one of the most important works of Russian historiography of the early 19th century. It represented an important source of material for subsequent generations of poets who wished to heighten the awareness of Russian history. A German edition of this monumental work was published at the same time. Karamzin, who was esteemed by his contemporaries as the founder of sentimentalism and as a national historian, made an equally meritorious contribution to the development of the modern Russian language. Karamzin's work for linguistic reform was an important stage in the evolution of modern literary Russian.

Although sentimentalism continued to dominate the literary scene in Russia at the end of the 18th and the beginning of the 19th century, with countless imitators of Karamzin describing the romantic adventures and sufferings of "poor" heroines on the pattern of his works, there were also literary works which continued the critical social tradition of Novikov, Fonvizin and Radishchev. Early realist writing reached a new climax in the works of the fabulist Ivan Andreevich Krylov.

Sumarokov, Ivan Ivanovich Chemnitzer and Ivan Ivanovich Dmitriev had already presented several collections of fables to the Russian people, but Krylov was the first to succeed in

giving this internationally popular genre a specifically Russian colouring. Krylov's peasants and anthropomorphic animals proved to be more than puppets; they were intimately tied up with Russian life. The defenceless sheep and smaller animals were just as much at the mercy of the powerful bear, the cunning fox and the mighty lion as the defenceless serfs were at the mercy of the all-powerful land-owners. Like other fabulists, Krylov also criticized general human frailties and vices such as phrasemongering and empty verbosity, envy and superciliousness, sycophancy and flattery, bragging arrogance and self-importance. Ample evidence of this is provided by his fables. They turned their attention to the chicanery of the tsarist bureaucracy and the sufferings of the working classes. In his works of social criticism, Krylov also made direct references to the eventful years of Russia's struggle against the Napoleonic invasion. His fable *The Wolf in the Dog-Run* is a lasting memorial to these years. Krylov's popular idiom and the life-like nature of the episodes and characters he describes were an important step on the way to classical Russian realism. As a poet, Krylov stood on the threshold of the new poetry of the 19th century.

The fundamental ideal of Russian literature in the 18th century corresponded to the image of man in European literature as a whole; it reflected the emancipatory trend of the Age of Enlightenment and anticipated the liberation of man from spiritual and material oppression.

11.

186 Russian peasant.
From Georgi, Beschreibung, St. Petersburg 1776

187 Inside a peasant's cottage.
Engraving by Geissler, ca. 1804

188 Beggars.
Watercolour by Ivan Alekseevich Yermenev,
ca. 1770. State Museum, Leningrad

189 Blind beggars singing.
Watercolour by Ivan Alekseevich Yermenev.
State Russian Museum, Leningrad

190 Peasants' repast.
Watercolour by Ivan Alekseevich Yermenev.
State Russian Museum, Leningrad

191 Estonian woman.

192 Armenian woman.

193 Kaluga woman
in winter dress.

194 Kamchatka woman.

195 Merchant from
Kaluga.
From Georgi, Beschreibung,
St. Petersburg 1776

196 Vasili Vasilievich Kapnist.
Painting by Vladimir Lukich Borovikovski. Late
18th century. State Russian Museum, Leningrad

ARCHITECTURE

ART OCCUPIES an important place in the cultural history of 18th century Russia. A new conception of art arose in the Age of Enlightenment with a secular character, replacing the church-bound modes of expression typical of the 17th century. The evolution and development of Russian national consciousness were of great benefit to the arts. The Petrine reforms, which were an important prerequisite for the social and cultural advancement of the country, were particularly important for this new style of art. This revival assumed major proportions from the middle to the end of the 18th century. The Academy of Arts in St. Petersburg developed into a national centre for the training of Russian artists, and produced outstanding masters. The excellent training they received there enabled them to express the social ideals of their times in consummate artistic form. The architects, for example, created great works of national architecture which were admired the world over. The classicistic style of architecture also had a significant influence on the development of sculpture, which reached great heights. Portrait-painting achieved great brilliance, in particular ceremonial and psychological portrait-painting. This art-form in the second half of the 18th century in Russia demonstrated the organic link between the concept of the human personality represented by enlightened thinkers and men of letters, and attempts to present the individuality and uniqueness of the human countenance in as life-like a way as possible. At the beginning of the 19th century, classicism as an

art movement was superseded by romanticism, which came into being in the course of a new stage of social development.

The far-reaching changes which took place in Russia in the late 17th and early 18th century also had a marked effect on building. It became particularly important to construct new towns and factories, as well as buildings for social and official purposes. Church and monastery buildings were also given a new look. A very important innovation was that detailed town plans were now used in Russia, with building being supervised by a state commission for the first time from 1709. Great parks and gardens were laid out in new ways and on an unprecedented scale. An entire code of building regulations, which were definitive for modern cities, resulted from Peter I's instructions regarding the promotion of massive construction in the cities, street alignment, fire precautions, the provision of parks and quays, drainage, paving, and street lighting at night. In this respect, the reign of Peter I marked a turning-point in the history of Russian architecture. For the first time in Russian history, an entire city—the later capital of the great Empire, St. Petersburg—was constructed after precise plans.

One of the architects working in Russia at the beginning of the 18th century was Ivan Petrovich Zarudny, an artist talented in many fields who was also renowned as a painter and sculptor. One of his major works was the Menshikov Tower in Moscow, which was built between 1704 and 1707 on the initiative of

Aleksandr Danilovich Menshikov on his own estate. Zarudny's design borrowed from the tradition of wooden tented roof church construction, thus giving the traditional sacred architecture a completely secular countenance. The tower clearly exhibited the transformation which was taking place in Russian society. The type of construction built by Zarudny for Menshikov was to have a considerable influence on all subsequent Russian architecture. In his capacity as a sculptor, Zarudny made several carved iconostases, for example in the Cathedral of St. Peter and St. Paul in the Peter and Paul fortress in St. Petersburg.

A start was made on building St. Petersburg immediately after the outbreak of the Northern War. It was part of the same Russian policy of reaching out to the West which was also being pursued both in the diplomatic and military spheres. St. Petersburg was not only intended as Russia's window to the West, but also as the latter's window to the tsardom. The proposed site, with its low-lying, muddy river-banks, was unsuitable for the founding of a large community. The original intention was therefore to construct only a port and a fortress there, but Tsar Peter was soon to decide to create the new capital of his Empire on that very spot. St. Petersburg was officially founded on 16th (27th) May 1703 when the foundation stone was laid of a fortress which was to bear the names of the Apostles Peter and Paul. During the first years of construction, the Swedish enemy was being fought in the immediate vicinity of the new city. Little is known, however,

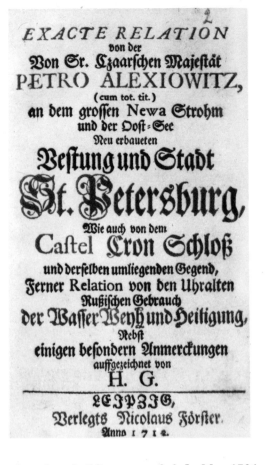

197 Title page from the Exacte Relation von der … Neu erbaueten Vestung und Stadt St. Petersburg …, *1712*

198 The Winter Palace in St. Petersburg at the time of Peter I. Engraving by Aleksei Fedorovich Zubov, 1717

about how building proceeded. In May 1704 the Kronschloss fortress was completed, thus securing the harbour on the seaward side. It was probably at this point that Peter ordered a more systematic approach to constructing the new city and recruiting the necessary workforce.

The Admiralty was the second major construction project in St. Petersburg. It was a large shipyard, but also played a defensive role. These two complexes determined the topography of the city centre from the outset. The next fortifications were built on the Neva, the Fontanka and the Moika in the form of wooden quays. Early engravings and city plans of St. Petersburg—whose accuracy cannot, it is true, be relied upon—show the fortified shipyard and Admiralty, the governor's palace, the Menshikov palace, the Peter and Paul fortress and, to the north, a large market and residential quarters for the workers. Later a larger complex was added in the form of the Tsar's residence, with its parks, and houses for the officers, engineers and craftsmen. Thus St. Petersburg gradually assumed the features of a city which, while its access from the sea was

blocked by the Kronschloss, was by no means totally protected from external threats. Only Peter's victory at Poltava in 1709 and the annexation of Livonia, Kexholm and Viborg by Russia in 1710 brought St. Petersburg the necessary protection. Rapid advances could then be made in expanding the city. In 1712 the Tsar made the decision which everyone had anticipated, and moved with his family from Moscow to St. Petersburg. The Senate and his aides had no alternative but to follow. This meant that St. Petersburg, founded so shortly before, had become the new metropolis of the Russian Empire.

The new imperial capital was built by the labour of many. Apart from the thousands of conscript labourers from all over the country, this included numerous foreign architects and master-builders from Italy, Holland, Germany, France, and other countries. But, with few exceptions, they began work only once the Peter and Paul fortress, the Admiralty and other complexes had already been built. No-one was in any doubt that the main initiative for the work of construction came from Tsar Peter himself. Feofan Prokopovich wrote: "It is fitting to acknowledge that he found a wooden Russia but created a golden one." Not infrequently, the untamed forces of nature had to be braved during construction, in the shape of fire, disease, flood and other plagues. Only a few months after the founding of the city, in September 1703, contemporary reports spoke of a "great gale" which buffeted "the new fortress, known as St. Petersburg … which was so

strong and lasted so long that it drove the water from the sea so high upon the land that it rose above head-height, and two thousand sick and injured people, who were not able to be brought away from there or to escape themselves in the panic, were drowned and mostly dragged out to sea as the waters receded". Three years later the Tsar himself reported of men and women sitting in trees and on rooftops "as at the time of the Flood". Wolves, too, were a cause for concern for the inhabitants of St. Petersburg. In 1714, for example, an entire sentry patrol is said to have been "devoured" by them, and "a few days later, a woman in broad daylight in front of Prince Menshikov's house".

The Italian architect Domenico Trezzini began work in the new city of St. Petersburg in about 1706. He had come to Russia after working in Denmark. He entered the service of the Russian Tsar, who ordered him to St. Petersburg immediately. Here Trezzini was to work for almost thirty years, until his death in 1734, during which time he completed numerous projects.

One of Trezzini's important constructions was the Cathedral of St. Peter and St. Paul in the Peter and Paul fortress, which was built under his supervision on the site of an earlier wooden cathedral. The ruler was particularly interested in the bell-tower, which he regarded as a symbol of his new residence. The cathedral and bell-tower were badly damaged in the fire of 1756 and had to be restored in the 1760s and 1770s. Another important work by

Trezzini in the Peter and Paul fortress was the gate dedicated to St. Peter (1717/18). But one of his finest works was the complex of twelve colleges (begun in 1722 and completed in 1742) which today houses the University of Leningrad. At the same time, Trezzini began work on an outline of the Aleksandr Nevski Monastery, and built the chapel in the north wing, which was dedicated in 1724. The early St. Petersburg, which was built of wood, did not survive long. The wooden houses were replaced by massive stone structures in rapid succession. Indeed, the Admiralty was rebuilt three times. Many fortifications were built in the first years of existence of the city, and after 1727 house-building was also stepped up dramatically.

During his visit to Germany in 1712, the Tsar also viewed, and greatly admired, the work of Andreas Schlüter in Berlin and Potsdam. During his visit to Russia, which lasted just over a year, Schlüter directed work on Peter I's castle in the summer gardens on the Neva, and on the fountains by the Fontanka, and completed work on the Orangeries in the summer gardens. He was evidently entrusted with super-

vising work in Kronstadt at the same time. Johann Friedrich Braunstein, who had come to Russia with Schlüter, worked in the tsardom for many years, and was particularly involved in the building of Petrodvorets, for which he drew up the first plans. One of Braunstein's most important works at Petrodvorets was the palace of Monplaisir, which was built between 1714 and 1725. Braunstein also worked in Tsarskoye Selo (today called Pushkin), where the first park was then being laid out.

Peter's last great visit to Europe influenced the building work in St. Petersburg which followed. This time it was French Baroque which captivated the Russian ruler. Even before he returned home, a horde of French artists had already set off for the Russian capital, led by the then famous architect Jean-Baptiste Le Blond. They were to concern themselves principally with extending the Tsar's pleasure grounds. In his letters from abroad, Peter insisted that plans be worked out quickly for his parks in St. Petersburg.

So far, Tsar Peter had had little luck with his architects. The genius Andreas Schlüter, who had fallen into disfavour in Berlin, the "Chief

Building Director" of the Tsar, whose orders were obeyed even by Trezzini, met an untimely death before he had made a proper start to his work. This served to arouse all the more curiosity in the new man who came to St. Petersburg in 1716, Le Blond, the "greatest engineer and architect ever in Russia" as a contemporary described him.

Le Blond visualized St. Petersburg as an enormous sea fortress similar to the "ideal cities" of the Italian Renaissance. When the Tsar returned, he walked through the city with Le Blond, the French master's plans in his hand, and quickly came to the conclusion that they were impracticable. The main flaw in Le Blond's plans for the city lay in the fact that they were too abstract, and did not pay sufficient attention to the natural features of the site.

Thus the hopes which the Tsar had placed in his new "general architect" were dashed. The ruler discharged him from the task of extending St. Petersburg and asked him instead to continue the work on Petrodvorets and on the large palace and parkland in Strelna. Le Blond died young in 1719. Several other foreign architects worked in St. Petersburg with Schlüter and Le Blond, and immediately after their deaths, including the Germans Gottfried Schädel and Johann Georg Mattarnovi, the Swiss Nikolaus Friedrich Härbel, and many others.

As Peter did not have an outstanding architectural genius at his disposal who was capable of drawing up systematic plans for the extension

of his capital, he at first refused to accept new plans and ordered work which had commenced to be continued as he had instructed. To this end, he stepped up the activities of the Building Commission which was directed by Ulyan Akimovich Sinyavin. The personal involvement of the Tsar in the building of St. Petersburg and its environs is clear from the more than one hundred plans in Peter's own hand which were found among his cabinet papers after his death.

In the twenties and thirties, St. Petersburg became a majestically beautiful city. The first Nevski Prospekt was designed as early as 1713, the year in which the Aleksandr Nevski monastery was founded. In the same year, a start was made on the construction of a second Prospekt, which betrayed the influence of Versailles and Paris. The new Nevski Prospekt showed similarities with the Avenue de Saint-Cloud and the Avenue de Paris. The Russian architects evidently drew on the plans of Le Blond during its construction. The most prominent of the Russian architects active after the death of Peter I were Zemtsev, Korobov and Yeropkin. Under their supervision, the castle banks were strengthened, paving and enclosure work undertaken, lighting improved and marshes drained, thus reclaiming land for construction.

The most famous architect in St. Petersburg in the 1720s and 1730s was Mikhail Grigorievich Zemtsev. Like Trezzini before him, he made a name for himself with his bell-towers. His high pointed towers proved not only to be beautifully proportioned, but also integrated well into the townscape of the low-lying city. Zemtsev built the St. Mary Church of the Nativity on the Nevski Prospekt, which later had to make way for the Kazan Cathedral, as well as the St. Simon Church in the Mokhovaya Ulitsa. The bell-towers of both cathedrals combined with the pointed spires from the time of Peter I to form the unique silhouette of early St. Petersburg.

Zemtsev's work in St. Petersburg from the mid-20s sparked off a period of intense activity. Zemtsev was responsible for work on the palace and the Aleksandr Nevski monastery; he was also the director of the School of Architecture. He carried out extensive work on the summer gardens, and was also in charge of work on the great "Italian Palace" on the east bank of the Fontanka, and on an administrative building on the Moika. One of the master's last great projects was the Anichkov Palace which lay on the west bank of the Fontanka, and was completed only after Mikhail Zemtsev's death.

Ivan Kuzmich Korobov was also an extremely busy architect. In 1717 he travelled to Holland and Flanders to familiarize himself more closely with shipbuilding and hydrotechnical construction there. In St. Petersburg he participated in the reconstruction of the Admiralty College from 1727 and drew up a plan for the entrance gate with its tower, which was crowned by a gilded steeple surmounted by a weather-vane in the form of a three-masted ship.

Petr Mikhailovich Yeropkin studied in Italy and returned to Russia in 1724. This versatile artist, who owned a large library of scientific works, showed a particular predilection for architectural theory and also translated Italian books on architecture. As a member of the State Building Commission, he elaborated plans for the development of the Admiralty island and that part of the city lying between the Neva and the Moika. He also produced plans for the western parts of the city. This gifted town-planner and architect fell into disfavour during the rule of Biron, against which he openly rebelled, and was executed in 1740.

The main achievement of Zemtsev, Korobov and Yeropkin lay in the way they redesigned St. Petersburg, based on a system of radiating streets. They embellished the face of the capital with ring-roads, parks and canals, and created important areas which could later be developed, from the middle to the end of the 18th century.

The new imperial capital put an end to the synonymity of Russia and Moscow which had existed since the 15th century. The new city on the Neva was, to Tsar Peter, a symbol of his work of reform. It was not without reason that he called the city his "Paradise" and sought invigoration and edification there in the brief respite allowed him from the vicissitudes of warfare. He issued countless decrees which favoured the expansion of St. Petersburg at the cost of other cities. An Academy was built in the new capital where there were glamorous celebrations, and foreign envoys built their

homes on the banks of the Neva. Peter's opponents in Russia complained that the new capital had golden shoes whilst the old one had to make do with bast.

St. Petersburg, the new metropolis on the periphery of the Russian Empire, occupied a key trading and strategic position, which was to become important not only in terms of economic geography, but also as a communications centre. The capital was popular with foreigners, since it was linked with the economic and cultural centres of Central and Western Europe by the Baltic and the regions on its shores, and acted as a magnet for the leading and ascendant forces among the Russian people: the nobility, the bourgeoisie, the lower urban classes and non-adscript peasants. Thus St. Petersburg, in keeping with the intentions of its founder, was truly the window to the West. It was no accident that, soon after the first piles had been driven into the swamp of the Neva Delta, other countries were gazing in wonder at the miracle in the North, a city which was conjured up out of a wilderness at the behest of the Russian Tsar and by the industry of the Russian people.

Important stimuli for the historical, linguistic and literary consciousness of the early Russian nation emanated from the new capital of St. Petersburg, the intellectual and cultural centre of the Empire. At the same time, the city presented a challenge to Sweden and England, and acted as an advance outpost of national defence. With the rise of the "Venice of the North" on the banks of the Neva and of the

Gulf of Finland, the position of the old imperial capital of Moscow also began to change; it was reduced to the rank of the second city of the Russian Empire and, as Aleksandr Pushkin later wrote, had to be content with playing "second fiddle".

The sudden spate of building activity which began in the early 1700s continued unabated in the middle of the century. The greatest projects of this period were, as before, palaces and churches, which served the need for representation of the imperial court and the aristocracy. Sumptuous, exquisitely-decorated palaces and splendid parks and gardens were designed, and embellished further by richly-ornamented sculptures. Despite the busy building programmes of Moscow and other Russian cities, the expansion of the new capital was clearly in the foreground. The Russian architects were trained at the School of Architecture in Moscow, and, from 1757, at the new Academy of Arts in St. Petersburg.

If Zemtsev was the busiest architect in Russia in the thirties, then the prodigious Rastrelli enjoyed this honour in the middle of the century; he completed many of the buildings begun by his predecessors, in addition to his own work. Bartolomeo Francesco Rastrelli was of Italian origin and had come to St. Petersburg with his father, the sculptor Carlo Bartolomeo Rastrelli, in 1716. He had received his first training from his father, who was proficient in many fields. In St. Petersburg, Bartolomeo Rastrelli was able to continue his education at the school of architecture in the Chancellery of

Construction, and to complete it in Italy. He was encouraged by the advisers of Empress Anna Ivanovna, and was then given ample opportunity to prove his talent as a young architect and as an assistant to older masters. Even in his early works, Rastrelli achieved stylistic elegance, sumptuous splendour and monumentality. After helping to reconstruct the Winter Palace, he directed the building of the castles of Mitau (Yelgava, 1738—1740) and Ruhenthal (Rundal, 1736—1740) in Courland. Empress Elizabeth appointed Rastrelli chief architect, and elevated him to the rank of a Russian count.

Rastrelli left his mark as an architect in almost all of the great cultural centres of Russia. The highpoint of his career began in the mid-forties with the construction of the great palace in Tsarskoye Selo, the Winter Palace and the Smolny Convent in St. Petersburg. His most remarkable achievement was his reconstruction of the Winter Palace, which served as a residence for the Tsar of Russia until 1917. The long complex of buildings with its impressive façade which was built overlooking the banks of the Neva between 1754 and 1762 is one of the most stunning examples of Russian baroque. Bartolomeo Rastrelli built or completed variations on this theme, on a smaller scale, in palaces for the nobility, such as the Anichkov Palace (1744—1750), the Vorontsov Palace (1749—1757), the Stroganov Palace (1751—1754), and others. He also directed work on the extensions to the castle buildings in Petrodvorets (1747—1752). The Smolny

Convent was not completed (1748—1760). The wooden palace buildings of the Kremlin in Moscow (1741—1744) and the summer residence in Lefortovo on the Yausa near Moscow have not survived. Rastrelli's conception of art was also expressed in the work of his many pupils and assistants, who built picturesque palaces, churches and triumphal arches. One such was the Moscow architect Karl Ivanovich Blank, who created the great tented roof crown of the Chapel of the New Jerusalem Monastery in Istra near Moscow after plans by Rastrelli.

Other architects did not find it easy to shine with their own designs, eclipsed as they were by the outstanding figure of Rastrelli. One person who did, however, succeed in this was Savva Ivanovich Chevakinski, who had been trained at the Naval Academy, where there was an architecture class. S. I. Chevakinski's most notable construction was the Nikolski Military-Naval Cathedral in St. Petersburg (1753—1762), which was built on a large square used for parades by the Navy. Apart from working as a naval administrator, Chevakinski also made an important contribution with his designs in Tsarskoye Selo, which were completed by Rastrelli.

Two of the most famous architects active in Moscow and its environs were Michurin and Ukhtomski. Ivan Fedorovich Michurin, a famous town planner, was involved principally in straightening major thoroughfares. In 1739 he published a detailed plan of Moscow, which is an extremely valuable document of the history of town planning in that city. In his capacity as an architect, Michurin also executed projects after plans by Rastrelli. Dmitri Vasilievich Ukhtomski, a pupil of Michurin, directed the execution of one of the greatest buildings in Moscow and its surroundings, the bell-tower in the monastery at Zagorsk, which had been begun by Michurin. At the same time, Ukhtomski himself completed numerous projects in Moscow. For example, in 1753 to 1766 he built the Red Gate, which was to be rebuilt several times in later years. His most important building project was the infirmary and hospital complex (1759). Ukhtomski also made a name for himself with the workshop school, or school of architecture, which he established in 1744. A series of gifted Russian architects was to graduate from here, including Kokorinov, Bazhenov, Starov and Kazakov.

Architects from the serf estate also won great acclaim around the middle of the 18th century. They included Fedor Semenovich Argunov, who built the great palace for Count Sheremetev by the Fontanka, and the fountain-house in St. Petersburg. Argunov also worked on other magnificent buildings for the Sheremetevs, such as the great country-house of the count's family in Kuskovo near Moscow.

The extent and intensity of building activity in Russia increased during the reign of Catherine II (1762—1796). As trade and industry grew, and education and science showed rapid development, so architects found themselves faced with new tasks. This was particularly true with regard to the construction of cities, which advanced considerably in the second half of the 18th century. In order to meet architectural demands, it was necessary to reorganize the very foundations of the previous administrative organs, and to this end a central Chancellery of Construction responsible for the whole tsardom was set up in 1762. Special councils worked alongside it, which were responsible for expanding St. Petersburg and Moscow and for the building of new cities. In 1763 Empress Catherine II issued an *ukaz* on the preparation of special plans for all cities of the Russian Empire, containing numerous directions for each *guberniya* on construction in the individual towns, which numbered about five hundred. Extensive surveying work was carried out throughout the country, which lasted more than twelve years, in order to implement the building programme. The surveying and planning of the two principal cities were in the foreground. In 1769 the plan for St. Petersburg, and in 1775 that for Moscow, were approved by the government.

These new programmes and plans also provided for the building of dwelling-houses and public buildings. The transition from the late baroque to the early classicistic style in architecture came as early as the 1760s and 1770s. The director of the central Chancellery of Construction, Ivan Ivanovich Betskoi, made a particularly important contribution to developing large-scale construction in Russia. But private as well as state building also made rapid progress. More and more aristocratic families built splendid palaces in the Russian cities, such as

those of the Yusupovs, Golitsyns, Sheremetevs, Razumovskis, and others of noble lineage. But they also built them on idyllic sites in the country. Majestic cathedrals also continued to be built.

Aleksandr Filippovich Kokorinov was one of the most important early classicistic architects in Russia. After being trained in Moscow, where he was a pupil first of Korobov and then of Ukhtomski, Kokorinov went to St. Petersburg in the early 1750s, where he built the home of the Academy of Arts, which clearly exhibited classicistic influence. The main part of the complex was built between 1765 and 1772, the remainder being completed by Yegor Timofeevich Sokolov after Kokorinov's plans in 1780—1784. The internal design of the building was completed only in the early

19th century. Kokorinov also worked as a professor of architecture after the Academy of Arts was founded.

Apart from Kokorinov, the French architect Jean-Baptiste Vallin de la Mothe also worked on designing the façade of the Academy of Arts; Ivan Ivanovich Shuvalov had engaged him as professor at the Academy in 1759. Before entering Russian service, Vallin de la Mothe worked in Italy and France for many years. He is best remembered for the "Little Hermitage" (1764—1767), and also helped to construct the wooden supports for the Admiralty, the so-called "New Holland".

The work of the architect Georg Friedrich Velten, one of the many assistants of Rastrelli, was also connected with the Academy of Arts. After the latter retired, chief architect Velten

became director of the Chancellery of Construction. He also taught at the Academy. He did much work on developing the land adjacent to the Winter Palace, adding the south pavilion of the "Hanging Gardens" to the north pavilion which Vallin de la Mothe had designed, and built the "Old Hermitage", a typical example of early classicism, on the banks of the Neva.

The techniques used in construction in St. Petersburg and other Russian cities were clearly expressed in the work of the Italian master Antonio Rinaldi. He entered Russian service during the reign of Empress Elizabeth and was initially employed as an assistant to Rastrelli.

The most important of Rinaldi's works were the Chinese Pavilion and the toboggan slide. The former (1762—1768) was a remarkable

203 Vologda,
in the north of European Russia. Wooden buildings
were typical of the town. From Bruyn, Reisen,
Amsterdam 1714

pavilion-like palace which was designed to be in harmony with the park, with the emphasis on elegance. This building already demonstrated what typified Rinaldi's work: his predilection for decorative interior design, such as parquet with insets, elegantly styled doors, stucco and small murals. These same embellishments were employed when he built the slide (1762—1774) not far from the palace. In his later works, Rinaldi favoured a stricter classicistic style, as is clear from the palace in Gatchina (1766—1781) and several buildings in Tsarskoye Selo.

The classicistic style found its most notable expression in the work of Bazhenov, Kazakov and Starov, who first made their mark in the sixties and seventies. Vasili Ivanovich Bazhenov was trained as an architect at Ukhtomski's School of Architecture. After graduating, he went to the University of Moscow, which he left for the Academy of Arts. After studying there for two years, he completed his training and travelled to France and Italy, returning in 1765. He had already been appointed professor in 1762 in his absence, and was elected a member of the Academy of Arts by virtue of the work he had accomplished outside Russia. But he was soon to fall out of favour with court circles, and in 1767 he felt obliged to leave St. Petersburg and move to Moscow. Bazhenov was very active during his Moscow period, his most important works being the reconstruction of the Kremlin Palace and of the palace complex in Tsaritsyno near Moscow. One of Bazhenov's assistants was Kazakov.

The new compositional devices used by Bazhenov when working on the Kremlin Palace were also employed during his work in Tsaritsyno, but only fragments have survived. These include the entrance gate, the semicircular palace, the reception palace (opera house), the kitchen wing with a gallery connecting the building with the palace pavilions, and a bridge traversing the street. The towered bridge with its great arches is one of Bazhenov's most eloquent creations. His greatest work in Moscow was the Pashkov House (1784—1786), which today forms part of the Lenin Library.

Shortly before the death of Catherine II, Bazhenov returned to St. Petersburg, where he designed a palace for the future emperor Paul. In 1799 he was appointed vice-president of the Academy of Arts. In this capacity he was occupied principally with plans for a basic reform of the Academy, and with the publication of an ambitious work on Russian architecture when he died suddenly on 13th August 1799. Bazhenov's role in the development of Russian architecture was a very important one. Under his influence, classicism reached its peak in the architecture of the Russian Empire, where it found practical application.

Matvei Fedorovich Kazakov was responsible, as Bazhenov's assistant, for much of the reconstruction work on the Kremlin buildings. He also helped with the work in Tsaritsyno. His greatest achievement was the Senate Building in the Moscow Kremlin (today the seat of the Supreme Soviet of the USSR). Not only was the Senate Building a completely new type of administrative centre; the University complex (1786—1793) designed by Kazakov was also a new type of building for educational purposes.

Kazakov also built numerous houses, hospitals and churches in Moscow, such as the Demidov Palace (1779—1791), the Golitsyn Hospital (1796—1801), the Church of the Metropolitan Philip (1777—1788) and the Cosmas-and-Damian Church (1791—1803), all in classicistic style. In 1801 he went into retirement, and during the last years of his life, despite his already failing health, he busied himself with collecting architectural drawings, which today constitute a valuable source of information on the history of Russian architecture.

The third great architect of Russian classicism was Ivan Yegorovich Starov. One of the earliest of his works were the buildings on the estate of Nikolskoye Gagarino near Moscow (1773). In 1774 Starov began the greatest project of his early career, the Holy Trinity Cathedral in the Aleksandr Nevski monastery in St. Petersburg. Apart from building the Cathedral, which had been begun in the reign of Peter I, Starov reconstructed the entire entrance to the monastery and created the large round square at the end of Nevski Prospekt where he built the entrance gate to the monastery. Between 1774 and 1780, Starov built the famous country palace of Taitsy near St. Petersburg. Starov's main works were accomplished in the eighties, for instance the Taurida Palace (1783—1789), which he built for Prince Po-

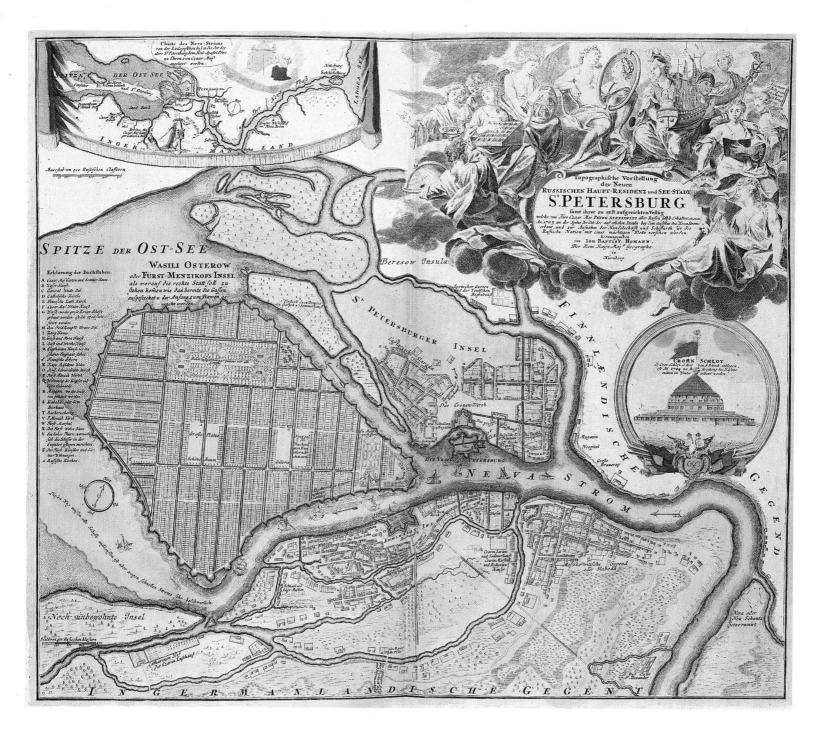

204 *The plan of St. Petersburg clearly shows*
the regular layout of the city. From the Atlas of
Johann Baptiste Homann, Nuremberg 1725.
Forschungsbibliothek, Gotha

205 *View from the Peter and Paul fortress*
to the palace on the banks of the Neva. Painting by
Fedor Yakovlevich Alekseev, 1794. State Tretyakov
Gallery, Moscow

206 *The Winter Palace was built in the style*
of Russian Baroque between 1754 and 1762 by
Bartolomeo Francesco Rastrelli. From Breton,
La Russie, vol. 1, Paris 1813

207 *The Fontanka in the Imperial Gardens of St. Petersburg. From Richter,* Ansichten, *Leipzig 1804*

208 *The country seat of Tsarskoye Selo became the property of Catherine I in 1710. The Palace and Catherine Park date from the mid-18th century, when Tsarskoye Selo became the summer residence of Empress Elizabeth. From Richter,* Ansichten, *Leipzig 1804*

209 *Petrodvorets, the Tsar's summer residence, was built between 1714 and 1728, and completed by Bartolomeo Francesco Rastrelli between 1747 and 1752. From Richter,* Ansichten, *Leipzig 1804*

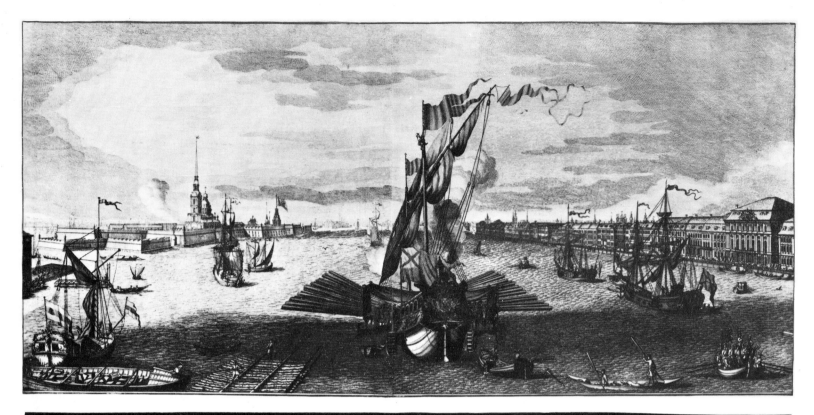

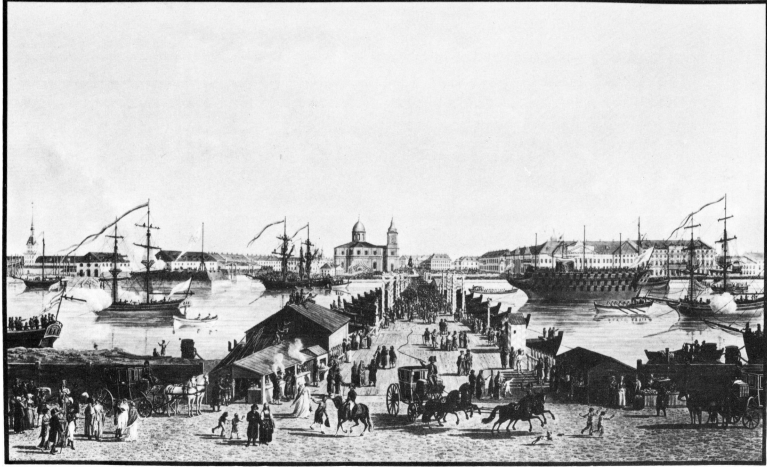

210 St. Petersburg; the Neva between
the Admiralty and the Academy of Sciences.
Engraving by Yelim Vinogradov, 1753

211 Celebrations on the Senate Square in
St. Petersburg on 12th May 1803 to mark the
100th anniversary of the city. Etching by Gabriel
Lory, 1803. Staatliche Museen Berlin,
Kupferstichkabinett

212 Moscow. View of the Voskressenski and
Nikolski Gate with the Tverskaya Ulitsa and
Neglinni Bridge. Painting by Fedor Yakovlevich
Alekseev, 1811. State Tretyakov Gallery, Moscow

213 View of a Moscow
gate. Engraving by
Geissler, ca. 1804

214 A Russian town.
Subsequent to the reforms
of Peter I, wooden
buildings gave way
increasingly to stone ones.
Engraving by Geissler,
ca. 1804

*215 The old Tsar's Palace in the Moscow Kremlin.
Engraving by Geissler, ca. 1804*

216 *Monastery of the Trinity and St. Sergius, Zagorsk, near Moscow. From Richter,* Ansichten, *Leipzig 1804*

217 *The Vasili Blashenny Cathedral was built by the architects Barma and Postnik between 1555 and 1561 to commemorate the capture of Kazan in 1552 under Ivan IV. From Richter,* Ansichten, *Leipzig 1804*

218 *Pashkov House in Moscow.*
It was built in the early classicistic style by Vasili
Ivanovich Bashenov between 1784 and 1786. Seen
from the courtyard, it is a typical country palace
with its gardens and magnificent gates, while the
main facade is that of a town residence. From
Richter, Ansichten, *Leipzig 1804*

219 Yekaterinburg.
Watercolour from Georg Wilhelm von Hennin's
Beschreibung der Werke im Ural und in Sibirien,
1735. State Museum of History, Moscow

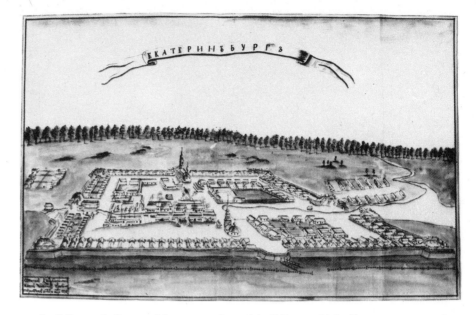

temkin in the style of Roman patricians' houses, and the Palace of Pella (1785–1789) which Emperor Paul had demolished. The Potemkin Palace is a unique construction combining castle buildings and towers, loopholes and an asymmetrical layout with classically austere, smooth white walls. Starov was forced to retire by Tsar Paul in 1798, and devoted the last few years of his life to teaching at the Academy of Arts, and to supervising the construction of the Kazan Cathedral. Apart from Bazhenov, Kazakov and Starov, several other important architects were active in the same period, the most famous of whom were Giacomo Quarenghi, Nikolai Aleksandrovich Lvov, Charles Cameron, Yegor Timofeevich Sokolov, Ivan Vasilievich Yegotov and Vikenti Frantsevich Brenna.

Giacomo Quarenghi soon made a name for himself as an outstanding expert on the architecture of antiquity and on the art of Andrea Palladio. He entered the service of Catherine II in 1780 at the age of 36, and soon occupied a similar position to that held by Rastrelli under Empress Elizabeth. During his first few years in the tsardom, Quarenghi closely studied the work of Russian architects, with particular reference to Bazhenov, Kazakov and Starov. The Italian master worked not only on the banks of the Neva, but also in Moscow and other Russian cities, as well as in the country. He sometimes adapted his plans for country palaces to suit buildings in the cities, one example being the St. Petersburg Bank Building (1783–1790) in the Sadovaya Ulitsa. The

most important buildings of Quarenghi were the complex of the Academy of Sciences (1783–1789) on the Neva, and his work on the Winter Palace and the Hermitage (1783–1787). In the early 19th century, Quarenghi directed the building of rows of shops at the corner of Nevski Prospekt and on the banks of the Fontanka, the Smolny Institute (which was adjoined to Rastrelli's baroque monastery complex in 1805–1808), the Catherine Institute and the hospital on Liteini Prospekt (1803–1805).

One of the country palaces built by Quarenghi for the nobility was the castle complex he constructed for Count Sheremetev in Ostankino near Moscow, which had its own theatre, on whose stage the owner had talented serfs rehearse and perform operas, ballets and plays. The example set by the Sheremetevs soon became fashionable, and towards the end of the 18th century countless members of the high nobility competed when building or rebuilding their town or country palaces in their attempts to design their residences in keeping with the classicistic tastes of the time.

Like the Italian Giacomo Quarenghi, the Scot Charles Cameron made a new home for himself in Russia. Cameron came to St. Petersburg in 1779 from Italy, where he had lived for many years. At that time he was already regarded as an outstanding expert on classical architecture. He built mainly in the suburbs of the new capital, for example in Tsarskoye Selo and Pavlovsk. He also worked for Count Razumovski in Baturino in the Ukraine. The com-

plex of buildings which Cameron annexed to the great palace was his most important assignment in Tsarskoye Selo: the agate rooms, the hanging gardens and a large gallery, which even today bears the name of the designer. Cameron built the palace and a few pavilions in Pavlovsk, including the Apollo colonnade, an open partial rotunda comprising a double row of Doric columns. The Pavlovsk parks were amongst the most beautiful in Russia at the end of the 18th century.

Serf architects played an important part in Russian architecture under Catherine II. The ostentatious country seat of Count Sheremetev near Moscow was designed largely by serf artists; the palace in Ostankino was built by Pavel Ivanovich Argunov, Aleksei Fedorovich Miranov and Grigori Yefimovich Dikushkin, all pupils of Fedor Semenovich Argunov. In Arkhangelskoye too, another aristocratic estate near Moscow, the serfs of Counts Golitsyn and Yusupov designed a superb complex of palace and parks, decorated with richly ornamented sculptures and embellished with terraces leading down to the river.

From the mid-1760s, Russian architecture was dominated by the classicistic style, and architectural work proceeded on an enormous scale. Many new cities emerged in the Russian Empire, including, in the south, Taganrog, Cherson, Yekaterinoslav (now Dneprepetrovsk), and others.

THE FINE ARTS

THE PROCESS of change and renewal which was clearly apparent in 18th century Russian architecture could also be perceived in other fields of creative art, such as graphics, painting and sculpture. Copperplate engravings dating back to the first ten years of the 18th century, which depict mainly battles and townscapes, are a living example of the direct link between art and real life. Peter I summoned many foreign drawers, copperplate engravers and artists to Russia, including Adriaan Schoonebeeck, who worked in Moscow from 1698 to 1705, and Pieter Pikaerdt, who worked in Moscow and St. Petersburg from 1702.

The most important Russian copperplate engraver at the beginning of the 18th century was Aleksei Fedorovich Zubov, a pupil of the Moscow armoury. His unusually large and detailed panorama of the city of St. Petersburg, which he carried out in 1716/17 and which covered a total of eight sheets, showed the generous scale and bustling activity of the young city. Another plate shows the victorious return to St. Petersburg of the Russian fleet. Zubov strove to achieve documentary accuracy and vividness in his work. His engravings were at the same time simple, precise and rich in content. Many of them give a vivid impression of life in Russia's young capital at the beginning of the new century. One of Zubov's contemporaries was the Russian engraver Ivan Adolski the Elder.

Portrait-painting was an important aspect of Russian art in the early 18th century. Even the first works from this period reveal the endeavour to find a new approach to portrait-painting and to portray people in a more realistic, up-to-date fashion. Realistic elements are apparent even in early portraits by Nikitin and Matveev. They had been sent to Italy and Holland respectively by Peter I to study painting. Ivan Nikitich Nikitin left a legacy of many portraits which reveal the originality of the artist. He also painted the Tsar several times in the early 1720s, and it is possible that he was responsible for the famous circular portrait of Peter I, which expresses the power of the great statesman and the unbending will of a unique figure. Peter was very fond of Nikitin, and gifted to him property not far from the Winter Palace. It is probable that Nikitin also painted the Tsar's Chancellor, Count Gavriil Ivanovich Golovkin, as well as a hetman.

But Nikitin was also able to depict other characters impressively, as can be seen from his small portrait of the Tsar's daughter Anna Petrovna (ca. 1720), which is remarkable for its careful choice of colouring. Nikitin was also responsible for the portrait of Tsar Peter on his deathbed (1725). It was obviously the work of only a few hours, but it captures quite remarkably the atmosphere of pomp and mourning. Nikitin also tried his hand at battle scenes, such as his paintings *The Battle of Poltava* and the *Battle on Kulikovo Field* show.

Andrei Matveevich Matveev executed murals in palaces and churches early in his career, but none of these has survived. His *Self-portrait with wife* (1729) won much acclaim. Matveev

was a very important figure in Russian painting in the 1730s. He was very prolific, and also directed the painting school which was attached to the Chancellery of Construction.

Eighteenth century Russia, which was now clearly in the ascendant, offered great scope to foreign artists, so that they continued to flock into the empire after the death of Peter I. Around the middle of the century, these included painters as famous as the brothers Georg Christoph and Johann Friedrich Grooth from Stuttgart. The latter spent many years in Russia, where he died. He was a painter of animals and, in particular, of birds. Other foreign painters included the portrait-painter Pietro Rotari, who chose many young women from the common people as his subjects. Others who worked alongside the Grooth brothers and Rotari included Giuseppe Valeriani, who had previously worked as court painter to Louis XV, Louis Toqqué, whose portraits did not always, however, win the approval of Empress Elizabeth, the Swedish portrait-painter Alexander Roslin, Johann Gottfried Danhauer, Georg Gsell and Louis Caravaque. The Italian Valeriani and his associates Antonie Peresinotti, Serafino Barozzi and Stefano Torelli set the tone in the forties. They represented French tastes in decorative painting, which was flourishing thanks to the ornately representative style which was customary under Empress Elizabeth.

The training centres which existed around the middle of the 18th century in the form of schools of painting and drawing, the Academy of Sciences, the University of Moscow and the Academy of Arts, which was founded in 1757, had an important influence on the artistic production of Russian painters in that period. The Academy of Sciences made a great contribution to the cultivation of Russian landscape painting and copperplate engraving, while great value was placed on training in decorative painting at the art schools. The serf brothers Aleksei Ivanovich and Ivan Ivanovich Belski, Ivan Firsov, Boris Sukhodolski and others all made a name for themselves as decorative artists.

The important Russian portrait-painters of the mid-18th century were Vishnyakov, Antropov and Ivan Petrovich Argunov. Ivan Yakovlevich Vishnyakov not only succeeded Matveev as director of the art school; he was also responsible for the excellent portraits of Sarah and Willim Fermor (1745), which are impressive examples of that period of Russian painting. The same is true of the works of Antropov. Aleksei Petrovich Antropov was a soldier's son who had been taught by Matveev. One of his best portraits dates from 1754, and shows A. M. Ismaylova, the first lady-in-waiting of Empress Elizabeth.

Other characteristic portraits show the Countesses M. A. Rumyantseva (1764) and A. V. Burlina (1763), and Princess T. A. Trubetskaya (1761). One of Antropov's gala portraits from the 1760s depicts Archbishop Silvester Kulyabka (1760), and shows a coarse, imperious, self-assured and pathologically ambitious prelate. In his gala portrait of Peter III, the artist showed the moral destitution of the unsightly, degenerate Tsar.

Ivan Petrovich Argunov, a talented architect and painter who was one of the serfs of Count Sheremetev, shared many features with Antropov. Apart from commissions to paint gala portraits, Argunov also depicted people from the society with which he came into contact as a painter, such as his painting of an unknown sculptor, possibly Fedot Ivanovich Shubin (1780s). Of his other major works, his portrait of Anna Nikolayevna, a foster-daughter of the Sheremetev family (1767), and of a *Peasant Girl Wearing National Dress* (1784), are particularly fine. The latter is one of the most beautiful works of this serf painter.

Russian painting flourished considerably in the second half of the 18th century, and this was also expressed in the depiction of historical scenes. The founder of this genre was Anton Pavlovich Losenko, whose drawings were an inspiration to many artists, including his pupil Ivan Akimovich Akimov, who worked at the Academy of Arts as a colleague of Losenko. Petr Ivan Sokolov created several works on themes from classical mythology, such as *Mercury and Argus* (1776) and *Daedalus tying on the wings of Icarus* (1777). Sokolov was an excellent draughtsman. The male nudes which he drew at the peak of his career are among the outstanding examples of 18th century Russian graphic art.

The heights which Russian painting achieved in the second half of the 18th century are especially apparent in the portraits of Rokotov, Levitski and Borovikovski. Fedor Stepanovich Rokotov made his name as early as the 1760s. His portrait of the famous poet Vasili Ivanovich Maikov was completed in about 1766. The *joie de vivre* and mocking spirit of the poet are presented with great conviction. At about the same time, Rokotov was working on a portrait of an unknown woman. In 1766 he moved to Moscow, where he worked as a teacher. His most successful portraits date from the next few years, and include his portraits of N. Y. Struyski, an unknown man in a three-cornered hat, A. I. Vorontsov, an unknown man in a pink robe, and others. All exhibit the keen powers of observation of this famous artist.

Rokotov's portraits from the eighties, such as those of V. Y. Novosiltsova (1780), P.N. Lanskaya (80s) and Y. V. Santis (1785) exhibit a further refinement of his technique. Those of Surovtseva and Surovtsev (end of the 80s) are among his late works, and are marked by deeper psychological veracity. The artist tried to express the intellect and inner being of his subjects.

Dmitri Grigorievich Levitski also made his name as a portrait-painter. He painted members of various classes of Russian society. Even in his early works, Levitski's attempts to present the human character in as concrete a form as possible are apparent. Numbered among these are the seven portraits entitled *Smolyanki* (1773—1776), which depict pupils of the Smolny Institute for young ladies. In the same period (1773) he painted Pavel Nikolae-

220 Ivan Zubov, Ismailovo. Copper engraving

221 Adrian Schoonebeeck, the sailing ship
"Prädestination". Copper engraving.
The Dutch artist was summoned to Russia by
Peter I as early as 1698.

vich Demidov and Denis Diderot. The Demidov portrait is an obvious example of gala painting, but also betrays the attempts of the artist to achieve realism. The entrepreneur Demidov, a passionate lover of flowers, stands beside a table on which lie a watering-can, an open book and some bulbs. In the background can be seen the Moscow home for foundlings, which was built with the aid of a generous donation from Demidov. Levitski depicted Diderot quite differently during the latter's visit to St. Petersburg in 1773/74. The great scholar appears as a man out of the ordinary, without a wig, with thinning hair and lines under his eyes. His face tells of creative talent, a strong intellect and a questioning mind.

Levitski's greatness was no less apparent in his depiction of women. He was able clearly to emphasize the individual traits of the various aristocrats. He portrays the Princess P. N. Golitsyna (1781) in all her beauty, using silvery-bluish, blue-green and violet shades to highlight her cold, haughty elegance. Countess P. F. Vorontsova is shown as an unassuming, attractive woman with a slightly mocking expression. The two paintings of Princess Lvova of 1778 and 1781 are in a similar style.

The vital, expressive characterization of his subjects also typifies Levitski's other paintings. One of his particular concerns was to portray the *joie de vivre* of his subjects. Thus his portrait of Bakunina is an attractive depiction of a woman radiating freshness and health. Other famous portraits by him are those of Ursula Mnishek and Anna Davya Bernucci (1782),

which present two totally different types of woman.

Levitski's portraits of male subjects painted in the 1780s made an equally strong impression. Attention was given by the artist to expressing the individual characteristics of the figures. Levitski painted the frivolous, empty-headed Aleksandr Dmitrievich Lanskoi, a favourite of Catherine II (1792), the clever courtier Aleksandr Vasilievich Khrapovitski (1782) and the morose Mark Fedorovich Poltoratski. He took particular care with the depiction of his friend, the architect Nikolai Aleksandrovich Lvov, whom he knew as a clever, talented figure in 18th century Russian society. His portrait of *Catherine II as Legislator* (1783) shows the Empress with a youthful face. Levitski's portrayal of the great ruler was the object of Derzhavin's ode *The Vision of the Mursa*. Levitski painted not only courtiers and aristocrats, but also public figures such as Novikov (1796/97), who numbered among his friends.

One of Levitski's pupils was Vladimir Lukich Borovikovski, son of a Ukrainian Cossack, who received his first training at the Mohyla Academy in Kiev. Borovikovski began his career as a painter of icons, but turned to Levitski's speciality at an early stage, and was soon regarded as a famous portraitist. He received commissions, not only at the Imperial Court, but also at the "Little Court" of Grand Duke Paul. In St. Petersburg, the artist became a freemason, and worked eagerly within the Free Society of Friends of Languages, Science and Art. Some of the best works by Borovi-

kovski are the portraits *Unknown Woman with Medallion* (1798), *Y. A. Naryshkina* (1799), *M. Y. Lopukhina* (1797), *G. R. Derzhavin* (1795) and *D. P. Troshchinski* (1790s). Stepan Semenovich Shchukin and Nikolai Ivanovich Tontsi also worked as portrait-painters at the end of the 18th century.

The life of the lower classes was also represented in 18th century Russian painting, as is apparent in genre painting, although this was not to develop fully until the 19th century. Nevertheless, some of its proponents attempted as early as the second half of the 18th century to gear painting towards presenting the way of life of the common people. One of these was Mikhail Shibanov, one of Potemkin's serfs. Little is known about Shibanov. He probably first gained prominence as an artist in the 1770s. His portraits of the Spiridovs and the Nestorovs date from this period. It was then, too, that he created his famous scenes from the life of the common people, *A Peasant's Repast* (1774) and *Wedding Ceremony* (1777).

Nor is much known about the life or work of the painter and drawer Ivan Alekseevich Yermenev, who graduated from the Academy of Arts, then painted portraits in Paris, where he witnessed the storming of the Bastille in 1789. This scene was the subject of one of his copperplate engravings. His watercolours depicting scenes from the life of Russian peasants won acclaim; they included *Blind Beggars Singing*, *A Peasant's Repast* and *Beggar*. These works very probably originated in the

1770s, i.e. before Yermenev's visit to France. His pictures contain an expressiveness unsurpassed in strength, such as is equalled in literature only by the peasant characters of Radishchev. A direct path leads from Yermenev to Russian realistic genre painting of the 19th century.

Interest in the plastic arts had increased considerably in Russia by the end of the 17th and beginning of the 18th century, especially in statuary. Prior to the 18th century, it was used mainly by the church for the decoration of frames for pictures of saints, iconostases, altar balustrades, church instruments, doors, etc. Being less ruled by the spirit of asceticism than painting, sculpture played an important role in secular life from an early stage. Thus one could find, in the homes of noblemen and rich merchants, useful articles made of wood, ivory and various metals and ornamented with carvings and engravings. In the early 18th century, goldsmiths in Moscow, and later in St. Petersburg, enjoyed a good reputation throughout Russia. Peter I revealed his taste for plastic art at an early age, and sent to Venice for large numbers of sculptures for his palaces and gardens; these can still be seen today in the Summer Gardens in Leningrad.

Thus in the early 18th century, decorative sculpture was widespread throughout Russia. Examples are the sculptures decorating the church at Dubrovitsy (1690—1704), at the Menshikov Tower (1705—1707), on the bas-relief of the Summer Palace in St. Petersburg (1714) built by Andreas Schlüter, and on the

interior decoration carved out of stone in Peter's chamber at Monplaisir by Nicolas Pineau, who worked in Russia from 1716 until about 1726. The carving of iconostases also continued in Peter's time, as that of the Peter and Paul fortress shows; it was designed by Ivan Petrovich Zarudny and executed by the woodcarvers Ivan Telegin and Tikhon Ivanov.

The Italian Bartolomeo Carlo Rastrelli, the father of the famous architect Bartolomeo Francesco Rastrelli, was a sculptor of some stature. Carlo Rastrelli accepted a proposal made by Tsar Peter and came to Russia in 1716 by way of France, where he had done mainly decorative work. He branched out considerably in the tsardom. Initially, he concentrated on sculpture, and on adding ornamentation to the cascades at Petrodvorets. Along with Andrei Konstantinovich Nartov, he worked on a model for a triumphal column which was to imitate the famous Trajan's column and keep alive the memory of the Northern War. Peter's death meant that the project was not realized, but the drawings survived. The column was to bear the legend, "The Russian Samson tears

asunder the Swedish lion at Poltava 1709". References were also to be made to other events from the war period, such as the capture of Riga and the founding of St. Petersburg, and Russian soldiers and peasants were also to be depicted on the base of the column.

During Peter's lifetime, Carlo Rastrelli worked very intensely on a portrayal of the great ruler. He took a mask as early as 1719, from which he made a wax bust. The famous bronze bust of Peter I, several copies of which were cast between 1723 and 1729, dates from 1723. Rastrelli also worked for many years on his equestrian statue of Peter, which was cast in bronze in 1745/46 after the artist's death. It was not until 1800 that Rastrelli's monument to Peter was erected in front of the Mikhailov Palace by Emperor Paul. Rastrelli made his statue of Peter larger than life. The monument was modelled on François Girardon's memorial to Louis XIV, but differed from the latter in the simplicity of its form and its deliberate monumentality. During the reign of Empress Anna Ivanovna (1730—1740), Rastrelli created the outstanding bronze statue *The Empress*

Anna Ivanovna and her Blackamoor (1741). Until his death in 1744, Carlo Rastrelli remained the most important sculptor in Russia.

In the mid-18th century too, the decorative aspect of Russian plastic art was very important. But much work was also done in other fields of plastic art, such as small sculpture. Lomonosov's friend Dmitri Ivanovich Vinogradov, a chemist and technologist, set up a porcelain factory in St. Petersburg, the third in Europe since the invention of European porcelain. Apart from services, vases, bowls and tobacco jars, many other articles were made, as well as small, remarkably elegant, statuettes. These articles were in many respects worthy of comparison with products from Meissen, Paris and Berlin. Many painters and sculptors were employed by the St. Petersburg manufactory. A school was also attached to it, at which skilled workers could be trained in many aspects of ceramics. The main subjects taught in the classes were drawing and modelling. The factory flourished greatly when Lomonosov became its director. His experiments and research into clay mixing, colouring and firing methods proved extremely successful.

The classicistic style was much more apparent in the field of sculpture than in that of painting in the second half of the 18th century. Although many sculptors were still occupied with decorating palaces, parks and public buildings, the sculpting of statues and busts became increasingly widespread as an independent branch of the art. Thus, three-dimensional portraits also flourished during this period.

One of the leading sculptors in this field was Fedot Ivanovich Shubin, the son of a non-adscript peasant from a fishing village near Kholmogory on the White Sea. His career bears much resemblance to that of the young Lomonosov. He went to St. Petersburg in 1759, where he was offered—probably on Lomonosov's recommendation—a place at the Academy of Arts, where he was a student from 1761 to 1766. On the basis of his talent and his excellent results, he was awarded the Great Gold Medal, which enabled him to complete his training abroad as a scholarship student of the Academy. He worked for three years in Paris and then for two years in Rome. On his way home to St. Petersburg in 1773, he also paid a short visit to London.

Even one of the first works created by Shubin after his return from abroad, the bust of Prince A. M. Golitsyn (plaster 1773; marble 1775), demonstrated the great talent of the artist. His bust of the Russian General Field Marshal Count Zakhar Grigorievich Chernyshev, who is represented as a courageous fighter, dates back to 1774. In a similiar vein, the artist made a bust of Field Marshal Count Petr Aleksandrovich Rumyantsev-Zadunaiski in 1778. The portrait of an unknown man and the bust of Countess M. R. Panina, whose expression is reminiscent of portraits by Rokotov and Levitski, also date from the 1770s. Shubin's busts of Empress Catherine II's adviser on foreign policy, Prince Aleksandr Andreevich Bezborodko (ca. 1798), and of Admiral Vasili Yakovlevich Chichagov (1791) have become especially well known. His bust of Emperor Paul (marble 1797; bronze 1798) was no less than grotesque, with its grimacing face and chest weighed down with medals. In contrast to this, Empress Catherine II, who was portrayed several times by F. I. Shubin, is presented as an ideal, as *Catherine II as Legislator* (1788—1790) amply shows. Shubin also made a bust of Lomonosov (1792). Shubin's last years were marked by material want and personal humiliation, to which he was subjected by the Court.

The sculptor Fedor Gordeevich Gordeev was of the same generation as Shubin. After graduating from the Academy of Arts, he worked in Paris, Rome, Pompeii and Herculaneum. When he returned home, he became a director of the Academy of Arts in St. Petersburg. The principles of classicism are clearly evident in Gordeev's work, for example in his tomb for Princess N. M. Golitsyna (1780), a marble bas-relief that betrays the influence of ancient culture. In later tombs, i. e. that for General Field Marshal Prince Aleksandr Mikhailovich Golitsyn (1788), one can already discern a different composition and pomp. Another tombmaker was Ivan Petrovich Martos, a Greek immigrant. His most significant works (such as the Minin and Posharski monuments in Moscow, 1804—1818) belong, however, to the 19th century. Martos' monuments to M. P. Sobakina (1782) and Y. S. Kurakina (1792) are very impressive. His figures are capable of expressing many emotions, and are the best examples from the late 18th century.

ПЕТРЪ ВЕЛИКІЙ
ОТЕЦЪ ОТЕЧЕСТВА ІМПЕРАТОРЪ ВСЕРОСІЙСКІЙ

One of the greatest Russian sculptors in the second half of the 18th century was Mikhail Ivanovich Kozlovski. Extensive journeys took him, too, to Paris and Rome, where he showed a great interest in ancient culture. When he returned to St. Petersburg, Kozlovski assisted in the decoration of the marble palace, and also worked on the great marble statue *Catherine II as Minerva* (1785), in which he glorified the Empress of Russia as the Goddess of Wisdom.

When he next visited Paris, Kozlovski was caught up in the revolutionary events of 1789, and it was here that he created *Polycrates bound to a tree* (plaster 1790), which depicts human suffering and the popular desire for liberty.

Kozlovski's later period of acitivity dates from 1790, i.e. after his return home. As before, the great artist was inspired by classical themes, as is evident from the great terracotta statuettes

which depict scenes from the *Iliad*. Just as striking was the group *Ajax defends the corpse of Patrocles* (bronze 1796). Kozlovski created outstanding works in the first few years of the new century, such as the bronze relief for the tomb of General Petr Ivanovich Melissino (1800) and the memorial to Countess S. A. Stroganova (1801/02). His greatest artistic success was the Suvorov monument in St. Petersburg (1801), which is an impressive portrayal of the great Russian commander. This monument counts amongst the most outstanding achievements of classicistic sculpture in Russia.

Feodosi Fedorovich Shchedrin, the son of a soldier, was born only two years before Kozlovski. He graduated from the Academy of Arts and subsequently worked in France and Italy. In St. Petersburg he designed the allegoric figures for the Grand Cascade at Petrodvorets. At the same time, Shchedrin worked on Kazan Cathedral (1804—1811) along with Gordeev, Martos and others. Much of Shchedrin's work dates from the 19th century, since the artist enjoyed a long life. His later works bore the stamp of a new stage in the development of Russian classicism. He became renowned principally for his plastic art, which glorified the victorious Russian naval forces. Ivan Prokofevich Prokofev was also involved in the ornamentation of the cascades at Petrodvorets. His main works, too, date from the 19th century; Prokofev was a famous portrait artist.

The name of Étienne-Maurice Falconet, who came to Russia in 1766 on Diderot's recommendation and was commissioned to erect a memorial to Peter the Great by Catherine II, is linked to an important chapter in the history of Russian sculpture in the second half of the 18th century. The model for the statue was completed as early as 1770. The monument was to rest on a large block of granite, which had to be transported to the place allotted to it. Contemporary observers gave vivid accounts of the arduous task involved in bringing the stone foundation to its site: a mighty granite block, found near the Finnish village of Ljachta, was chosen as a base "instead of another on the island of Kronstadt, on which Peter the Great had sometimes sat and amused himself with his naval officers ... About one eighth of this stone (from the village of Ljachta) was visible above the ground, where it lay sunk in yellowish sandy, limey soil alone, and with no stony ground or stones round about. When the earth was removed from round about it in winter, and when it stood free in a trench, it was found to be 24 feet thick, 21 feet wide and 42 feet long. Its weight is estimated at 2,200,000 pounds by the cubic method of calculation." The enormous stone was transported to the riverbank and loaded onto a large boat: "When they pumped the water out of it, only the front and rear ends lifted up, but the centre, on which the load rested, remained under water. This bending caused many boards to break free, and water rushed in. All hands were called to the pumps, and with the help of large stones, which were laid on both sides of the vessel, it (the water) was finally made to recede ... and thus it (the boat) was sailed up the lesser Neva and down the great Neva." The journey by river covered a distance of twelve versts. The bronze cast for the great monument to Peter was made between 1775 and 1777, but it was not erected until 1782.

Falconet's monument with its inscription "Petro Primo—Catharina Secunda" was an enormous achievement. The "famous and learned statuarist" had been supported during the creation of his masterpiece by his "pupil" Mademoiselle Marie-Anne Collot, who had come with him to the Russian capital. Falconet's monument to Peter played an important part in the development of a Russian national consciousness, and had a lasting influence on subsequent generations of artists and poets, as is illustrated by Aleksandr Pushkin's famous work *The Bronze Horseman.*

224 *Ivan Nikitich Nikitin,*
Peter I, *ca. 1720. State Russian Museum,*
Leningrad

225 *Ivan Nikitich Nikitin,*
Portrait of Tsarevna Praskovya Ivanovna, *1714.*
State Russian Museum, Leningrad

226 Fedor Stepanovich Rokotov,
Portrait of V. N. Zurovtseva, *between
1785 and 1790. State Russian
Museum, Leningrad*

227 Andrei Matveevich Matveev,
Self-portrait of the artist with his wife, Irina
Stepanovna, *1729 (?). State Russian Museum,*
Leningrad

228 *Ivan Yakovlevich*
Vishnyakov, Empress
Elizabeth, *1743.*
State Tretyakov Gallery.
Moscow

229 *Ivan Yakovlevich*
Vishnyakov, Sarah Eleonora
Fermor, *ca. 1750.*
State Russian Museum,
Leningrad

235 Vladimir Lukich Borovikovski,
Portrait of O. K. Filippova, 1790. State Russian
Museum, Leningrad

236 Vladimir Lukich Borovikovski,
Portrait of V. S. Vasilyevna, 1800. State Tretyakov
Gallery, Moscow

237 Vladimir Lukich Borovikovski,
Portrait of Prince Aleksandr Borisovich Kurakin.
State Tretyakov Gallery, Moscow

Following pages:

238 Fedot Ivanovich Shubin,
Self-portrait. State Russian Museum, Leningrad

239 Petr Drozhdin,
Portrait of the artist Aleksei Petrovich Antropov
with his son and wife Yelena Vasilyevna.
State Russian Museum, Leningrad

Previous pages:

240 *Ivan Petrovich Argunov,*
Portrait of an unknown woman in Russian national
dress, *1785. State Tretyakov Gallery, Moscow*

241 *Aleksei Petrovich Antropov,*
Portrait of a hetman of the Don Cossacks, Fedor
Ivanovich Krasnoshchenko, *1761. State Russian
Museum, Leningrad*

242　Mikhail Shibanov,
Peasants' repast, *1774. State Russian Museum,*
Leningrad

243　Mikhail Shibanov,
Wedding festivities, *1777. State Tretyakov Gallery,*
Moscow

244 *Mikhail Shibanov,*
Portrait of Count Aleksandr
Matveevich Dmitriev-Mamonov,
1787. State Russian Museum,
Leningrad

245 *Fedot Ivanovich Shubin,*
Prince Aleksandr Mikhailovich
Golitsyn. *Plaster 1773; marble,*
1775. State Russian Museum,
Leningrad

246 *Fedot Ivanovich Shubin,*
General Field-Marshal Count
Petr Aleksandrovich Rumyantsev-
Zadunaiski. *Marble, 1770*

247 *Fedot Ivanovich Shubin,*
Paul I, *marble, 1800. State*
Russian Museum, Leningrad/
Palace Museum, Pushkin;
Academy of Sciences of the USSR,
Moscow

248 *Fedot Ivanovich Shubin,*
Bust of an unknown man. *Marble,*
1770. State Tretyakov Gallery,
Moscow

249 *Fedot Ivanovich Shubin,*
Mikhail Vasilievich Lomonosov.
Plaster, bronze and marble, 1792/93.
State Russian Museum, Leningrad

250 *Mikhail Ivanovich Kozlovski,*
Polycrates. *Bronze, 1790. State Tretyakov Gallery,
Moscow*

251 *Marie-Anne Collot,*
Étienne-Maurice Falconet. *Bronze, 1768. École des
Beaux Arts, Paris*

252 *Marie-Anne Collot and Étienne-Maurice
Falconet,*
Monumental head of Peter I, *model for the
memorial to Peter. Bronze. Hermitage Museum,
Leningrad*

253 *Étienne-Maurice Falconet,*
Monument to Peter I in St. Petersburg, *bronze,*
1775–1777, erected in 1782. Engraving from
Richter, Ansichten, *Leipzig 1804*

254 *Bartolomeo Carlo Rastrelli,*
Anna Ivanovna and her Blackamoor. *Bronze, 1741.*
State Russian Museum, Leningrad

255 Peter I's crown.
State Museums of the
Moscow Kremlin,
Armoury

256 Three-part service
from Solvychegodsk,
late 17th century.
Solvychegodsk armoury

257 Dish and knives.
Late 17th century.
Solvychegodsk armoury

260 *Ice chutes on the Neva. Popular festival during Butter Week. Engraving by Geissler, ca. 1804*

261 *All the fun of the fair. Engraving by Geissler, ca. 1804*

Following page:

262 *Fireworks and illuminations displayed in front of the Imperial Summer Palace in Moscow on New Year's Day, 1749. Etching, Berlin, privately owned*

THEATRE AND MUSIC

THE BEGINNINGS of theatre in Russia go back to the pre-Petrine era, when there were many links with German dramatic art. The first detailed accounts of theatrical performances in Russia date from the reign of Tsar Aleksei Mikhailovich (1645–1676). At the sovereign's command, the German pastor of the Protestant parish in the Moscow foreign quarter, Johann Gottfried Gregorii, assembled a new theatrical troupe which performed religious and secular plays for the Imperial Family and other state dignitaries. A theatre was established for this purpose in the village of Preobrazhenskoye. The first performance took place on 17th October 1672. The Tsar appeared at this event with his complete retinue and royal household, and although the performance lasted all of ten hours, it nonetheless won the approval of the Tsar. An auditorium was soon constructed in the Kremlin itself, and the performances transferred there. Gregorii and his troupe were at pains to perform their plays in Russian as well as in German. The Court Theatre was disbanded following Aleksei's death in 1676, but it was to reappear just a few years later.

The main contributors to the cultivation of drama at the end of the 17th century in Russia were cultured representatives of aristocratic families such as the Dolgorukis, Sheremetevs and Golitsyns. Peter's sisters, Sofia Alekseevna and Natalya Alekseevna, were also active as actresses and playwrights. By the same token, Biblical dramas were presented at the theological academies in Kiev and Moscow. Peter's famous associate, Bishop Feofan Prokopovich,

also wrote and staged secular plays. During his first trip abroad in 1697–98, Tsar Peter himself had become better acquainted with the dramatic art of the West, and had attended several theatrical performances. The resulting impressions reinforced the monarch's intentions of establishing a permanent theatre in Russia. Thus in 1702, despite the fact that the hostilities with Sweden were at their peak, a theatrical company led by Johann Christian Kunst came to Moscow at the behest of the Tsar. The actors in this travelling company were German students. They performed in a building erected in Red Square for the purpose by Peter. The performances laid great emphasis on the presentation of tableaux, as evidenced by the scenery, mechanical devices, machinery for the simulation of flight, and so on. There were two performances per week. The German texts of the plays were rendered into Russian by translators from the diplomatic *prikaz*. These included *Scipio Africanus, Don Pedro, Don Juan, Bajeset, Tamburlaine, Le Médecin malgré lui*, and others. Operatic intermezzi with arias were sometimes included. In Moscow, as elsewhere, the clown was a popular and permanent feature on stage.

Peter regarded the Moscow theatre not only as a place of entertainment and edification; his main motive for its establishment was educative, in other words, he saw the theatre as a medium for the propagation of his plans for reform. With this in mind, he instructed the director of the theatre, Johann Christian Kunst, to train young Russians as professional actors.

This transformed the theatre in Red Square into a school of drama, and before long Russian actors were treading the boards.

The operatic intermezzi, which were intended as light relief during the plays, required the collaboration of musicians and orchestras. To this end, Peter engaged a group of musicians from Hamburg. In imitation of his example, aristocratic dignitaries employed orchestras which were often made up of serfs; we know of such orchestras in the palaces of Menshikov, Golovkin and Prokopovich. The ladies of aristocratic society were particularly concerned to ensure that regular concert performances took place. One important group of musicians was constituted by Swedish prisoners of war, who created a niche in Russia for military music and musical choirs in particular. Thus orchestral music began gradually to establish itself along with the theatre in its role as a primary requirement of opera and ballet. From this time on, the pleasures of music ceased to be a rarity at the Imperial court and in the palaces of the high dignitaries of the realm.

In the theatrical performances of the Petrine period more and more plays came to the fore which contained clear references to current political events, such as the Streltsy uprisings and Russian victories over the Swedish enemy. Actors were granted the right to carry a sword and thereby advanced to a position of social privilege. When the Imperial Family and the administration of the state moved to St. Petersburg in 1709, the Russian theatre also gained a new centre for its activities in the young capi-

tal. Here, as well as the German theatre there was a Russian stage on which primarily contemporary conflicts were portrayed. Theatrical performances continued in Moscow as before, with a high degree of amateur participation, and plays written by Russian playwrights were staged. For instance, Fedor Shurovski, a student at the school of surgery, wrote the play *The Glory of Russia* in honour of the coronation of Empress Catherine I in 1725, whilst Feofan Prokopovich contributed his tragicomedy *Vladimir*, in which he poured scorn on the ignorance of priests and monks, whom he portrayed as wanton gluttons and tosspots.

Theatrical and concert life began to flourish at the Imperial court in the period following Peter's death. A court orchestra under the direction of Hübner had already arrived in St. Petersburg during the last years of the great Tsar's life, and had introduced chamber music to the imperial palace. At the same time there were ballet troupes and other orchestras with German, Russian and Italian dancers, musicians and actors. Italian virtuosi headed by Cosimo, the "famous Musico Buffo", appeared at the celebrations held to mark the coronation of the Empress Anna. A court theatre was established in the Summer Garden; in winter,

performances were held in one wing of the Winter Palace. The Court Director of Music at this time was Francesco Araya, who also composed many operas. In accordance with the taste of the age, it was primarily stories of fantastic wizardry and romantic adventure which were presented on stage; one example was Araya's play *The Power of Love and of Envy*, the text of which was translated into Russian by Trediakovski. When the opera was performed in 1737, the Great Chorus of forty members, and four military bands, took part. Araya wrote 17 operas between 1735 and 1763 alone. The main heroes of his works were Harlequin and Pantaloon. The musical intermezzi and dances which were interpolated during the performance provided a pleasant diversion during the action, which could last for hours.

The groups of strolling players found in Germany also gained admittance to the world of the Russian theatre after Peter's death. Thus in 1739, the famous Karoline Neuber brought her troupe to St. Petersburg, where they performed comedies and burlesques and earned great applause. However, when Empress Elizabeth ascended the throne in 1741, the French theatre came into its own. Theatre-goers assembled in the opulent court theatre built by Bartolomeo Carlo Rastrelli, where they were seated in magnificent boxes rising in four tiers above the stalls. Every week during the long winter season, the brilliant pleasures of the French theatre were supplemented by one French and one Russian play, and occasionally an Italian opera augmented the glory of the

263 *Theatre Square in St. Petersburg.*
From Breton, La Russie, vol. 1, Paris 1813

264 *Variation of the dramatic form of*
Shakespeare, written by Catherine II.

265 *Empress Catherine II of Russia.*
The monarch, whose interests were many and
varied, was also active in the field of literature.
Copper engraving by Johann Heinrich Lips.
Hermitage Museum, Leningrad

Court Festivals. The performances had an added attraction in the form of interpolated ballet scenes.

The French theatre, and French literature, gave Russian actors and poets a great deal of inspiration and example, which resulted in much imitation. For instance, students at the Land Cadet Corps in St. Petersburg formed an amateur theatre at the instigation mainly of Melissino, Svistunov and Osterwald; this was the germ which was to grow into the future National Theatre. Student cadets also appeared increasingly at court, where they also participated in performances of ballet. Empress Elizabeth took a lively interest in the work of these student actors. The Russian dramatist Sumarokov, a former student of the Land Cadet Corps, made a great contribution as a playwright to the performances by these cadet actors.

Around the middle of the century attempts to create a national theatre began to appear elsewhere. In Yaroslavl, Fedor Grigorievich Volkov, a merchant's son, and his brother Grigori Grigorievich put on shows in a barn together with some of their friends; these soon attracted the attention of the *voyevoda*, Musin-Pushkin. A public theatre was established soon thereafter. Fedor Volkov had studied in Moscow and St. Petersburg, where he had become well acquainted with German and Italian drama. He inaugurated the Yaroslavl theatre with the drama *Esther* and the pastoral idyll *Evmon and Berfa*, for which he also wrote the music. The performances of the actors not only satis-

fied the audience, but they were applauded throughout Russia. Empress Elizabeth soon came to hear about Volkov's reputation; in 1750, she issued an *ukaz* summoning Volkov's company, with its scenery and costumes, from Yaroslavl to St. Petersburg, where they earned generous applause for their performances. The Empress also saw to the further training of the young actors; the Volkov brothers and their friends were offered the chance to enter the Cadet Corps and to complete their training. For his part, Fedor Volkov forged links with a number of dramatists and provided support during the training of the famous actors Ivan Afanasevich Dmitrevski and Yakov Danilovich Shumski.

Fedor Volkov was not only the founder of the national Russian theatre, but also the first Russian operatic composer. The title of his opera was *Tanyushka, or The Fortunate Encounter*. It received its premiere in 1756, which is regarded as the year of the foundation of the permanent Russian National Theatre. The first director of the theatre was the versatile classicist poet and literary theorist Aleksandr Petrovich Sumarokov. The theatre of 1756 still exists today; it is now the Pushkin Theatre in Leningrad.

Russian dramatic art took a further step forward during the reign of Catherine II. Plays became a permanent feature of the theatrical programme under Catherine. Private theatres in provincial cities and in the homes of the nobility also boasted a wide repertoire and had no reason to fear comparisons with theatres

abroad. Nearly all the plays in the classical repertoire of the time were performed, including many by important Russian dramatists, such as Petr Alekseevich Plavilshchikov, Tatyana Mikhailovna Troepolskaya and Sila Nikolaevich Sandunov. A high standard of performance was also achieved by theatres in which the performers were serfs, like the outstanding operatic singer Praskovya Ivanovna Zhemchugova-Kovaleva, who was in the service of the Counts Sheremetev. Russian poets portrayed the wrongs and injustices which were prevalent in the tsardom in impressive fashion in their stage works. Like Peter I, Catherine II saw the theatre as a school for the education of the nation, which she tried to use to serve her own ends. Alongside Volkov, whose services to the Russian theatre earned him elevation to the nobility, Yevstignei Ipatovich Fomin distinguished himself as a composer. The popular comic opera *Miller, Wizard, Quack and Matchmaker* was written by him. The virtuoso violinist Ivan Yestafevich Khandoshkin also made a name for himself as a composer.

Theatre and music underwent an important upsurge in Russia during the Age of Enlightenment, which was characterized by the definition and development of national cultural values. Russian actors, musicians and poets turned to the theatre and to music and enjoyed great success, making a considerable contribution, in the 18th century, to the evolution of the creative powers of the peoples living in the tsardom.

CHRONOLOGICAL TABLE

1645—1676
Tsar Aleksei Mikhailovich (Peter I's father)

1648—1654
Re-unification of Russia and the Ukraine

1676—1683
Tsar Fedor Alekseevich (Peter I's step-brother)

1682—1725
Tsar Peter I Alekseevich (the Great), Emperor from 1721

1682—1689
Regency of Sofia Alekseevna (Peter I's half-sister)

1689
Treaty of Nerchinsk with China
Sofia deposed. The 17-year-old Peter takes over the government. The co-regency of his cretinous half-brother Ivan (V) remains meaningless until the latter's death (1696).

1700—1725
The Petrine reforms result in important changes in social, political and cultural life, but do not destroy the existing order with its system of serfdom. Resistance is expressed in the conservative opposition. The hopes of the opponents of reform come to rest on Peter's incompetent son Aleksei (d. 1718).

1700—1721
Russia allied with Denmark and Saxony-Poland against Sweden in the Northern War for vital access to the Baltic. Russia suffers a crushing defeat at the Battle of Narva (30th November 1700).

1704—1711
Social rebellion among the Bashkirs

1705—1706
Uprising of poor town-dwellers, conscripts and lower-ranking Cossacks in Astrakhan and the surrounding area

1707—1708
Rebellion led by Kondrati Bulavin on the Don and in the Ukraine

1709
Sweden decisively defeated by Russia in the Battle of Poltava in the Ukraine, thus losing its position as a European great power.

1711
King Charles XII of Sweden incites the Ottoman Empire to war against Russia, which is defeated in the Prut campaign.

1721
30th August: Peace of Nystad (Finland) ensures Russian predominance on the Baltic. Russia becomes an Empire and the Tsar assumes the title of Imperator.

1722—1723
Russia at war with Persia

1725—1727
Empress Catherine I (Peter I's wife)

1727—1730
Emperor Peter II Alekseevich (Peter I's grandson)

1730—1740
Empress Anna Ivanovna (Peter I's step-niece)

1740—1741
Emperor Ivan VI Antonovich

1741—1761
Empress Elizabeth Petrovna (Peter I's daughter)

1756—1763
Russia's participation in the Seven Years' War greatly increases her power.

1762
5th January—28th June: Emperor Peter III

1762—1796
Empress Catherine II (Peter III's wife, the former Princess of Anhalt-Zerbst)

1768—1774
Russia at war with Turkey

1773—1775
Peasants' revolt led by Emelian Pugachev in the Urals and Volga region. Foreign peasants, Cossacks, workers and non-Russians demand the abolition of serfdom and of the nobility. Pugachev, who claims to be Tsar Peter III, is executed in Moscow (1775).

1783
Annexation of the Crimea

1787
Catherine II's journey to the Crimea, accompanied by the German Emperor Joseph II, provokes a declaration of war from Turkey.

1787—1792
Russia allied with Austria in the war against Turkey

1788—1790
Russia at war with Sweden

1796—1801
Emperor Paul Petrovich

1801—1825
Emperor Alexander I Pavlovich

BIBLIOGRAPHY

There is no room here for a complete list of the specialist literature in essay form. The following bibliography lists those surveys, collections and monographs which provide important guidance on the subject and contain comprehensive bibliographical information.

ALEKSEEV, M. P.: *Zur Geschichte russisch-europäischer Literaturtradition.* Berlin, 1974.

ALPATOV, M. A.: *Russkaya istoricheskaya mysl' i Zapadnaya Evropa XVII–pervaya chetvert' XVIII veka.* Moscow, 1976.

AMBURGER, E.: *Beiträge zur Geschichte der deutsch-russischen kulturellen Beziehungen.* Giessen, 1961.

AMBURGER, E.: *Geschichte des Protestantismus in Russland.* Stuttgart, 1961.

AMBURGER, E.: *Geschichte der Behördenorganisation Russlands von Peter dem Grossen bis 1917.* Leyden, 1966.

AMBURGER, E.: *Ingermanland.* 2 vols., Cologne, Vienna, 1980.

ASEEV, B. N.: *Russki dramaticheski teatr XVII– XVIII vekov.* Moscow, 1958.

Die Aufklärung in Ost- und Südosteuropa. Cologne, Vienna, 1972.

Der Bauer Mittel- und Osteuropas im sozialökonomischen Wandel des 18. und 19. Jahrhunderts. Cologne, Vienna, 1973.

Ein bedeutender Gelehrter an der Schwelle der Frühaufklärung: Dimitrie Cantemir (1673–1723). Berlin, 1974.

Beförderer der Aufklärung in Mittel- und Osteuropa. Freimaurer, Gesellschaften, Clubs. Berlin (West), 1979.

Beiträge zur Geschichte Peters des Grossen. Edited by H. L. C. BACMEISTER, 3 vols., Riga, 1744–1784.

BELYAVSKI, M. T.: *M. V. Lomonosov i osnovaniye Moskovskogo universiteta.* Moscow, 1955.

BERKOV, P. N.: *Istoriya russkoi zhurnalistiki XVIII veka.* Moscow, Leningrad, 1952.

BERKOV, P. N.: *Literarische Wechselbeziehungen zwischen Russland und Westeuropa im 18. Jahrhundert.* Berlin, 1968.

BERKOV, P. N.: *Problemy istoricheskogo razvitiya literatury.* Leningrad, 1981.

Die Berliner und die Petersburger Akademie der Wissenschaften im Briefwechsel Leonhard Eulers. Edited by E. WINTER, 3 vols., Berlin, 1959, 1961, 1976.

Biblioteka Petra I. Leningrad, 1978.

Briefe von Christian Wolff aus den Jahren 1719–1753. Ein Beitrag zur Geschichte der Kaiserlichen Akademie der Wissenschaften zu St. Petersburg. St. Petersburg, 1860.

BUCHHOLZ, A.: *Die Göttinger Russlandsammlungen Georgs von Asch.* Giessen, 1961.

Buch- und Verlagswesen im 18. und 19. Jahrhundert. Berlin (West), 1972.

CHEREPNIN, L. V.: *Russkaya istoriografiya do XIX veka.* Moscow, 1957.

CLENDENNING, P. and E. BARTLETT: *Eighteenth Century Russia: A select Bibliography of works published since 1955.* Newtonville, 1981.

CRONIN, V.: *Katharina die Grosse. Eine Biographie.* Düsseldorf, 1978.

DANILEVSKI, V. V.: *Russkaya tekhnicheskaya literatura pervoi chetverti XVIII veka.* Moscow, Leningrad, 1954.

DERBOV, L. A.: *Obshchestvenno-politicheskiye i istoricheskiye vzglyady N. I. Novikova.* Saratov, 1974.

Die deutsch-russische Bewegung und Leonhard Euler. Edited by E. WINTER, Berlin, 1958.

Deutsch-slawische Wechselseitigkeit in sieben Jahrhunderten. E. Winter zum 60. Geburtstag. Berlin, 1956.

DIDEROT, D.: *Bildungsplan für die Regierung von Russland.* Berlin (West), Basle, 1971.

DMITRIEV, Y.: *Cirk v Rossii.* Moscow, 1977.

DÖPMANN, H.-D.: *Die Russisch-Orthodoxe Kirche in Geschichte und Gegenwart.* Berlin, 1977.

Dokumenty i materialy po istorii Moskovskogo universiteta vtoroi poloviny XVIII veka. 3 vols., Moscow, 1960, 1962, 1963.

Dokumenty stavki E. I. Pugacheva 1773–1774 gg. Moscow, 1975.

DONNERT, E.: *Politische Ideologie der russischen Gesellschaft zu Beginn der Regierungszeit Katharinas II.* Berlin, 1976.

DONNERT, E.: *Johann Georg Eisen (1717–1779). Ein Vorkämpfer der Bauernbefreiung in Russland.* Leipzig, 1978.

EICHHORN, C.: *Die Geschichte der St. Petersburger Zeitung 1727–1902.* St. Petersburg, 1902.

ELIZAROVA, N. A.: *Teatry Sheremetevykh.* Moscow, 1944.

EVSINA, N. A.: *Arkhitekturnaya teoriya v Rossii XVIII veka.* Moscow, 1975.

FEDOSOV, I. A.: *Iz istorii russkoi obshchestvennoi mysli XVIII veka. M. M. Shcherbatov.* Moscow, 1967.

FEYL, O.: *Beiträge zur Geschichte der slawischen Verbindungen und internationalen Kontakte der Universität Jena.* Jena, 1960.

FIGUROVSKI, N. A.: *Leben und Werk des Chemikers Tobias Lowitz (1757–1804).* Berlin, 1959.

FLEISCHHACKER, H.: *Mit Feder und Zepter. Katharina II. als Autorin.* Stuttgart, 1978.

FONVIZIN, D.: *Der Landjunker und andere satirische Dichtungen und Schriften.* Berlin, 1957.

FROESE, L.: *Ideengeschichtliche Triebkräfte der russischen und sowjetischen Pädagogik.* Heidelberg, 1956.

Genesis und Entwicklung des Kapitalismus in Russland. Berlin, 1973.

Geschichte der russischen Kunst. Vols. 5 and 6, Dresden, 1970, 1976.

Geschichte der russischen Kunst. Dresden, 1975.

GESEMANN, W.: *Die Entdeckung der unteren Volksschichten durch die russische Literatur.* Wiesbaden, 1972.

GITERMANN, V.: *Geschichte Russlands.* Vol. 2, Hamburg, 1949.

GRABAR, I.: *O russkoi arkhitekture.* Moscow, 1969.

GRASSHOFF, H.: *Antioch Kantemir und Westeuropa.* Berlin, 1966.

GRASSHOFF, H.: *Russische Literatur in Deutschland im Zeitalter der Aufklärung.* Berlin, 1973.

GRASSHOFF, H., A. LAUCH and U. LEHMANN: *Humanistische Traditionen der russischen Aufklärung.* Berlin, 1973.

GRASSHOFF, H., H. RAAB, E. REISSNER and M. WEGNER: *Russische Literatur im Überblick.* Leipzig, 1974.

GRAU, C.: *Der Wirtschaftsorganisator, Staatsmann und Wissenschaftler Vasili N. Tatishchev (1686–1750).* Berlin, 1963.

GROH, D.: *Russland und das Selbstverständnis Europas.* Neuwied, 1961.

HASSELBLATT, J.: *Historischer Überblick der Entwicklung der Kaiserlich-Russischen Akademie der Künste in St. Petersburg.* Leipzig, 1886.

Herder-Kolloquium 1978. Weimar, 1980.

HINZ, W.: *Peters des Grossen Anteil an der wissenschaftlichen und künstlerischen Kultur seiner Zeit.* Breslau, 1933. (Also in: *Jahrbücher für Geschichte und Kultur der Slaven 8* (1932),

pp. 349–447; *Archiv für Kulturgeschichte 23* (1933), pp. 162–169).

HÖSCH, E.: *Die Kultur der Ostslaven.* Wiesbaden, 1977.

Illyustrirovannaya istoriya SSSR. 3rd edition, Moscow, 1980.

Istoriya Akademii nauk SSSR. Vol. 1, Moscow, Leningrad, 1958.

Istoriya estestvoznaniya v Rossii. Vol. 1, Moscow, 1957.

Istoriya Moskovskogo universiteta. Vol. 1, Moscow, 1955.

Istoriya Moskvy. Vol. 2, Moscow, 1953.

Istoriya russkoi literatury. Vol. 1, Moscow, Leningrad, 1958.

Istoriya SSSR. Vol. 3, Moscow, 1967.

KELDYSH, Y. V.: *Russkaya muzyka XVIII veka.* Moscow, 1965.

KISLYAGINA, L. G.: *Formirovaniye obshchestvenno-politicheskikh vzglyadov. N. M. Karamzin 1785–1803.* Moscow, 1976.

Klassenkampf und revolutionäre Bewegung in der Geschichte Russlands. Berlin, 1977.

KOMKOV, G. D., B. B. LEVSHIN and L. K. SEMENOV: *Geschichte der Akademie der Wissenschaften der UdSSR.* Berlin, 1981.

KOPELEVICH, Y. C.: *Osnovaniye Peterburgskoi Akademii nauk.* Leningrad, 1977.

KRASNOBAEV, B. I.: *Ocherki istorii russkoi kultury XVIII veka.* Moscow, 1972.

KRASNOBAEV, B. I.: "Russkaya kultura XVIII veka. Predmet i zadachi izucheniya", in: *Istoriya SSSR.* 6/1976, pp. 29–45.

KRUMBHOLZ, J.: *Die Elementarbildung in Russland bis zum Jahre 1864.* Wiesbaden, 1982.

Kultura i iskusstvo petrovskogo vremeni. Leningrad, 1977.

KUNTZE, G.: *Studien zur Geschichte der russischen satirischen Typenkomödie 1750–1772.* Frankfurt-am-Main, 1971.

KURMACHEVA, M. D.: *Peterburgskaya Akademiya nauk i M. V. Lomonosov.* Moscow, 1975.

KUZMINA, V. D.: *Russki demokraticheski teatr XVIII veka.* Moscow, 1958.

LAUCH, A.: *Wissenschaft und kulturelle Beziehungen in der russischen Aufklärung. Zum Wirken H. L. C. Bacmeisters.* Berlin, 1969.

LEHMANN, U.: *Der Gottschedkreis in Russland. Deutsch-russische Literaturbeziehungen im Zeitalter der Aufklärung.* Berlin, 1966.

Literatur im Epochenumbruch. Funktionen europäischer Literaturen im 18. und beginnenden 19. Jahrhundert. Berlin, Weimar, 1977.

LOMONOSOV, M. V.: *Ausgewählte Schriften in zwei Bänden.* Berlin, 1961.

Lomonosov, Schlözer, Pallas. Edited by E. WINTER. Berlin, 1962.

M. V. Lomonosov v portretakh, illyustratsiyakh, dokumentakh. Moscow, Leningrad, 1965.

LUPPOV, S. P.: *Istoriya stroitelstva Peterburga v pervoi chetverti XVIII veka.* Moscow, Leningrad, 1957.

MADARIAGA, I. de: *Russia in the Age of Catherine the Great.* London, 1981.

MASSIE, R.: *Peter the Great.* London, 1981.

MATTHES, E.: *Das veränderte Russland.* Frankfurt-am-Main, Berne, 1981.

MAVRODIN, V. V.: *Krestyanskaya voina v Rossii v 1773–1775 godakh. Vosstaniye Pugacheva.* 3 vols., Leningrad, 1961, 1966, 1970.

D. G. Messerschmidt. Forschungsreise durch Sibirien 1720–1727. Edited by E. WINTER. 5 parts, Berlin, 1962, 1964, 1966, 1968, 1977.

MOHRMANN, H.: *Studien über russisch-deutsche Begegnungen in der Wirtschaftswissenschaft (1750–1825).* Berlin, 1959.

MOISEEVA, G. N.: *Drevnerusskaya literatura v khudozhestvennom soznanii i istoricheskoi mysli Rossii XVIII veka.* Leningrad, 1980.

MOROSOV, A. A.: *Michail Wassiljewitsch Lomonossow 1711–1765.* Berlin, 1954.

MÜHLPFORDT, G.: "Deutsch-russische Wissenschaftsbeziehungen in der Zeit der Aufklärung (Christian Wolff und die Gründung der Petersburger Akademie der Wissenschaften)", in: *450 Jahre Martin-Luther-Universität Halle-Wittenberg.* Vol. 2, Halle, 1952, pp. 169–197.

MÜHLPFORDT, G.: "Lomonosov — Sein Werden und Wirken in der Welt der Aufklärung", in: *Wissenschaftliche Zeitschrift der Universität Berlin. Mathematisch-Naturwissenschaftliche Reihe 11.* 1962, No. 4, pp. 623–642.

MÜHLPFORDT, G.: "Leipzig als Brennpunkt der internationalen Wirkung Lomonosovs", in: *Studien zur Geschichte der russischen Literatur des 18. Jahrhunderts.* Vol. 3, Berlin, 1968, pp. 271–416, 576–599.

MÜHLPFORDT, G.: "Lomonosov und die mitteldeutsche Aufklärung", in: *Studien zur Geschichte der russischen Literatur des 18. Jahrhunderts.* Vol. 2, Berlin, 1968, pp. 135–231, 401–427.

NICHIK, V. M.: *Iz istorii otechestvennoi filosofii kontsa XVII — nachala XVIII veka.* Kiev, 1978.

N. I. Novikov i obshchestvenno-literaturnoye dvizheniye ego vremeni. Leningrad, 1976.

Novye cherty v russkoi literature i isskustve XVII — nachala XVIII veka. Moscow, 1976.

Ocherki istorii Leningrada. Vol. 1, Moscow, Leningrad, 1955.

Ocherki istorii SSSR. "Period feodalizma", "Rossiya v pervoi chetverti XVIII veka. Preobrazovaniya Petra I", "Rossiya vo vtoroi polovine XVIII veka", "Narody SSSR v pervoi polovine XVIII veka". Moscow, 1954, 1956, 1957.

ONASCH, K.: *Liturgie und Kunst der Ostkirche in Stichworten.* Leipzig, 1981.

Ost und West in der Geschichte des Denkens und der kulturellen Beziehungen. Festschrift für Eduard Winter zum 70. Geburtstag. Berlin, 1966.

OVCHINNIKOV, R. V.: *Manifesty i Ukazy E. I. Pugacheva.* Moscow, 1980.

PAVLOVA, G. E. and A. S. FEDOROV: *Mikhail Vasilievich Lomonosov.* Moscow, 1980.

PEKARSKI, P.: *Nauka i literatura v Rossii pri Petre Velikom.* 2 vols., St. Petersburg, 1862 (reprinted Leipzig, 1972).

PEKARSKI, P.: *Istoriya Imperatorskoi Akademii nauk v Peterburge.* 2 vols., 1870, 1873 (reprinted Leipzig, 1977).

PESHTICH, S. L.: *Russkaya istoriografiya XVIII veka.* 2 vols., Leningrad, 1961, 1965.

Petr Veliki v inostrannoi literature. St. Petersburg, 1872.

POSOSOSHKOV, I. T.: *Kniga o skudosti i bogatstve.* Moscow, 1951.

PROKOPOVICH, F.: *Sochineniya.* Moscow, Leningrad, 1961.

PUSHKIN, A. S.: *Gesammelte Werke.* Vol. 5, Berlin, Weimar, 1965.

RADISHCHEV, A. N.: *Ausgewählte Schriften.* Berlin, 1959.

RADISHCHEV, A. N.: *Reise von Petersburg nach Moskau.* Berlin, 1952, Leipzig, 1982.

A. N. Radishchev v portretakh, illyustratsiyakh, dokumentakh. Leningrad, 1961.

A. N. Radishchev und Deutschland. Beiträge zur russischen Literatur des ausgehenden 18. Jahrhunderts. Berlin, 1969.

Reiseberichte von Deutschen über Russland und von Russen über Deutschland. Cologne, Vienna, 1980.

Reisen und Reisebeschreibungen im 18. und 19. Jahrhundert als Quellen der Kulturgeschichtsforschung. Berlin (West), 1980.

RICHTER, L.: *Leibniz und sein Russlandbild.* Berlin, 1946.

Rossiya i SSHA. Stanovleniye otnoshenij 1765–1815. Moscow, 1980.

Rossiya v period reform Petra I. Moscow, 1973.

RUEHL, L.: *Russlands Weg zur Weltmacht.* Düsseldorf, 1980.

Russisch-deutsche Beziehungen von der Kiewer Rus bis zur Oktoberrevolution. Berlin, 1976.

Russische Bibliothek. Edited by H. L. C. BACMEISTER, 11 vols., Riga, Leipzig, 1772–1789.

Russkaya kultura XVIII veka i zapadno-evropeiskiye literatury. Leningrad, 1980.

Russkiye povesti pervoi treti XVIII veka. Moscow, Leningrad, 1965.

Russko-germanskiye nauchnye svyazi mezhdu Akademiej nauk SSR i Akademiej nauk GDR 1700–1974. Moscow, 1975.

Russland und Deutschland. Stuttgart, 1974.

SAKHAROV, A. M.: *Istoriografiya istorii SSSR. Dosovetski period.* Moscow, 1978.

August Ludwig von Schlözer und Russland. Edited by E. WINTER. Berlin, 1961.

SCHROEDER, H.: *Russische Verssatire im 18. Jahrhundert.* Cologne, Graz, 1962.

SCHÜTZ, W.: *Michail W. Lomonossow.* Leipzig, 1970.

SHTRANGE, M. M.: *Demokraticheskaya intelligentsiya Rossii v XVIII veke.* Moscow, 1965.

SIEVERS, L.: *Deutsche und Russen. Tausend Jahre gemeinsame Geschichte.* Gütersloh, 1980.

SMOLITSCH, I.: *Geschichte der Russischen Kirche 1700–1917.* Vol. 1, Leyden, 1964.

STÄHLIN, K.: *Aus den Papieren Jacob von Stählins. Ein biographischer Abriss zur Kulturgeschichte des 18. Jahrhunderts.* Berlin, 1926.

STANYUKOVICH, T. V.: *Kunstkamera Peterburgskoi Akademii nauk.* Moscow, Leningrad, 1953.

STIEDA, W.: *Johann Albrecht Euler in seinen Briefen 1766–1790. Ein Beitrag zur Geschichte der Kaiserlichen Akademie der Wissenschaften in St. Petersburg.* Leipzig, 1932.

Studien zur Geschichte der russischen Literatur. 4 vols., Berlin, 1963, 1968, 1968, 1970.

Svodny katalog russkoi knigi, 1725–1800. 3 vols., Moscow, 1963, 1964, 1966, supplementary volume 1975.

TETZNER, J.: *H. W. Ludolf und Russland.* Berlin, 1955.

TOLSTOI, D. A.: *Ein Blick auf das Unterrichtswesen Russlands im 18. Jahrhundert.* St. Petersburg, 1884.

TOLSTOI, D. A.: *Das Akademische Gymnasium und die Akademische Universität im 18. Jahrhundert.* St. Petersburg, 1886.

TOLSTOI, D. A.: *Die Stadtschulen während der Regierung der Kaiserin Katharina II.* St. Petersburg, 1887.

TROITSKI, S. M.: *Russki absolyutizm i dvoryanstvo v XVIII veke.* Moscow, 1974.

TROYAT, H.: *Peter der Grosse. Biographie.* Düsseldorf, 1981.

VERNADSKI, G. V.: *Russkoye Masonstvo v tsarstvovaniye Yekateriny II.* Petrograd, 1917 (reprinted Vaduz, 1970).

VIRGINSKI, V. S.: *Tvortsy novoi tekhniki v krepostnoi Rossii.* Moscow, 1957.

VISKOVATOV, A. V.: *Istoricheskoye opisaniye odezhdy i vooruzheniya Rossijskikh voisk.* 4 parts, St. Petersburg, 1899.

F. G. Volkov i russki teatr ego vremeni. Moscow, 1953.

VSEVOLODSKI-GERNROSS, V. N.: *Russki teatr vtoroi poloviny XVIII veka.* Moscow, 1960.

WINTER, E.: *Halle als Ausgangspunkt der deutschen Russlandkunde im 18. Jahrhundert.* Berlin, 1953.

WINTER, E.: *Frühaufklärung.* Berlin, 1966.

WINTER, E.: *Ketzerschicksale.* Berlin, 1979.

Wissenschaftspolitik in Mittel- und Osteuropa. Wissenschaftliche Gesellschaften, Akademien und Hochschulen im 18. und beginnenden 19. Jahrhundert. Berlin (West), 1976.

WITTRAM, R.: *Peter I. Czar und Kaiser.* 2 vols., Göttingen, 1964.

WOLFF, C.: *Eigene Lebensbeschreibung.* Leipzig, 1841.

ZAPADOV, A. V.: *Russkaya zhurnalistika poslednei chetverti XVIII veka.* Moscow, 1962.

ZHIDKOV, G. V.: *Russkoye iskusstvo XVIII veka.* Moscow, 1951.

ZIEGLER, G.: *Moskau und Petersburg in der russischen Literatur (1700–1850).* Munich, 1974.

ZUBOV, V. P.: *Istoriografiya estestvennykh nauk v Rossii. XVIII vek — pervoi poloviny XIX veka.* Moscow, 1956.

SOURCES OF ILLUSTRATIONS

ADN-Zentralbild, Berlin 116, 130
Klaus Bergmann, Potsdam, 36, 37
Bibliothèque Nationale, Paris 34, 35
Deutsche Fotothek, Dresden 33, 38, 39, 43, 46, 47, 62/63, 66, 70, 74, 80, 83, 85, 92, 98, 103, 117, 118, 121, 159, 198, 206, 210, 211, 230, 236, 245, 251, 262
Deutscher Verlag der Wissenschaften, Berlin 2, 115, 200
Deutsches Museum, Munich 95
Deutsche Staatsbibliothek, Berlin 53
Volkmar Herre, Leipzig 31, 139—143, 146, 186, 187, 191—195, 213, 214, 215, 253, 260, 261
Hochschulbildstelle, Halle 67, 78, 88, 112, 114, 123, 125, 127, 128, 129, 154, 158, 160, 166, 172, 188, 197, 201, 202, 203, 216, 217
Sabine Hüthel, Leipzig 31, 144, 145
Musée d'Art et d'Histoire, Geneva 82
Novosti Press Agency, Moscow 24, 205, 212, 231, 233, 234, 237, 238, 243, 256, 257, 258
Carin Plessing, Leipzig 40, 44, 54, 68, 81
Gerhard Reinhold, Leipzig 64
Eberhard Renno, Weimar 20, 141, 204
Wolfgang G. Schröter, Leipzig 65
Staatliche Bücher- und Kupferstichsammlung, Greiz 1, 21, 22, 51, 52
State Hermitage, Leningrad 252
State Historical Museum, Moscow 27—29, 30, 58—60, 93, 170, 185, 219
State Russian Museum, Leningrad 84, 188—190, 196, 223, 224, 225, 226, 227, 229, 232, 238, 239, 241, 244, 246, 247, 249, 254
State Tretyakov Gallery, Moscow 171, 228, 248, 250

The publisher is obliged to Joachim Petri, Leipzig, for the provision of all photos not included in this list.

Illustrations were taken from the following books:

Ascher, Abraham: *Der Kreml.* Wiesbaden, 1975.
Breton, Jean-Baptiste Joseph: *La Russie ou moeurs, usages et costumes.* 6 vols., Paris, 1813.
Bruyn, Cornelis de: *Reisen door klein Asie, Palestina en over Moskovien door Persie en Indie.* Amsterdam, 1714.
Büsching, Anton Friedrich: *Magazin für die neue Historie und Geographie.* Part 1. Halle, 1767.
Fleischhacker, Hedwig: *Mit Feder und Zepter. Katharina II. als Autorin.* Stuttgart, 1978.
Geissler, Christian Gottfried Heinrich/Friedrich Hempel: *Malerische Darstellungen der Sitten, Gebräuche und Lustbarkeiten bei den russischen, tatarischen, mongolischen und anderen Völkern im Russischen Reich.* Leipzig, 1804.
Geissler, Christian Gottfried Heinrich: *Strafen der Russen.* Leipzig, 1805.
Geissler, Christian Gottfried Heinrich/Johann Richter: *Spiele und Belustigungen der Russen aus den niederen Volksklassen, dargestellt in Gemälden.* Leipzig, 1805.
Georgi, Johann Gottlieb: *Beschreibung aller Nationen des Russischen Reiches.* St. Petersburg, 1776.
Gruber, Johann Gottfried/Christian Gottfried Heinrich Geissler: *Sitten, Gebräuche und Kleidung der Russen in St. Petersburg, dargestellt in Gemälden.* Leipzig, 1805.
Gruber, Johann Gottfried/Christian Gottfried Heinrich Geissler: *Russische Volksvergnügungen.* Leipzig, 1805.
Hempel, Friedrich/Christian Gottfried Heinrich Geissler: *Russische Völker und Völkerstämme.* Leipzig, 1805.

Hösch, Edgar: *Die Kultur der Ostslaven.* Wiesbaden, 1977.
Isbrand-Ides, Evert: *Driejaarige Reize naar China.* Amsterdam, 1704.
Korb, Johann Georg: *Diarium Itineris in Moscoviam.* Vienna, 1700.
Makogonenko, I. P.: *A. N. Radishchev v portretakh, illyustraciyakh, dokumentakh.* Leningrad, 1961.
Olearius, Adam: *Vermehrte Moscowitische und Persianische Reisebeschreibung.* Schleswig, 1656.
Richter, Johann (ed.): *Ansichten von St .Petersburg und Moskau.* Leipzig, 1804.
Richter, Johann/Christian Gottfried Heinrich Geissler: *Sitten, Gebräuche und Kleidung der Russen.* Leipzig, 1805.
Sakulin, P. N.: *Die russische Literatur.* Potsdam, 1927.
Steller, Georg Wilhelm: *Beschreibung von dem Lande Kamtschatka.* Frankfurt/Main, 1721, Leipzig, 1774.
Struys, Johann: *Drie Reysen durch Italien, Griechenland, Liefland, Moscou …* Amsterdam, 1678.
Weber, Friedrich Christian: *Das veränderte Russland.* Part 1, Frankfurt/Main, 1721.
Weber, Johann Philipp Balthasar: *Die Russen oder Versuch einer Reisebeschreibung nach Russland und durch das Russische Reich nach Europa.* Ed. by Hans Halm, Innsbruck, 1960.

INDEX OF PLACES AND NAMES

ERICH DONNERT

RUSSIA IN THE AGE OF ENLIGHTENMENT